MARKED CARDS
CARDS
AND
LOADED
DICE

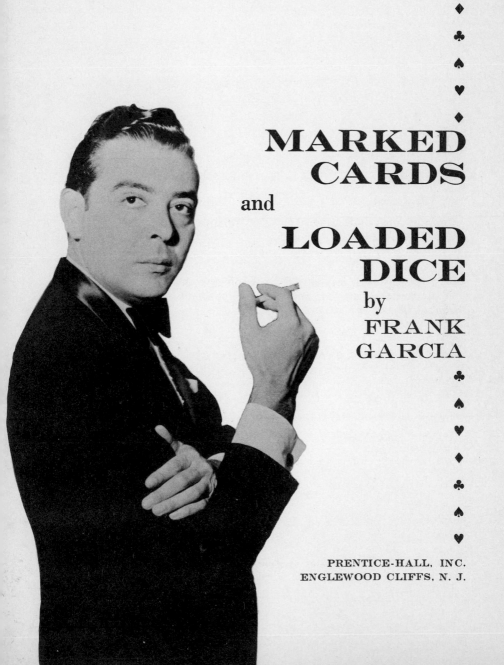

MARKED CARDS

and

LOADED DICE

by
FRANK
GARCIA

PRENTICE-HALL, INC.
ENGLEWOOD CLIFFS, N. J.

Printed in the United States of America

55709-T

DEDICATION

AFFECTIONATELY DEDICATED TO MY THREE-YEAR-OLD SON, FRANK
NICHOLAS, WHO DID HIS BEST TO DISTRACT ME.

ACKNOWLEDGMENTS

Above all, I wish to acknowledge the lifelong help, encouragement and inspiration of my parents, Nicholas and Felipa Garcia.

I want to thank my good friend, Henry Lee, who has helped make this book possible.

To Dai Vernon, Jay Ose and Francis Carlyle, I owe a heavy debt of gratitude for their technical advice and assistance.

And I want to thank particularly Deputy Chief Inspector Joseph L. Coyle, Captain T. J. Meyer and Detective Richard Gallagher of the New York City Police Department for their unstinting cooperation.

Last, but far from least, for *Marked Cards and Loaded Dice* would have been sadly incomplete without him, I want to thank Randi, my photographer.

CONTENTS

♠
♥
♦
♣
♠
♥
♦

CHAPTER I

THOSE "FRIENDLY" GAMES

♠
♥
♦
♣

At home

IT'S A FRIENDLY LITTLE HOME in a friendly little housing develop-
ment in a friendly Midwest city. Sitting around the baize-covered card
table in the basement rumpus room, half a dozen neighbors are playing draw poker.

You've heard similar conversation thousands of times. *I'll stay. . . .
Raise. . . . Dammit, I've got to fold. . . . Three cards, and baby,
be good to me.*

With five-cent chips and a limit, nobody can get badly hurt. Just
another friendly little Saturday night session of the boys. . . .

Friendly?

Let's kibitz this game more closely.

Keep your eyes particularly on Joe Lawrence, the lucky host, and
Bill Adams, who almost never takes a pot. We can forget the others.
They're just four guys, playing average, uninspired poker.

Right now, Joe is dealing. He's a bluff, red-faced auto salesman,
quite a card himself, the other fellows think, and he makes a production
of standing up as he deals. It's what brings him his luck, he says, and
the other players laugh. That's Joe for you!

Fact is, Joe is a card cheat. Like most amateurs, he isn't a very good
one. He hasn't mastered the sleight-of-hand arts of palming cards or
switching decks. Nor does he know anything about "smudging," "nail-
nicking" or "glim-working," larcenous little refinements of the game
which I will tell you about later.

1

But in a "novelty" store which dispenses crooked gambling equipment, Joe picked up a deck of Bicycle Back cards for $5. He was willing to pay that much because the backs are cleverly marked to reveal the value of each card. (For an extra $1, he could have gotten a deck marked for suits, too.)

Now, so fumblingly that any professional gambler would spot him on the first hand, Joe is trying to get back a modest dividend on his investment. He stands up to deal because he can more easily read the backs as he passes out the cards, and his obvious intentness is almost laughable.

To any pro, his erratic pattern of betting would be an equally telltale admission that he is engaged in "paper work," as marked cards are called in the gambling underworld. Sometimes, he folds quickly for no apparent reason. Then, next time, though a couple of the other players stay in with their original deals, indicating that they have strong hands, Joe is a tiger. He raises and raises—and wins.

Of course, Joe is as obvious as a five-aoe hand, but if *you* were his friend and neighbor, would you suspect him? Most amateur card-players are honest and take it for granted that the games they play in private homes and at lodge rooms and veterans' halls are honest, too.

Oh-oh

Joe has just won another big pot, and Bill Adams, grumbling that he never has any luck, helpfully pushes the chips toward him. As he draws back his hands, palms down, toward his lap, a chip drops onto the table. "Gosh, my hand must be sweaty," he apologizes.

Actually, Bill is a cheat, too. He is a "check copper" who steals a few chips whenever he can from the winners' pots. So Bill is trying to cheat Joe, and Joe is trying to take the house with marked cards.

Just another friendly little Saturday night session of the boys. . . .

On the town

After a quarter of a century as a traveling salesman, Jack Andrews takes his fun where he finds it. Tonight, as luck would have it, just after receiving a wire for $1,000 against his drawing account, he runs into another businessman he has seen around the hotel lobby for a couple of days.

"Little game up in Suite 810 later if you're interested," the stranger says. "A lot of laughs and fairly fast action."

"Hope it's seven-card stud," Jack tells him. "That's *my* game."

"Say, that's funny!" the stranger exclaims. "Just what we're playing."

"I'll be there by 10:00," Jack promises.

To me, hotel suites all have pretty much the same slickly professional but cold decor—and so do the card games that are played in them. If Jack had asked me, I would have advised him to stay away. But he didn't, of course, and now it's 11:00 P.M. in Suite 810, and maybe I was wrong. Let's have a look.

From his pile of chips, Jack has apparently been winning consistently. There's a peculiar rhythm to seven-card stud, almost like an intricate dance step. *Draw-and-look-and-raise-and-bluff-and-only-drop-if-you-have-to.* Jack has mastered it, he's a good player, but not *this* good.

It's a syndicate operation, I'm convinced, and they're just fattening Jack for a $1,000 kill. How?

This girl who wanders around the suite (you know the type that wanders around hotel suites) could be reading Jack's hand as she serves him drinks and then signaling one of the players.

I watch her awhile.

No, that's not it. She *is* just serving drinks for her $25 night's pay, and she's worth it. Between her rather obvious charms and all the whisky she pours into Jack, she is a first-rate distractor. Sex and whisky *and* cards don't mix.

Maybe it's Jack's lobby friend who steered him into the game. He and one of the other players are "quarreling" so unnecessarily that I suspect they have some set of signals. Perhaps a sending-receiving set attached to each other by wire under the table. The sender signals his hands almost like a telegrapher, and the other player receives by little jerks of the wire attached to his pants leg.

Dammit, I dropped my cigarette case. Picking it up, I got a quick look under the table. Nothing suspicious there. There isn't even a peep-hole on the wall, that quaint, ancient but still-serviceable device for peeking at the victim's hands. No, I guess we're back to marked cards as the master "paper workers" employ them. They read them so fast that you would never suspect they are reading, and they lose often enough so they don't seem infallible.

Suddenly, Jack rips out an oath. "Luck" has been steadily turning against him, and the last big pot began eating into his own money. He's a little drunk now and nasty.

"I want fresh cards!" he demands. "There's something peculiar here."

"Check!" the steerer agrees quickly. "I'm leery, too. Let's send down to the cigar stand in the lobby for a new deck."

That's it! How could Jack know that, only a few days ago, a playing card "salesman" loaded the cigar stand with 50 new decks at a ridiculously low wholesale price the proprietor couldn't resist? They were all marked, of course.

The "fresh deck" comes up, and Jack nods owlishly. Nobody's going to put something over on him! Let us pass over the next half hour in merciful silence. Jack loses the rest of his $1,000 and writes a check for another $200 in losses which his friend, the steerer, generously "tears up" (after carefully palming it in favor of a blank piece of paper). It will be presented for payment at the bank at 9:00 A.M. before Jack wakes up and fuzzily wonders whether maybe he was taken.

Supposing the syndicate hadn't had the forethought to preplant its marked decks? Then the bellboy would have brought up an honest deck—and Jack's friend, casually reaching for a cigarette, would have switched it for a marked deck already in his pocket.

One of a dozen ways (which I intend to describe as we go along) they're *bound* to take you when you get into a "friendly" game with strangers.

In the barracks

"Hey, fellows! Pass the word. Big game in our barracks tonight."

In every GI camp, every Navy, Air Force or Marine outfit, those are *trouble* words. Oh sure, you think the game is honest, and maybe, just *maybe,* it is.

You think so because they're your own dice? Where did you get them? More than one operator in uniform has given loaded dice to a patsy or left them someplace in the barracks where they would surely be found.

Casually, after somebody else has organized the game and introduced the phonies, he will casually drop in for the kill.

That's precisely what is happening tonight in Barracks K. Some 30 men are huddled in a huge, shouting circle, ten of them playing actively, the other 20 "off bettors" wagering with or against the throwers.

For one meek-looking recruit, the transparencies come up 7 and *11* with amazing obedience! He runs up a quick killing of about $80 and quietly bows out of the game. But, wait a minute.

Did you spot that almost imperceptible gesture as he rolled the dice in both hands before his last throw? He was "palming out" his loaded transparencies and "palming in" a pair of legitimate dice. Thus, he departed both with $80 and the evidence of how he had "won" it.

Whether they are transparencies, "belly shapes," or the misspotted dice known as "Ts," crooked dice work flimflams our servicemen out of untold millions of dollars yearly. This really makes me angry. If, as I have, you've seen some of the dreary outposts of our defense, you can sympathize that men gamble to escape the deadly boredom.

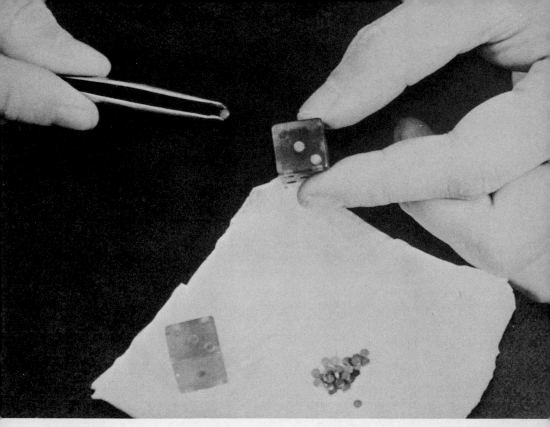

Figure 1. With tweezers, author is inserting tiny tungsten loads into holes drilled into side of dice. Tungsten is one of the most effective weights now used to "gaff" dice.

Figure 2. First step in a basic technique for switching dice. The author is "helpfully" picking up the dice, preparatory to handing them to victim. Right hand has a pair of dice palmed.

Figure 3. Notice author's retracted thumb. Actually, he is tucking dice between thumb and palm while bringing forward the crooked dice with his first two fingers. Right hand releases palmed dice. Picking up regular dice, author locks them for switch.

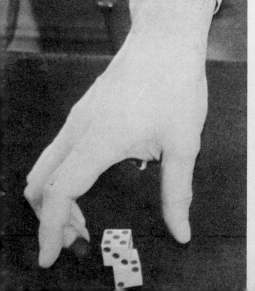

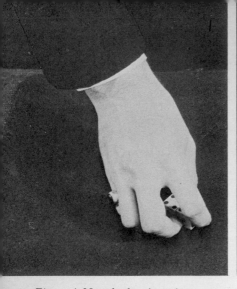

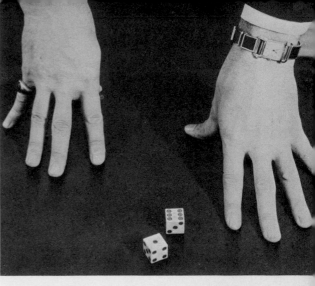

Figure 4. Now he has just about completed switch. Honest dice are secured between thumb and palm, and crooked dice are about to be dropped onto the table.

Figure 5. Move completed. Do you notice something peculiar about position of one hand? The thumb is concealed—because it is holding the dice switched out of the game.

Figure 6. As he prepares to deal, author's right thumb manipulates bottom card so that he can "pike" or "peek" it.

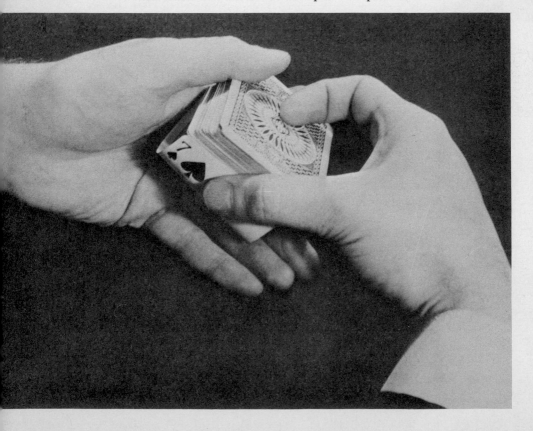

Perhaps they shouldn't, but they do, and at least they deserve a fair roll for their money!

Just as bad as the "mittmen" who switch crooked dice in and out of the game are the side-bet vultures who trap the innocent with sucker odds. Now that the recruit has left, the dice are honest again in Barracks K, but the bets aren't. Listen:

"Even money he can't make his eight!" (The correct odds are 6 to 5.)

"Three bucks to a deuce that he won't ten." (Rightly, a 2 to 1 bet.)

"His point's an easy five—but I'll put up ten bucks against $15 that he doesn't make it." (A rank steal! The odds are 3 to 2 against the tosser making a five, *not* 2 to 3.)

And so, unfortunately, it goes wherever there are lonely soldiers, sailors, Marines and Air Force men trying to kill bleak hours by a game of chance that isn't chance at all. One of my chief purposes in writing this book is to alert these lambs in uniform—and their parents, sweethearts and friends back home—to the colossal fraud that is being perpetrated on them.

In saying this, I do want to add one optimistic bit of qualification. The Defense Department, the generals, the admirals and the lesser brass are keenly alert to the problem. They are doing all they can to suppress crooked gambling. The best way, of course, is through education of the intended victims, especially our thousands of innocent teenagers, away from home for the first time in their lives. I hope this book will, to some extent, contribute to that necessary, worldly information.

A brief message from Garcia

In the following chapters, I propose to show you in detail how almost all crooked card and dice tricks are worked. I make my living doing this. As The Gambling Investigator, I am retained by hotels, steamship lines, casinos and private clubs to expose sharpers—at very comfortable fees, because my profession is very small, exclusive and confidential.

It is also a calling full of excitement and surprises. From the wideopen towns like Phenix City, where every night is Saturday night, to gamble-crazy Las Vegas, you name the card, craps or wheel game and I daresay I have tested it for its honesty.

In pursuit of my calling, I've rolled the dice in those murderous games that float weekly from one plush hotel suite in New York to the next, just ahead of the police. I've played blackjack in the back rooms of social clubs where the action can be just as ruthless. I've played aboard ship, on planes, in military installations, even in the back seat of a chartered bus coming back from a salesmen's convention.

More than once I had been threatened with a "working over," but I have found fun as well as excitement (and profit) in my strange profession. Sometimes, for example, when I find cheats are using a deck with the high cards marked, I switch in my own "cooler" in which only the *low* cards are marked. I don't like hustlers, so for a couple of hands I get a malicious pleasure out of watching them sweat, squirm, rub their eyes—and drop big pots to me.

Then, not to press my luck, especially if they have a bodyguard sitting in, I switch decks again, thus leaving no evidence, collect my winnings and depart to report to the client who has retained me. The hustled hustlers, I know, will be arguing more loudly than a husband-wife bridge team over who pulled what bonehead play.

I would *like* to be able to report, from my observations, that there are comparatively few crooked gamblers and that your chances of being taken by them are minute. Actually, however, it is my experience that there are tens of thousands of men—and women—who live *solely* by cheating at cards or dice, plus many more "amateur" crooks who infest "friendly" games.

Of course, as I have found when I talked this way on TV and on lecture tours, honest people are reluctant to believe such harsh facts. They like to think other people are honest, too, which is commendably charitable but dangerous in the extreme at the card table.

So first, if I may, I will attempt a nationwide survey of the extent of crooked gambling and explain what it means to *you*.

CHAPTER II

♠
♥
♦
♣
♠
♥
♦

ANY HONEST GAME IN TOWN?

♣
♠
♥
♦

FOR PURELY PERSONAL REASONS, such as your age, ulcers and alimony complications, if any, you may rate the eternal follies of mankind in different order. But, surely, your list must include pretty girls, good food, plenty of money, strong whisky—and gambling. It would be presumptuous for me to sermonize about gambling, so all I say is, It's *here* and apparently here to stay.

The average deck of 52 cards, plus its jokers, each card being 3½ inches long, would extend 189 inches. Now, take pencil and paper and multiply 189 x 60,000,000. (This is the average number of packs manufactured and sold yearly just in the U.S., according to the Association of American Playing Card Manufacturers.)

Next, convert the total into miles, and you will come up with the impressive figure of 178,977.27 miles. (At least, I did.)

Thus, laid end to end as statisticians pixieishly present their results, the decks bought yearly by our card-loving public would make seven bridges around the world at the equatorial circumference, with about 5,000 miles left over. A difficult trick, even for a master prestidigitator, I concede, but I think you read my message.

Bar none, with both men and women, cardplaying is far and away the biggest participant sport in the country. Three out of four Americans play cards or play at cards.

Surveys show that practically 'nine out of ten homes boast at least one deck of cards, and most are probably two- and three-deck families. Even television can't distract us from cut, shuffle and deal. As a matter of fact, more cards are played in homes with TV than in those without it. And despite inflation, an estimated 100,000 couples still play penny-ante, or "poor man's poker," every Saturday night.

When the cops come marching in

Nine out of ten players, or so they say, engage merely in those "friendly" games at home or at a neighbor's home—and there's the rub, as we have already seen! By police definition, a "friendly" game is one in which no homicide, assault or fraud is *known* to have occurred, which is a rather negative endorsement when you come to think of it.

Interestingly, people prefer canasta, contract bridge, pinochle, poker and solitaire in that order. Numbers six through ten on the card parade are rummy, 500, auction bridge, hearts and gin rummy. Running a close 11th is cribbage, which is particularly favored only in New England and the Far West.

(The reason is probably that mariners find it easy to play, two-handed, in restricted quarters. During their long voyage under the Arctic icecap, the crew of the atomic submarine *Nautilus* kept their minds diverted with cribbage.)

Among men, the preference is for poker, pinochle, canasta and contract bridge, in that order. The ladies genteelly go for canasta, contract bridge, solitaire (old maids' solace?) and rummy.

Now I want to make a rather brash statement, and please don't throw in your hand until you have heard me out.

Forget sex, game, gentility or geography. *Wherever* cards are played, there is flagrant cheating!

Forget, too, for the moment, the notorious spots like Miami, Covington, Ky., and the rackets-controlled games that flourish through New Jersey, Pennsylvania, Tennessee and points west. In these, it would offend the deepest ethical principles of the crooked gamblers to let you leave unplucked.

Oh, those clever Egyptians!

No, I am talking about the "friendly" games, so-called, which may be neighborhood, club, convention, hotel or fast "pickup" action while traveling. They may be cards, craps, even loaded tiddlywinks or marked dominoes! Yes, I can steer you to a place where you can purchase a set of dominoes, unobtrusively marked with tiny imperfections, for $125.

And there's nothing in the least new about all this. In Chicago, the Natural History Museum possesses several pairs of bone or soapstone dice, which look remarkably like present-day "ivories," though they were discovered in ancient Egyptian tombs. They are loaded to throw twos and fives.

Sadly, a card or dice cheat doesn't have to be particularly talented to take the average, trusting player. As a matter of fact, most of the crooks whom I personally know have mastered only one or two cheating methods. Patiently, they sit through a long game, losing frequently and waiting for the big pot, the kill, to cheat and win. They get away with it, night after night, only because several factors are running heavily in their favor.

First, with very few exceptions, there hasn't been a worthwhile, up-to-date book exposé on gambling in years. One of my favorites, *Gambling and Gambling Devices,* by a repentant thief named John Philip Quinn, was published back in 1912. Another, which I found even more difficult to obtain for my gambling library, *Sharps and Flats,* by John Nevil Maskelyne, came out in 1894.

Would you believe it? Many of the "exposés" I read today are taken right out of Quinn and Maskelyne! They expose antiquated, even *extinct* forms of cheating that would be scorned today by the cheapest three-card-monte swindler furtively operating in the doorway of a vacant store.

What's a compact between friends?

I would expect the professional gambler to know all the more common tricks, though, on occasion, he can be fooled too. After all, it is his business to use not only his eyes but also his sense of touch, smell and hearing to detect various kinds of cheating.

He knows, for example, that the glass ashtray or highly polished compact, placed *so* casually on the table, is a "shiner" that will reflect kings, queens and aces to the dealer who is a "glim worker." He listens for a certain kind of phony dealing which is too fast for him to detect with his eyes. If his nose is keen, he can actually smell cards that have been doctored with a preparation to facilitate false dealings. (All these "gaffs," as the cheats call them, will be described more fully as we go along.)

On the other hand, if you have spent your time more virtuously than learning how to steal money across a card table, you can scarcely be expected to know these tricks. But, I must add, you *will* lose your money!

Thus, public ignorance and trust play into the hands of the cheats. But that isn't all. Another advantage going for these strange persons who work so desperately hard to avoid work, is the existence of a shady, coast-to-coast industry manufacturing cheating devices of every conceivable variety thought up by the larcenous mind of man.

These tricks (many of them custom-made to the gambler's specifications) range from "shiners," cleverly designed into finger rings and cufflinks, to elaborate "hold-out" machines, which are prosthetic-like contraptions strapped to the player's arm and concealed under his shirtsleeve. They include $350 electronic sending-receiving sets, delicate tools with which the do-it-yourself cheat can mark and "strip" cards to his own liking and many other "gaffs" which an honest person wouldn't dream of suspecting. For obvious reasons, few of these devices are inexpensive, and some of them cost as much as $1,200.

Just the manufacture and sale of marked cards is almost an industry in itself. There are eight or more major makers and retailers, three of the largest being located right in the heart of New York City. I know. I have shopped in them. According to reliable sources, an estimated 100,000 such decks are printed yearly, and the crooks make as much as $20,000,000 annually in using them.

Where do you get all this cheating paraphernalia? Throughout the country, in most any large-sized city, you will find "joke" and "novelty" shops, many of which are merely fronts for peddling the stuff. Of course, first you will have to win the confidence of the proprietor.

Surprisingly, there also is a flourishing mail-order business in supplyng crooked devices to crooked men and, now that I have been able to get my name on the list, I regularly receive catalogues from the Middle West and the West Coast.

All these fraudulent cards, dice, tools and other cheating gear are sold with the pious reservation, "Only for exposé or entertainment purposes." Sometimes, I think half the country must be magicians—and the other half dead set on "exposing" them.

But there is a corollary fraud, too. Much of the wares represent dated, overpriced junk, and the amateur crook who aspires to take his neighbors may well find that, first, the supply houses have taken him. A little later, I will spell out exactly how the professional cheat swindles the amateur cheat.

But it requires little imagination to guess how the shrewd purchasers employ these tricks. Many are employed in big factories and make more money out of one game than they could from a week's honest work at time-and-a-half. Many have infiltrated veterans' posts. (Certainly, they're veterans themselves; they hustled every payday during their 20-year hitches!) Many are floaters who work conventions, ships, planes and hotels for the hit-and-run dollar.

Beware the "businessman"!

Unfortunately, many, many persons are determined to believe that such high-wide-and-crooked gambling went out with the old-fashioned faro dealers who wore stovepipe hats and worked the Mississippi River steamboats a century ago. Actually, nothing has changed, except that gambling has become treacherously refined.

By today's standards, the old-timers were rather crude in their operation and absurdly obvious in appearance. I have rubbed cards with many of them, and the only Gaylord Ravenals, the only waxed mustaches I have ever seen are in the costume movies.

Figure 7. Here is one variation of a one-handed "peek," which is especially good for black-jack.

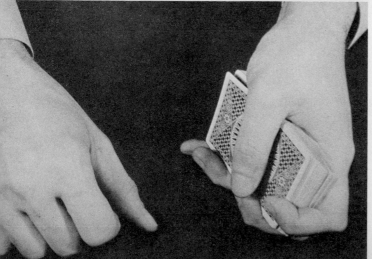

Figure 8. Another variation of the one-handed "peek." Notice the squeezing grip which enables "mechanic" to simultaneously "peek" four top cards from the rear.

No, the present-day cheats are "businessmen" who dress quietly and talk softly. They make a point of handling the cards clumsily, even dropping them occasionally. They are courteous, almost diffident and deadly. Only when they relax among themselves do they employ their special vocabulary, a ripe, wonderful form of trade talk that has undertones of Broadway, the race tracks and the underworld.

But this is a private language that they never share with outsiders. As part of my work, I've had to learn it, of course. You will be amused, I think, if you glance through my glossary at the end of the book—and it may also come as an eye-opener to find how many contemptuous definitions they have for an honest man.

Unlike the Klondike Sals historically associated with gambling, today's women cheats are well mannered and fashionably dressed in outfits that are restrained in cut and color. Many seem to be respectable, suburban-type ladies. In fact, there is a new and disturbing trend among women gamblers.

More and more, I find, they include housewives and working girls who obviously don't *need* the money. Rather, they are willing to degrade themselves for the excitement and the opportunity to realize tax-free windfalls which they can spend on fur coats, jewels and winter cruises. I have had some very uncomfortable experiences in exposing them.

Never trust a grandmother!

Matter of fact, my friend and mentor, John Scarne, the great authority on crooked card and dice gambling, swears that he knows a 75-year-old grandmother who cheats regularly at gin rummy. She is what is known to the profession as "a peeker," "a glimpser" or "a glim worker." Each hand, she steals a look at the next card while picking up her own.

"When you are gambling, you shouldn't trust your *own* grandmother," John advises. "Where it involves money and gambling, they're all out to get you!"

From my own experience, particularly with the ladies, as I shall set forth, I couldn't agree more.

Another friend of mine, the late Sergeant Audley Walsh, of Ridgefield Park, N.J., a brilliant small-town cop, spent more than a quarter of a century and thousands of his own dollars to become a nationally known authority on crooked gambling. Time and again, I remember, Audley used to caution me:

"Don't gamble at all! But if you do, then stay clear of strangers, and watch out for those 'friendly little' games!"

A hair from the horse's tail

I wish every skeptic could have had the opportunity, as I did, to browse through Audley Walsh's "Chamber of Gambling Horrors." His $35,000 collection included about 8,000 decks of cards (some of them dating back to the 1600s), 2,000 pairs of dice, dozens of faro boxes, carnival wheels, roulette wheels, chuckaluck cages and whatnots. Save for a few antiques, they were all completely phony.

The cards represented the most artistically executed "paper work," the dice always (or never) rolled seven, the various wheels were manipulated by friction brakes, electricity, electronics or a hair from a horse's tail to stop wherever the operator desired, which naturally wasn't where the patrons had their money down.

Surprisingly, the old-fashioned horse's hair wheel has one great virtue that the most advanced electronic gadgets do not possess. On seeing trouble approach, the operator quickly snaps off the hair, thus disposing of the evidence. Neat and no need to cry, "Hey, rube!"

Figure 9. Audley Walsh, late New Jersey policeman, who was one of country's greatest authorities on crooked gambling, with part of his "Chamber of Horrors" collection of "gaffed" devices. Everything in this photo is crooked!

In ten minutes, Walsh himself could fix any deck of cards, any wheel or any *bingo* layout (which gives you something to think about if you like that innocent-seeming card-and-disc game). But the sad thing, as he said to me, was that men calling themselves "gamblers" were greedy enough to tamper with the wheels.

Even on an "honest," nonfixed carnival wheel, the odds are 120 to 1 against the player!

Yes, in barefaced cheating or in odds so grossly unfair that it comes down to cheating, Americans are being stolen blind every year. Though some of the individual "grifts" are penny-ante operations, the total pot divided by the gamblers is incredibly large. According to the estimates of federal officials, the "handle" or total take from all forms of gaming may run as high as $47 *billions* annually.

To many persons, this figure will sound preposterous. However, *The Nation,* a respected magazine, devoted an entire issue to the fruits of its own investigation and, from my own observations all over the country, I couldn't agree more with the shocked conclusions of the editors:

"Professional gambling today is the most lucrative, most destructive and withal most widely tolerated form of crime in the country. . . . Each year the revenues that pour into the coffers of Gambling Inc. are used to bribe elected officials, to oil political machines and to corrupt police and other law-enforcement agencies on a scale so staggering that it has not yet been truly measured."

You can't *win if—*

When you translate this into terms of your own pocketbook, there is only one answer, short of legal, honestly controlled gambling. You simply *must* learn to protect yourself, and get a fair share, a fair deal, a fair price for your money.

You won't do that if you try to buck impossible house odds.

You won't do it if you shoot craps with a professional who knows the "Greek roll" (about which more later), the correct odds and all the sucker bets.

You won't do it if you try to play cards with a "mechanic" who has mastered the various false cuts, shuffles and deals.

You certainly won't do it if you bet by "system," hunch or dream book.

"Systems," hunches, dreams are all for the birds—that is, for "the pigeons," as the pros scornfully call suckers. Mathematicians (and I don't mean those shabby characters who calculate the racing form over a cup of coffee in the Automat) say flatly that *no* system will safely conquer a game of pure chance. I appreciate how tempting some of them seem, but remember, *No* system works.

The little tailor and the ghostly voice

Except that millions of misguided bettors naïvely, superstitiously persist in playing them, I would prefer to ignore dreams and hunches altogether. What *I* think of them (especially when they come up against a crooked operation that is a match for a dream any time) is summed up in one of the classic stories told and retold among gamblers themselves.

Once upon a time, there was a little New York tailor who sold his shop for $1,500 and struck out bravely for Las Vegas to make his fortune on the roulette table.

The first night, his "system" cost him $1,200, and he was prudent enough to cash in his remaining chips and start driving right home. Maybe, he thought, he could put the $300 down on another shop and start tailoring anew.

Suddenly, driving through the desert with not a car in sight, he heard a voice behind him.

"Go ba-ack," commanded the ghostly whisper. "Tu-urn a-around. Go ba-ack, I sa-ay."

The tailor looked in the back seat, lifted the hood, even looked under the car. There was no one any place. It was a true voice. So he returned to Vegas and, as soon as the casino opened, bought $200 worth of chips.

"Put it a-all on the red," he heard. He looked around, but none of the other players seemed to have overheard the instructions.

"I sa-aid the re-ed," the voice repeated impatiently.

With a resigned shrug, the tailor shoved out all his chips just in time. The ball landed on the red, paying 2-to-1. Now he had a $400 stake.

"Put it a-all on 35," the voice directed. As he hesitated, the voice said sharply, "I sa-aid 35." Again, the little tailor won, and $400 times 35 now gave him a bankroll of $14,000. He was in business!

Right through till early morning, every time he heard the voice he played and, when it came down to the closing bet, only he and the harassed croupier still were at the table. But by now, the tailor almost owned the casino, and so the pit man and the manager strolled over to watch the action.

"Put a-all the mo-oney on the double-0," the voice ordered.

Unhesitatingly, the tailor pushed a mountain of chips onto the double-0.

The croupier blinked. He looked imploringly toward the pit man who glanced toward the manager, who made a barely perceptible signal.

The wheel spun, the ball bobbled. It dropped onto the double-0. Then, just as mysteriously as the voice had come to the tailor out of nowhere, the ball climbed up—and dropped onto No. 17.

The little tailor started crying and then, for the last time in his life, he heard the voice once more.

"Ah, nu-uts!" it whispered disgustedly.

The story may be apocryphal, but I prefer to believe it. Even a power from the spirit world cannot beat Vegas.

Win or lose, I lose

Almost from boyhood, I have been observing and practicing every form of card trick I ever heard or read about, because you can't expose them unless you can duplicate them.

For the secrets of some, gamblers have offered me considerable sums of money, but I'm not in the business of coaching cheats. There is a school for crooked gamblers in Chicago—let them matriculate there.

However, I do take pupils when I am convinced of their honesty and, as I write this, I am giving card-trick lessons to a retired Nevada croupier, temporarily down on his luck. He assures me piously (and I believe sincerely) that he merely intends to go into show business as a magician.

When I told him that I plan to reveal almost everything I have learned, he was incredulous. "You're going to expose all kinds of 'gaffs,'" he asked. "Aren't you afraid the boys will work you over?"

Yes, within the bounds of libel, I am going to tell as much as I can. *No,* I'm not particularly afraid of being beaten up, though it is a possibility. It's not that I am a hero, but I *despise* crooks of all kinds. My own Dad was let in "on a sure thing" as soon as he landed on the docks of New York from his native Spain many years ago. The sure thing, of course, was a swindle that took all his hard-earned dollars.

If a person enjoys a game of cards, I think he is entitled to expect an *honest* game. I know I like to play myself every once in a while— and I don't always win. (Of course, my situation *is* a little peculiar. If I do win, I have to accept suspicious, sidelong glances as I rake in the pot. And if I don't, I'm sure to hear, "So *you're* an expert!")

The way I feel is this. There is only a handful of *real* pros in my profession, and they are getting along in years. I want to make sure that their fine work doesn't go for naught by adding what little I can to the education of the public.

But even if you learn as much from this book as I hope you do, I foresee no technological unemployment. The "gaffs" keep changing, and I must keep up with the new ones. The criminal I may expose today in Bridgeport, Conn., will work as a shill in Omaha, Neb., till he gets up another stake. And there are so many naive, trusting card players everywhere!

So, I say, if you gamble and lose, that's your business. If you gamble and get cheated, then it becomes *my* business.

Now let me tell you about some of the more common tricks by which you may be victimized. They are widely used because they can be mastered fairly easily, and most crooked gamblers are plain lazy.

CHAPTER **III**

♠
♥
♦
♣
♠
♥
♦

BEWARE THESE COMMON TRICKS!

♣
♠
♥
♦

IN CROOKED GAMBLING, as in all professions, there are varying degrees of mastery and even genius—and there are also bums.

The best way to cheat at the card table is by the use of decks that have been premarked subtly and artistically, so subtly, in fact, that even another cheat cannot spot the markings unless he knows precisely what he is looking for. To explain marked cards requires many illustrations, and I will devote a later chapter to them.

In a more humble way, there are two techniques by which cards can be marked *during* play, and the odds are uncomfortably close that you may be victimized by these "gaffs," as the crooks call them.

First, many frauds scratch or prick the cards with various implements so they can identify them by *touch*. Second, there are what I call the "chemists and cosmeticians" of the cheating profession, who employ a number of concoctions in "smudgy moves" to identify the cards by *color*. In either case, only the high cards need be marked.

The ladies, bless 'em

Primitively, cards were slightly burred on the edges with a fingernail that had been sharpened to a tiny point. Though I have found in my research that the "nail punch" is an ancient fraud, the technique still is used widely today by those gamblers naturally blessed with sharp, long nails that attract no suspicion—the lady larcenists, as we shall see.

Men cheats, however, were soon forced to devise artificial punches, consisting of tiny metal points affixed to the first joint of the right

20

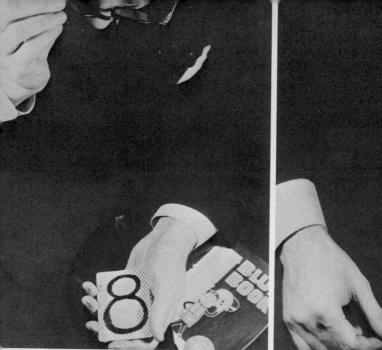
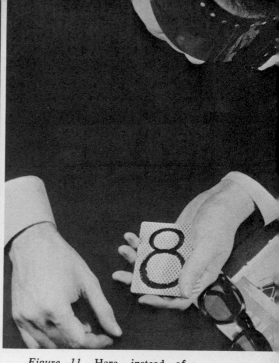

Figure 10. With luminous "readers," a new form of marked cards, you can't lose. Large figure "8" on back of card becomes visible only after author has donned tinted glasses.

Figure 11. Here, instead of wearing tinted glasses, author is using a doctored eyeshade to get the same results.

Figure 12. The notorious "hump" system for marking cards. In top card, notice the "hump" near right-hand corner; in bottom card, right at the corner. "Hump" at corner usually signifies an ace. Other bulges running leftward along top of card or down the side progressively indicate King, Queen, Jack, etc.

Figure 13. Three places where part of design can be blocked out to show value or suit are indicated by arrows. Compare with the untampered portions of the design.

thumb. With them, in the gambler's argot, they "blister," "punch" or "hump" the aces and court cards.

At the modest price of three for $3, you can purchase thumb pricks today from the gaming supply houses, along with the special adhesive tape necessary to attach them. You can also pay considerably more. I happen to possess a solid gold punch, custom-made to my own specifications, which cost me $10.

More refined, but unfortunately more ostentatious in sophisticated circles, is the "poker ring." This seemingly ordinary finger ring conceals on its underside a needlepoint only 1/64th of an inch in length. As the player holds his cards, he can mark any of them by casually pressing them against the needle with either thumb.

One difficulty in "punching" is that, during fast play, the operator may miss the card he is trying to mark. This drawback was remedied by a famous gambler (now retired and living in Rhode Island) who devised the *double* punch. He invented a punch with two points so that, if one missed the intended card, the second point would surely prick it.

However, there is an even graver obstacle in all the pricking techniques. The gambler cannot see the marks on cards being held by the other players. He only feels them when he is handling the deck himself.

Thus, "punching" can be fully utilized only by "second dealers." These are artists who can keep holding back the top card for themselves or their confederates (if touch tells them it is a high one) while dealing "seconds," the cards under the top, to the other players.

You can tell a crooked deck by its color

For crooks with less supple fingers, the discovery of "shade work" represented a marvelous advance in the art of marking while the game was in progress.

Originally, the cheat carried a blue aniline pencil in his pocket and, occasionally rubbing the point on his finger, furtively deepened the tint on blue-backed cards. This method is described by an early English authority, who felt compelled to add an unhappy tribute to American enterprise:

"Across the water, superior intelligence soon concocted a coloured paste which would answer the purpose much better. Scooping a hole in a piece of cork, the cavity was filled with the composition, and the cork was sewn inside the lower edge of the waistcoat. In this position, the colour was convenient to the hand.

"The idea thus conceived has been improved upon until one may say that this method has reached perfection in the form of appliances

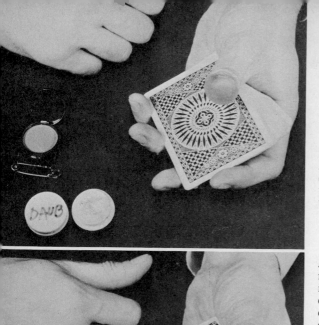

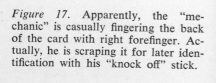

Figure 14. Author preparing to mark card with "daub," a pasty concoction that will give it almost imperceptible tint. Notice his left thumb.

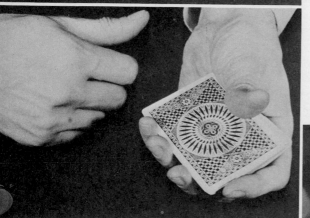

Figure 15. With left thumb, he has now daubed the top card. "Mechanics" conceal daub in match books, tie clips, cufflinks—even behind their ears. So beware the player who fiddles nervously with jewelry or plucks at his ears during play.

Figure 16. Notice the tiny strip of sandpaper affixed to first finger of right hand. This is a "knock off" or "sandtell" stick to mark cards by roughing the edges or backs.

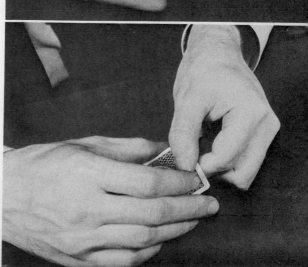

Figure 17. Apparently, the "mechanic" is casually fingering the back of the card with right forefinger. Actually, he is scraping it for later identification with his "knock off" stick.

known as 'shading boxes.' These implements of chicanery are little nickel-plated boxes which are completely filled with the coloured composition. In the center of the lid is a slot through which the colour is pressed. The finger being passed over this slot takes up a little of the colour."

Soon, shading boxes came in pairs (for both red and blue coloring), their bases prepierced with holes so they could be sewn inside the vest or under the flap of a side pocket. The composition was a mixture of melted olive oil, stearine, camphor and the particular dye, from which the superfluous oil had been kneaded out with a knife. The great virtue of the paste was that merely rubbing the card on the table would remove it, thus destroying the evidence.

Ah, the wonders of twentieth century chemistry!

Since this wry tribute to Yankee enterprise in the last century, American gamblers have maintained their acknowledged leadership in "cosmetic" cheating.

Thanks to continuing research in chemical laboratories, the game supply houses today offer improved colored concoctions exotically named at reasonable prices and a remarkable variety of colors. There is even a *luminous* daub visible only with the aid of luminous glasses or visor. Considering its chemical intricacy, it seems most modestly priced at $3.50 per box. But I am sure that it doesn't work too well.

Some gambling experts maintain that "shade work" is a dying art, but the current catalogues I receive from game supply houses flatly disprove this. The houses are briskly competing with each other for the patronage of the "cosmeticians," and have sharply cut their prices to the neighborhood of $2 to $4 per box or bottle.

For example, one house located in New York gravely describes its "daub" as a concoction "used primarily for preparing cards while giving a demonstration" (!) and then boasts:

"Our DAUB is absolutely different and superior to any of the daubs sold by other houses and we know from expressions from customers that this daub has no equal. It is applied by touching the container with the finger tip and then pressing the card on the position desired. The color will match perfectly and will never dry out. It is not GREASY, therefore will not smear. Priced the same as others ask for common daub."

That is, $2 for the red· or blue daub and "also furnished in GREEN as this color is used at times under colored lights" (all three for $6).

But, ah, softly cries another supply house that lurks modestly behind a postoffice box number in a certain California town:

"Our Instant Shading Daub has met with great success. It will not show on the fingers, will not flash on the cards, is not greasy and is absolutely permanent when applied. Our Daub is toned down, making it impossible to apply too much. We guarantee our Daub to be the best you have ever used."

How to tell a "shade worker"

Can one possibly improve on perfection? Yes, advertises this same house. By paying only $1 more (or $3 per box) for its Golden Glow Daub. This goo is ecstatically described as "the finest one color Daub ever manufactured for use on red, blue, green, brown or any colored back cards, with or without white border. Golden Glow Daub is different from all others as it leaves a delicate golden smoky glow shade on the card which is very hard to detect."

How far we have progressed from such primitive markings as "the ashtray smudge" and "Chink Ink"! But ancient as these latter tricks are, they are still occasionally used, and you should be alert to them.

If you find yourself playing with a heavy smoker, watch carefully as he puts his cigar into the ashtray. Just possibly, he may mark the cards by rubbing a bit of ashes onto them. On the other hand, "Chink Ink" (sometimes called Monte Tell) is an early form of daub that is applied to the *edges* of cards. You can now purchase it in black, blue or red.

Whichever his particular technique, new or old, the "shade worker" is difficult for the amateur to expose. Sooner or later, since he always knows the disposition of the high cards, he may betray himself by his betting, if he is greedy. That is, he will drop when seemingly he has a good hand, and stay with a mediocre one (which he, of course, knows is good enough to win).

But if he is an experienced, self-disciplined shade man, you are in for trouble! He will play a tightly conservative game, dropping a number of small pots and conserving his powers of divination for the kill. Even if you suspect his betting pattern, you can't challenge him, for it is only a clue and not evidence.

Unless you have the skill to palm several of the high cards for later inspection, I can only offer this advice: *Just stop playing with him.*

Sometimes, you can smell trouble

There is still a different breed of "cosmeticians" who employ concoctions not to mark cards but to facilitate crooked dealing. Their favorite brand is applied to the aces to make them slippery.

Thus, when the dealer starts to cut the deck, he taps its side in a seemingly clumsy gesture as he picks up the cards. This causes a break at one of the aces. A few such cuts, a series of shuffles, and presto! Eventually, he works all four aces together where he wants them to be, either at the top or bottom.

Some supply houses claim to have "secret" formulae compounded "by our own chemists." This is false, as well as unethical, advertising. They have merely bought automobile wax, perhaps thinned it to make it more bland like cold cream, then relabeled it in a jar about the size of a shotglass.

And, of course, priced it for a fantastic markup.

While this gaff is extremely efficacious, there are two ways by which you may detect it. If the paste has been improperly applied, the cards will be slightly discolored. And, do you remember, I mentioned earlier that gamblers sometimes employ their sense of smell to detect trickery? If your nose is keen, you will sniff a faint, gasoline-like aroma.

The downfall of "Suitcase Charlie"

Of course, in "nail-punching," "thumb-pricking" and all the "smudgy moves," the goal is theft of the pot. Thus, many years ago, to a now-forgotten cheat, there came an inspiration classic in its simplicity. Why not bypass the tedious techniques that take time to master, he reasoned, and steal the pot *direct*.

"I care not who *wins* the pot, so long as I 'cop' the checks (or chips)," was his slogan. So his form of naked larceny became known as "check copping." That is, "copping" or stealing the checks, chips and coins right off the table even when he loses the pot.

This was accomplished originally by an ordinary bit of beeswax concealed in the palm. The "check copper" would helpfully push the chips and coins toward the winner, at the same time affixing several of them to the underside of his hands. As he withdrew his hands, palms down, he would drop the loot unnoticed into a pocket.

Today, better than beeswax, packets of prepared check cop are available for $3 in strip form which the crook then cuts into small discs or squares. And still better, because of its invisibility, is a liquid form at the same price.

Matter of fact, if a crook is broke, he can make his own. Once, I remember, when I was keeping tabs on a character known as "Suitcase Charlie" for professional reasons, I dropped in unexpectedly at his little furnished room in Brooklyn and surprised him in the act.

Charlie had pinned one end of a roll of adhesive tape to his bureau, the sticky side facing the ceiling, and was heating the underside with a match. As the gum started to bubble, he scraped it off with a razor. When he saw me, he shrugged disgustedly.

"Here, take it," he said. "If you're sitting in tonight, there won't be any percentage for me, anyhow."

To veteran players, "check coppers" become obvious after a few hands. They are constantly reaching into their pockets, ostensibly for gum, cigarettes or matches, actually to transfer their loot from the lap to a pocket. Experienced ones can perform this maneuver in a moment, but the St. Vitus dance with the hands always gives them away.

By and large, "coppers" are crooks too stupid, lazy or slow-fingered to master more refined tricks and, as you can imagine, they command little status among crooked gamblers. "Suitcase Charlie" was no exception and, on one occasion, I recall, he distinguished himself by committing the most unpardonable mistake in the cheating profession. He got drunk on the job.

During the evening, he kept solicitously pushing the pots toward the various winners, making a good commission for himself each time. Though he didn't win once, in his deplorable condition he forgot to grouse, as "check coppers" should to divert any suspicion.

Worse, he even forgot to drop his loot into his pocket.

So, despite his losses, the pile of chips and coins in front of him kept growing instead of dwindling till it became obvious to all the other players.

"How come you haven't taken a pot all night—but you have more chips than when you started?" one challenged him.

For a moment, there was silence. Then "Suitcase Charlie" thought fast. That is, for him and especially in his condition.

Glaring right back at his accuser, he exclaimed in outrage, "Why, *you* fellows must be fattening me for a kill!"

By unanimous request, Charlie then departed from the game.

Now, from such chicanery, let's turn in contrast to one of the true *artists* of the profession. He operated well before my time, for which I am most grateful. I am sure he would have fooled me, as he did his contemporaries.

CHAPTER **IV**

TRIBUTE TO A FORGOTTEN ARTIST

"The very finest holdout the world has ever seen is that known as the Kepplinger or San Francisco. This machine in its latest forms is certainly a masterpiece. Yet so little appreciation has the world for true genius that the inventor of this marvellous piece of apparatus is practically unknown to the vast majority of his fellow-men."—Sharps and Flats

In the almost seven decades since the worldly-wise British author, John Nevil Maskelyne, wrote this sad tribute, the same unkind obscurity has dogged P. J. (*The Lucky Dutchman*) Kepplinger. Though he has been called "a notorious master cheat and cardsharp," in this chapter I want to offer my own nosegay of appreciation.

Kepplinger was far more than a pre-eminent hustler; he invented and daringly operated the most complicated, ingenious and successful contraption in the history of crooked gambling. And, transcending the mean souls around him, he displayed the dedication of the *artist*.

With his creation, which has been well described as "a complexity of strings, wheels, joints, tubes, pulleys and working parts," he could have taken the innocents night after night, to his immense profit, till in the palsy of age he could no longer manipulate his apparatus.

But he scorned such easy pickings, instead playing "hard" games with cheats of equal eminence, and, even in these, he scorned ordinary prudence.

Kepplinger could not bring himself to allow his masterpiece to lose at least occasionally, even on some of the smaller pots, which would

28

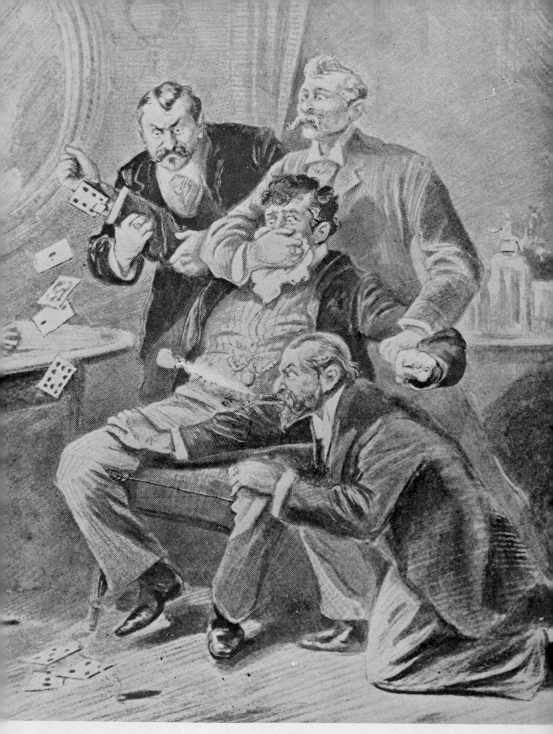

Figure 18. "Trembling with fury and rage, he tugged and snarled, but it was of no avail—the secret was out!" Kepplinger, master of the holdout machine, being mugged by other gamblers who muscle in on his invention.

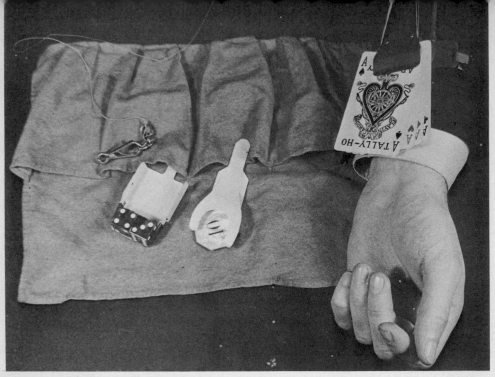

Figure 19. Card holdout machine in retreating position. (In actual use, of course, machine would be worn under sleeve and the withheld card would not be visible.)

Figure 20. Holdout machine in "sneaking" position as it feeds withheld card into player's hand. Also illustrated are other devices to "cop" or switch dice and to steal poker chips.

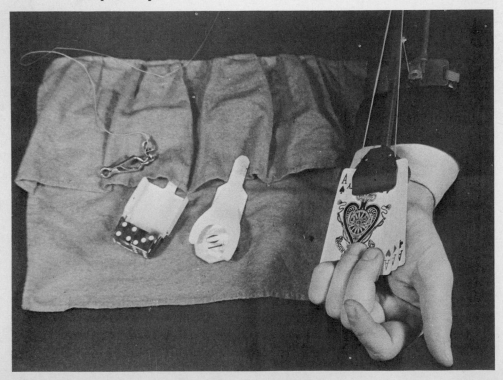

have allayed suspicion. And thus, alas, he suffered the fate of so many proud, high-souled artists who will not compromise with practicality. He was exposed.

This ain't just history, brother!

But to understand the brilliancy of Kepplinger's achievement, the tragedy of his fall, you first must know something about holdouts.

And, I hasten to add, this is no mere essay on antique cheating, *for holdouts still are being used today*. I doubt you would run up against another Kepplinger, though "Smoky Joe," whom I will tell you about in a minute or two, is a superb current master of the machine.

Most probably, you would encounter a cheaper mechanic operating a cheaper machine, and you should know what to look for. Let me fill you in first on the background so you will understand these clever contraptions.

Back in the eleventh century, many historians believe, one S'eun Ho, Emperor of China, invented the first playing cards to entertain his many wives and possibly to unburden himself of their fatiguing attentions. By the twelfth century, I'll wager, the Chinese, being alert people, were already devising the first fumbling holdouts, for these devices practically insure victory. Certainly it is a curious coincidence that the "Heathen Chinee" in Bret Harte's fable of crooked poker was a holdout artist.

In essence, this technique allows you to abstract the high cards, conceal them on your person or under the table and then reintroduce them into play whenever you need them. A man who has one or two aces comfortably stashed in his sleeve plays a relaxed, happy, successful game of cards.

If by chance the ancient Chinese overlooked this excellent device, the rakehells of well over a century ago certainly did not. However, their holdouts were manual rather than mechanical.

A dropped card and a dropped gambler

In an era when men's clothing, with its frilled cuffs, ruffled and pleated shirtfronts and wide-cuffed jackets, was simply tailor-made for crooked gambling, the cheats stored "coolers," or previously prepared decks, all over their persons.

Casually straightening a cuff or toying with a ruffle, they introduced them into the play at will. In time, however, it got so that even if a gamester *sincerely* reached for a pinch of snuff, he was immediately suspect. Obviously, more ingenuity was called for on the part of the crooks.

The first reputed mechanical holdout is described by the great French conjurer, Jean Eugène Robert Houdin, famed for his mechanical magic effects and the first illusionist to use electromagnetism. In his auto-biography, written more than a century ago, Houdin reported the exist-ence of a cuffbox large enough to hold a complete pack of doctored cards. *"La boite à la Manche,"* as he termed it, was concealed in the forepart of the coat sleeve—along with a pair of pincers large enough to grasp an entire deck.

As he picked the legitimate pack off the table, Houdin explained, the gambler pressed his forearm down lightly. The pressure ejected his hidden, prepared pack into his hand, and also activated the pincers to seize the honest deck and deposit it in the cuffbox. Presumably, of course, none of the other players noticed the cheat had the burly right arm of a weight lifter.

Only once, when the pincers failed and an extra card fluttered onto the table, was the fraud exposed—and the unlucky gambler shot in the ensuing duel. At least, according to Houdin's story.

As a matter of fact, there is considerable skepticism among historians of fakery whether Houdin really *saw* this monster holdout or was merely passing on gaming rumor of the period. At any rate, the machine was far too unwieldy and erratic for general use.

It was the increasing popularity of poker (in which even one good card supplies an enormous advantage) that attracted the better minds of the cheating world to the possibilities of a workable holdout.

A penny, a bug, an awl

Probably the first successful technique was devised by a player, his name now lost, who had two peculiarities. He always played with his back to the wall and always seemed to tire early in the game, frequently yawning and stretching his arms.

Actually, he would palm a card and, in stretching, tuck it behind his coat collar. Another yawn and stretch would bring it back into play.

Once detected, of course, this elemental holdout was forever useless, though to this day a variation called the *coup de cuisse* is practiced widely. In this maneuver, the card held out is deposited under the knee. Thus, any casual-seeming movement such as hitching the chair backward or forward or adjusting the trouser legs, *which allows the hands to drop below the table,* should make you immediately suspicious.

Now and then today, cheats even use "the bug," probably the world's first table holdout. This device consists of a bit of watchspring attached to a shoemaker's awl and a penny, the latter serving as the base. Then the awl is stuck into the underside of the table so the spring lies flat, projecting slightly beyond the table edge toward the cheat.

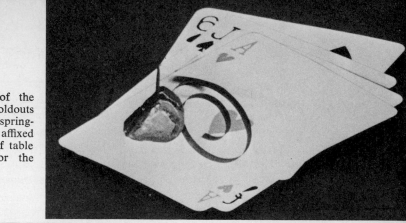

Figure 21. One of the most primitive holdouts is the "bug," a spring-like contraption affixed to the underside of table to hold cards for the "mechanic."

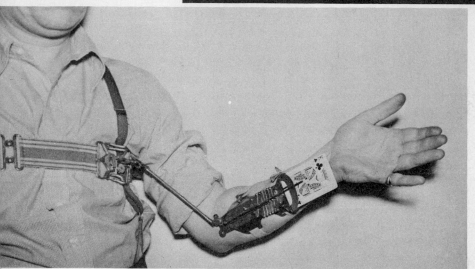

Figure 22. Audley Walsh demonstrates the "gamblers'" or chest holdout. He takes a deep breath, and the King of Clubs is retracted into his sleeve.

Figure 23. Now Audley Walsh exhales, and the chest holdout sneaks the King into his palm. The chest holdout represents a refinement on Kepplinger's original invention.

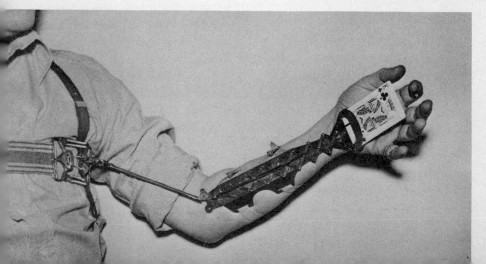

The operator, covering his cards with his hands, held them near the table edge so that he could thumb the desired ones between the spring and table. With a similar maneuver, he later brought them back into his hand. (The so-called "suction table holdout," which is often advertised today, is merely an inferior variation of the same gadget, a suction cup and paper clip being substituted for awl and watchspring.)

Pass a card through the table, partner

As the Age of Invention flowered in America, the misguided Goodyears and Edisons of crookdom kept pace with the more prosaic and honest inventions, devising many strange contraptions for the card cheat.

Some were as simple as the ring holdout (still being used) for bighanded players. This is merely a thin blade of bone affixed to any finger ring so that a card may be held snugly against the palm. Some were as complicated as the "Chicago poker table" and the "check-slot" combination holdouts. These were ordinary round poker tables equipped with check slots for depositing the players' chips. With a squeeze of the hand, the slots would disappear into the table, leaving a holdout for cards.

The "check-slot combination" table possessed a superb additional advantage. There was a narrow slit beneath the playing surface through which one confederate could pass a card clear across the board to his partner without detection!

Gradually, either because they were too simple or too complicated, most of these devices fell into disfavor. However, you should remember, every so often old and forgotten "gaffs" are revived for use against a new generation of innocents.

A spider on the coat

Next, thinking cheats began concentrating on vest and sleeve holdouts. The first vest work was accurately and derisively christened "the breastplate," because it covered most of the operator's chest. He was burdened down almost like a medieval knight.

Later, for both vest and sleeves, there were lighter devices worn within the crook's clothing. These consisted primarily of a "sneak" (which grasped the heldout cards) and attached cords that ran from the "sneak" down to the operator's shoe.

As he moved his foot, the tightening on the cord forced the "sneak" to the edge of his vest or sleeve seam where the card was affixed to it. As he relaxed the pressure by moving his foot again, an elastic cord retracted the "sneak" inside his clothing.

More simply, the "coat spider" and vest holdout (attached by sharp springs to coat sleeve or vest) were merely spring blades that pinioned the held-out cards. However, they were stationary holdouts, much like the "bug" table holdout.

Simplest of all was the cuff pocket tailored into the coat sleeve at the underside of the seam joining sleeve and cuff. Holding the pack in his left hand, the crook inserted his little finger between the cards he wanted and the rest of the deck. Then he raised his left arm so the cuff pocket was level with the deck. Next, ostensibly putting down his cigar or reaching over to count his chips, he reached toward his left side with his right arm. This shielded his left hand which was pushing the desired cards into the cuff pocket.

Later, after he had dealt and allowed the other players to discard and draw to fill their hands, he again made the screening movement with his right arm to "examine" his own hand.

During this maneuver, his left hand extracted the heldout cards from the cuff pocket and dropped them on the top of the deck. Then, discarding, he openly drew the cards he had held out!

However, in all such manipulations of what one writer has sadly called these "deadly implements known as playing cards," there still were snags.

With the vest holdout, for example, the hand had to be drawn over the breast to insert and extract cards. This is a most obvious movement which requires very strong misdirection on the part of the operator, or the other players will spot it. With the cuff pocket, there was often difficulty, as you can readily imagine, in extracting the cards. Even the later addition of a finger-operated slide that literally *threw* them into the player's palm was not foolproof.

Three ounces of deviltry

"Jacob's Ladder," forerunner of all mechanical sleeve holdouts, represented a wholesome step forward. First, there was a sturdy base plate fastened on the underside of the forearm. To one end of the plate was attached a small pair of tongs connected by a rod to a lever.

Merely by pressing on the table, the operator squeezed the lever which activated the rod which pushed out the tongs almost to the edge of the sleeve cuff. When he lifted his arm, thus releasing the pressure on the lever and rod, an elastic band retracted the tongs.

But, again, there were technical difficulties. The cheat had to wear a suspiciously large shirt cuff to conceal his apparatus, and then sometimes the cards snagged in the cuff, causing embarrassment or worse to the player.

Some of these objections were gradually overcome through refined arm and foot pressure machines, adapted both to sleeve and vest work. In fact, one cheater's helper of the Victorian era perfected a three-ounce machine worn halfway down the vest. With pressure of only ¾ of an ounce, the device threw out additional cards behind those already in the crook's hand.

"There are no plates, and no strings, to pull on and no springs that are liable to break or get out of order," he advertised in triumph of this pioneer effort in miniaturization. "This machine is worth fifty of the old style Vest Plates for practical use, and you will say the same after seeing one."

True, perhaps. Yet enough distressing malfunctions persisted—in a risky business that could not tolerate malfunctions—to make prudent gamblers hesitate.

Enter our hero

It was then, in 1888, that P. J. (*The Lucky Dutchman*) Kepplinger, a heavy-set, hard-eyed gambler, embarked on his phenomenally lucky streak in San Francisco.

To this day, because cheats rarely keep diaries or give interviews, no one knows how many weeks, even months, Kepplinger had worked furtively in a hotel room to perfect his masterpiece. But the results are a matter of historical record.

"He sat like a statue at the table," says a contemporary account. "He kept his cards right away from him, he did not move a muscle as far as could be seen. His opponents could look up his sleeve almost to the elbow, and yet he *won*."

These were, remember, card cheats every bit as accomplished as Kepplinger, wise to all the tricks known up to that time, but they couldn't catch him. One gambler, forced out of a game by the master's "luck," once *thought* that he detected "an unnatural movement." After hours of further scrutiny, he was no wiser—and still a very heavy loser.

Finally, three of Kepplinger's professional victims abandoned all pretense of genteel finesse. One night, they kept the game going until all the players except they and Kepplinger had departed. On the pretext of getting a cigar, one of them left the room, locked the front door, doused the outside gaslights and then returned.

A real-life Rube Goldberg

Casually, a second dropped out of the game, got his hat and, apparently leaving, walked behind Kepplinger.

"Then, suddenly and without a moment's warning, Kepplinger was seized, gagged and held hard and fast," says a writer of the period.

As one player held the writhing Kepplinger in a mugger's grip, his two confederates pawed over the bulky body. Finally, in his right sleeve, they uncovered "the most ingenious holdout ever devised."

"Trembling with fury and rage, he tugged and snarled, but it was of no avail—the secret was out! In less time than it takes to tell, however, they let him loose and then and there a compact was made to keep the 'find' a secret for their mutual benefit."

In briefer modern words, they muscled in. At the price of his life, *The Lucky Dutchman* had to construct a Kepplinger for each of them.

His device consisted of a base plate firmly secured to his right sleeve and a cover for it which was anchored to a false cuff. Both were concealed by a second, outer sleeve. The cord which worked the holdout slide ran up to a pulley at his elbow joint. Then, between elbow and shoulder, the cord passed inside a telescopic tube (which could be adjusted to the length of the player's arm).

At the shoulder joint, there was another pulley, and the cord there was joined to a flexible tube of coiled wire which ran down to the knee. Here was yet a third pulley. From it the cord now ran out through an opening in the seam of the right trouser leg and was attached to a hook which projected out of the left trouser leg at the knee.

By very slightly spreading his knees, Kepplinger tightened the cord, thus forcing the holdout slide out through the false cuff into his hand. Bringing his knees together, bending the cards slightly so they could conform to the curve of the cuff, he let the slide retract with the held-out cards.

A Paderewski of poker

"The act is so rapid that the closest watch will not detect the manipulation," an observer wrote when the secret was finally out. "It is beautifully constructed and is absolutely noiseless.

"It is controlled by a natural movement not calculated to excite suspicion and unlike other holdouts has no pneumatic apparatus to get out of order and betray the operator by either frequently pressing his arm to his side or making some other motion that might attract the attention of the other players."

Actually, Kepplinger was a brilliant performing artist, a Paderewski of poker, a Van Cliburn of cards for, right in full sight of the other players, there *were* some six "unnatural" movements he had to make as he sat down at the table.

First, the pulley at his right knee was detachable from a spring-catch socket. Otherwise, the cord running down his body would have been so tight that he couldn't stand erect, and he would have hobbled to the table like Nomad the Hunchback. So the pulley had to be attached.

Then, he had to manipulate two tiny spring clips to open the holes in the seams of both trouser legs to allow the cord to pass from his right to left leg. Three more movements followed. He pulled the cord through the right seam. He found the hook lying flat against his left leg on a pivot and turned it outward. He attached the cord to it.

And after the game, all had to be done in reverse order!

Nonetheless, for more than a year, Kepplinger and his three unwanted partners never once were detected and, actually, the secret came out by ironic accident.

In Chicago, one of the partners, a character named Heller, was arrested in a routine police gambling raid. He pleaded so piteously for an opportunity "to change my shirt," even offering a bribe, that the police not unnaturally became suspicious. They dragged him to the stationhouse, searched him and found the Kepplinger.

Again, they refused his bribes and pleadings and summoned in the reporters to announce their discovery. REVELATIONS OF WONDERFUL DEVICE FOUND ON GAMBLER CAUSE SENSATION, the newspapers cried.

Of course, the imitators immediately got to work, and there were some refinements in the master's creation. The best was chest control, incorporated into the Sullivan holdout, so that simple inhalations and exhalations controlled the "sneak." Can't stop a man from *breathing,* can you? But the fundamentals of the Kepplinger, in all their deadly complexities, have remained unchanged down to this day.

No dying art!

Because the device is expensive, complicated and utterly damning if you are caught with it, many gambling authorities will tell you that the holdout is rarely used today.

Admittedly, to become an accomplished "machine man," a gambler must be more than a mere "hustler," as the profession calls lower-echelon operators. He must be a "mechanic," which is a considerable step upward, and no average "mechanic" at that.

Mastery of the holdout requires at least a month of dedicated, daily practice even if you are a "mechanic," and then, even more important, the exercise of rigorous self-control during play. A man who can summon and dispatch aces at will often suffers a dangerous, giddying sense of power, as Kepplinger's own downfall illustrates so sadly.

Properly, to avoid suspicion, the holdout should be used most sparingly, only three or four times during the course of a big game, and never in a small game, because the risk just isn't worth it. Holding out just *one* card is sufficient to beat any honest game. In fast, smart play, it is sometimes necessary to hold out two. Beyond that is madness and by no means "lump-proof," as the professionals say. That is, you run the serious risk of detection and a beating up.

Nonetheless, from my own knowledge, I must completely disagree with those who profess to believe the holdout is archaic.

For example, if you are willing to spend several hundred dollars and wait several months, right now in England you can obtain a "Martin," Rolls-Royce of contemporary holdouts, custom-built to your specifications. And, if you are too impatient or impoverished, you can send your height and arm length (cuff to armpit) to a certain supply house and obtain any of five different holdout machines ranging in price from $125 to $155. (In all cases, cash on the line and no refund or exchange privileges.)

Also available, for "machine men" with modest aspirations, is an arm pressure machine made of aluminum, brass and steel and attached to the forearm. The device is *not* a "Martin" and you can obtain it for a mere $75.

Beware "Smoky Joe"!

Obviously, then, holdouts are still being widely used, or they wouldn't still be made in such large numbers.

The fact that they can be purchased for as little as $75 proves that mediocre gamblers—the ones *you* are most likely to meet—still use them. Even in the big, "hard" games throughout the country, I know, top gamblers resort to the device, despite the danger of detection, when the pot seems worth the risk.

Matter of fact, I have personally met one of the two or three top holdout men in the world today. "Smoky Joe," so nicknamed because he is a chain smoker, operates regularly through the Midwest, at Las Vegas and on the West Coast, and despite his shady reputation, no one has been able to expose this latter-day Kepplinger.

Not long ago, with three confederates, "Smoky Joe" decided to test his machine against a notorious gambling house in Lexington, Ky. First, one of his associates took a job as a lookout man and later as a dealer in the house to study its operations.

Some nights, he reported back, no-limit blackjack was played so, on such an auspicious evening, "Smoky Joe" dropped in. After some hours, he departed—with $270,000 of the house's money.

Aside from such hit-and-run holdout operations, there is one major city, to my own knowledge, where the "machine men" cluster in notoriously large numbers. Inasmuch as a bit of poetic justice is involved, I am pleased to report that the city is—San Francisco!

Thus, obscure as he may be to the laity and even, in too many cases, to members of his own profession who owe him so much, Kepplinger has become a prophet *with* honor in his own country.

CHAPTER V

BIG GAME TONIGHT!

NOW THAT WE'VE DISCUSSED some of the common forms of cheating, I think you might enjoy accompanying me, as my unseen partner, on one of my professional assignments. At the moment, you know as much as I do. A "hustler" or "mechanic" (remember the distinction?) has worked himself into an honest card game, and our mission is to expose him. Got your hat and coat?

The scene is the third-floor rear of what New Yorkers call a brownstone; the one-time home of an affluent Victorian family that has been converted into a discreet private gambling club for rich men. They are largely Wall Streeters, business executives and the lucky grandsons of successful men who want fast, no-limit action and get it in a peculiarly cruel form of five-card stud.

The betting is "progressive." That is, they open at $1, but each succeeding bet doubles, $2, $4, $8 and so on. A player can lose $100 almost before he has decided to stay, and dropping $1,000 on the evening's play is not unusual.

Not the kind of stakes you and I would play for but, otherwise, this could be *your* game in *your* own home, club or lodge—including the presence of a cheat.

I am introduced as a Chicago tool-and-die executive in town on business, and as the game gets underway, I shuffle clumsily and overbet a little to disarm the crook, whoever he is. You see, the rather stuffy House Committee, which retained me, wouldn't tell *me* the name of the suspected player. My job—that is, your job and mine—is to find

41

him independently and, if the evidence is tangible like marked cards, palm it for corroboration.

Mr. Hemingway, I presume?

We are playing around a big, old-fashioned, specially built card table of carved mahogany with ivory chips decorated with the club's emblem. Even the baize table covering seems a richer green, like Irish grass, and the smoke from the imported $2 Havanas that come in club-stamped cellophane wrappers doesn't make your eyes smart. An elderly, white-coated Negro presides over a portable bar and sandwich table and carves ham, turkey or roast beef to order. You see why I like my work?

If this were a pickup public game at some resort, convention or hotel, I would try to single out the cheat through the gambling under-world's code of mutual identification. "How's the rabbit (sucker) business?" I would ask. Or, perhaps, "Do you know Mr. Hemingway (or Mr. Hennessy)?"

If he answered that the rabbit business was fine or that Mr. Hemingway was indeed a dear friend, he would be establishing himself as a fellow sharper. From that point, with a little further harmless-sounding chitchat, two professionals who have never previously met can signal whether they will play together to take the innocents.

Obviously, though, a crook who had managed to insinuate himself into a rich, closed game like this one doesn't want another Hemingway around. He won't declare himself, so we will have to go at it another way. Let's study the intent faces around the table and see if they give us any clues.

First, Abner W. Jensen, a banker, cold and uncommunicative as his name and occupation would make you think. He plays with mechanical precision, rarely bluffing, almost never wasting a chip unless he has a high hole card. In the argot of card cheats, he is "an 86-er," or tight sucker.

A candidate for Gamblers Anonymous

Alongside him there is Horton Pillsbury III, his face reflecting the strained, haunted mind of the compulsive gambler. For such sad men, the psychiatrists have many explanations: they are tempting or testing fate, displaying insecurity in that they are trying to prove something to themselves, hungering for excitement or the easy dollar. In my lay opinion, all this comes down to the death wish.

Let's make a mental note that we later suggest to the House Committee that Horton join Gamblers Anonymous, a rescue organization much like Alcoholics Anonymous. Unless someone helps him soon, Horton will be dipping into the family trust funds. In fact, the desperate way he bluffs, I suspect he has been dipping already and in the mixed-up way of most gambler-embezzlers, is trying to recoup at the table.

Then there is Arthur Diehl, a rich young magazine editor, who plays smoothly and evasively, rarely bumping but occasionally bluffing, so he is difficult to figure out. And, finally, John Carter, a Wall Street broker, who seems blessed with that masculine form of feminine intuition we call "card sense." Instinctively, he *feels* the right time to stay, the right time to throw in.

Well, what do *you* think?

Most suspect, wouldn't you say, are Pillsbury, with the temperament and probably the motive to cheat, and John Carter, whose apparent X-ray eyes disturb me a little? On the other hand, we mustn't overlook the enigmatic Diehl and Jensen. The best cheats are the last ones whom you would suspect.

The House Committee has given us playing money, so for an hour we can lose and enjoy it, simultaneously disarming the crook, whichever one he is, and trying to discover his modus operandi.

How to tell a "cooler"

Thus, I draw optimistically to a pair of jacks (with another already showing in Jensen's hand), fail to call one of Pillsbury's obvious bluffs, even buck Carter when he has aces showing.

Meanwhile, not very hopefully, I look to see if anyone is using "the mechanic's grip." This is the so-called telltale way in which a professional holds the deck as he "bottom deals" or otherwise manipulates the cards. No, as I had thought, this technique is too dexterous for these men.

Most probably, don't you agree, we are playing with marked cards. But how were they marked, and how were they slipped into the game?

If they are professionally, premarked cards, we have a tedious job ahead of us. I will have to palm two or three so we can study them later at our leisure. (Once, even when I *knew* a deck had been marked, I studied it a whole week before discovering the actual markings.)

How would you say such a deck could be slipped into a tightly controlled, honest game? If you think it over for a moment, you will realize there are only two possibilities.

First, the cards might have been planted in advance with our Negro guardian of cards, chips, Scotch and sandwiches. One look, however, at our waiter's honest, alert face convinces me that he couldn't be either bribed or bamboozled into accepting such a deck. You agree?

Second, during the progress of the game, the cheat could have introduced a "cooler," or "cold deck" of marked cards. I hadn't mentioned it to you, but I have already eliminated this possibility—by my sense of touch.

Let me explain. An honest deck, passing through a succession of sweaty hands, becomes warm. When a switch is made, the new deck actually feels cool to the touch for a hand or so.

Betting the rabbit to show

(That is why, in their sometimes forthright way, gamblers call them "coolers" or "cold decks.")

Well, we have made some progress. If the cards are honest, they are somehow being tampered with right at the table. But there are so many techniques for doing this (as you may remember from the earlier chapter on "smudgy moves") that we might have to play for several nights before pinpointing the particular one.

However, I have a hunch. The players are (or were) gentlemen, so I doubt any of them learned the cheating business from the ground up. Most probably, the "gaff" is so simple I might almost overlook it.

Patiently, I wait for my deal. As I stack the cards, preparatory to shuffling, I casually turn the edge of the deck toward the overhead light. There! Do you remember the trick? I know it now. But still I can't figure who is using it.

Pillsbury? He plays with such illogical desperation that he reminds me of a compulsive gambler who was once being taken in a rigged game. When a friend tried to persuade him to drop out, he protested, "I know I'm being cheated—but I'm $2,000 in the hole and, besides, it's the only game in town!"

The "lucky" Carter or Arthur Diehl, both of whom handle the cards so expertly? Or even ice-water Ab Jensen? The way Ab usually plays, I think of "Conservative Welchie," a notoriously cautious gambler. When Welchie goes to the dog tracks, they say, he is *so* conservative that he always bets the rabbit for show. But we mustn't forget Ab.

Right now, I have a feeling about one of these gentlemen. For this hand, I decide to concentrate on him. Will you forgive me if I don't tell you his name? I have to put a good amount of "work" into my deal to make him betray himself—if I'm right.

While my pigeon (I think) is marking the cards in a certain way, I must resort to a more advanced technique of cheating. Later, we will discuss in some detail how a good gambler, by picking up the discards in the right order and shuffling off according to various formulas, can arrange the deck to his own liking. For now, so that we can get on with the story, just take my word for it. It *can* be done!

What's in the hole?

Not to clutter the action, I stack the deck to force out the other three players with a sorry assortment of treys, sixes and eights and nary a remotely possible flush or straight for them to pin any false hopes on. They all throw in.

As the first card, I give myself an ace in the hole and charitably do the same for my suspect. Next, showing, I give him a king and myself a queen.

He can hardly wait to raise, and I just stay along with him.

Second card showing is a queen for him, a nine for me. Again, he pushes forward a stack of chips, and I just call the bet. I want him to believe that I am staying for the future, not betting on my hole card.

"Third card," as they say in stud poker (which really means the fourth card dealt), adds another queen to his hand, an ace to mine. Now showing, he has K-Q-Q and I have Q-9-A.

Neither of us holds a possible straight or flush, but he *could* have a possible three queens or kings and queens paired. (Of course, I know better.)

I raise.

With my hole card, my best possible is a pair of aces. Casually, my arm rests on the turned-down card so he can't see it.

Now the payoff. A seven for him, making his hand K-Q-Q-7. A queen for me, adding up to Q-9-A-Q. On the board, we both have pairs of queens showing, and I am ace-high over his king. With my hole card, my best possible hand is a pair of aces or nines to back up the queens that show.

However, earlier in the hand, I had purposely dealt two nines showing to the dropouts. His only worry is whether my hole card is an ace.

And now the payoff . . .

If I don't have it, he takes the pot because (as I know) he has a holed ace that matches my ace showing, and his next highest card is a king over my queens.

In other words, his only concern is whether one of the two aces unaccounted for is my hole card. I have stacked him a hand in which he *should* invest heavily.

There is already more than $100 in the pot, and I push forward

another $100 worth of chips. Under the "progressive" betting rules of
the house, he has to cover with $200. Quickly, he reaches for the chips.

As he does, I lift my left arm and for the first time let him see my
turned-down hole card.

Little beads of sweat suddenly dot his forehead. He hesitates, then
throws in without even seeing me.

I was right! He read my hole card and knew that I had aces paired.

Clumsily, I spill my drink onto the cards, and immediately the
Negro attendant produces a fresh deck for play. (I could have merely
palmed the marked aces and substituted new ones, but the cheat would
have spotted them.)

The House Chairman wanders casually past our table, and I give
him a prearranged signal. He raises his hand for silence.

"Gentlemen, I have an unfortunate announcement. Mr. Garcia is
not what he seems. He is a professional gambling investigator retained
by us because of suspicion that there has been cheating in this game.
This he has now confirmed."

For a moment you could have heard a palmed card crash to the
floor.

Who dun it?

Except for an involuntary raising of his eyebrows, Diehl remains impassive. Carter dabs his sweating face with a monogrammed silk handkerchief. Angrily, Pillsbury slams his hand on the table, and the chips
rattle.

"How dare you!" he blusters to the House Chairman. "I'm resign-
ing."

Eyes narrowed thoughtfully, Ab Jensen cuts him off. "Be quiet,
Horton. He hasn't accused you—yet."

All of them stare challengingly at me.

"If you gentlemen will forgive me," I say apologetically, "all of you
displayed a rather erratic pattern of betting. That is, you often dropped
when *I* thought you should have stayed, and many times stayed with
little showing.

"An in-and-out game like that *might* mean that you were using
marked cards, but three of you were so obvious about it that I eliminated
you."

"Can you prove anything?" Ab Jensen demands.

I call for the old deck I had spilled my drink on. Quickly, I deal out
five draw poker hands, face down, and study them briefly.

"The cheat used a paste preparation called Chink Ink to 'pike' or mark the edges of the four aces with a faint tint," I explain. "If we turn over our hands now, we will find that Mr. Pillsbury, Mr. Jensen and myself each has an ace, and the fourth is at the bottom of the deck."

I turn over my hand and the deck. Slowly, the other players display their hands. The aces are where I had said they would be.

"Since no one has left the table," I add, "the cheat must have the Chink Ink still on him. Does anyone object to being searched?"

"Yes!" Face twitching, Ab Jensen, the *too* conservative player, rises so hastily that he knocks over his chair and almost runs from the room.

CHAPTER VI

♠
♥
♦
♣
♠
♥
♦

WHAT EVERY GI MUST KNOW

♠
♥
♦
♣

AS PART OF MY EFFORTS to expose crooked gambling, I have traveled thousands of miles and lectured to tens of thousands of U.S. Air Force GIs through France, Luxembourg, Germany, Scotland and as far north as the bleak Argentia and Harmon AF Bases in Newfoundland.

I hope I taught them something because *I* learned a great deal from them.

Despite the most vigilant efforts by the authorities, gambling—*every* kind of gambling—flourishes stubbornly among these young and often naive servicemen. It isn't the fault of the military. Take any men's dormitory, any fraternity house on any college campus right in the States, and you will probably find exactly the same thing.

Between ages 17 and 25, young men know, or think they know, more about the world than they will ever know again in their lives. Psychologically, they are ripe for plucking, and are they plucked!

You have to feel especially sorry for the GI victims of the card, dice and catch-penny cheats who swarm in and near every military establishment. Many of the latter are professional civilian gamblers, some are crooks in uniform, all operate on one principle. They know that the GIs, many of them away from home for the first time in their lives, are lonely and bored. In the excitement of gambling, they try to forget their lingering ache for home and the old, familiar faces up and down the block.

That is why I particularly despise those crooked male camp followers who victimize the GIs. Even to other cheats, they are shameless, heartless in capitalizing on homesickness and gullibility.

Old gaffs never die

And, professionally, most of them are mediocre operators who know only one or two "gaffs," or cheating methods, which usually are as dated as a World War I Jenny.

For example, not far from Düsseldorf, a group of GIs was clustered around a fast-talking sergeant who kept shuffling and dealing half a dozen cards face down on a bunk. The trick was to pick out the ace of clubs from among the six cards. One by one, the GIs put down their $1, $5 and even an occasional $10, miscalled and sadly departed.

Did my eyes deceive me!

Most professional gamblers will tell you that six-card monte is extinct today, and the "gaffed" set of monte cards in my own collection is more than half a century old. But right in front of me, a new crop of lambs was being shorn with very old scissors.

The trick? Simply cards that had been misspotted with false indices. Held one way, the ace of clubs *was* the ace of clubs, and the GIs accurately "tracked" it as the operator slapped his half dozen cards face down on the bunk. But when they called it, he exposed another card and, by holding it by the other end, transformed a "four of diamonds" into the "ace." (See figures 24, 25, 26, 27.)

I would have felt some slight respect for that sergeant if he had been working the *three*-card monte gaff, a slightly more modern version which at least requires dexterity. Two red and one black ace are shown and then moved rapidly back and forth to confuse the victim who has to call the red ace. He never does call it because of a move known among gamblers as the "hype."

The operator holds one ace in his left hand and the other two in his right hand, picking up the two cards with his thumb, first and second fingers. Thus held, either the top or bottom ace can be first released and, after a fast series of such "hyping" moves with either hand, the sharpest-eyed victim will become confused.

I remember Paris . . .

But "hyping" demands considerable practice and, in all my military travels, I found only one three-card monte game!

Matter of fact, many of the "gaffs" have nothing to do with either cards or dice. They are catch-penny tricks, played for drinks, dinner (or as much as the GI has on him), and all are premised on our great national weakness.

Figure 24. Here are six different cards, wouldn't you agree?

Figure 25. By some curious manipulation, they are now— six Aces.

Figure 26. If you study this photo, the explanation of six-card monte is obvious.

Figure 27. Moral: Always make sure that every card shown is fully exposed.

Say to any American—especially a GI—"Bet you *can't!*" and his red, American blood boils indignantly. "Bet I *can!*" he roars back. And the trap is sprung.

It was AF pay night in a Parisian bistro favored by American servicemen, and the place was jumping with *vin,* mademoiselles and that frightful French interpretation of rock 'n' roll that loses everything but the noise in translation.

A heavy-set hangar man elbowed his way roughly to the crowded bar. "No sweat (No trouble), friend," another AF enlistee said as he was jostled. The hangar man ignored him. He slammed his palm on the bar for silence.

"I got a real wad, you pikers!"

"Moxnix," a noncom said. "So what?"

"Moxnix! I'll bet you can't break what I slap down."

"Bet I *can!*"

"Me, too, big mouth!"

"And me!"

Within a minute, half a dozen GIs had laid $100 in bets on the bar, and their stocky challenger covered them. Then, slowly, he extracted from his pocket not a $1,000 bill, a $500 or a $100.

He dropped a nickel on the bar!

Not one of the six GIs had the five pennies to break it.

The match on the Rhine

In detecting cheats, I covered some three dozen AF bases which ranged from military establishments for almost 10,000, including dependents, down to forlorn little radar outposts that would almost break your heart. Here 15-men details lived behind barbed wire with two German police dogs, and the nearest town was 30 kilometers away, a small town at that.

The type of "gaff," I discovered, varied with the size of the post. Now and then, in some of the small details, a few men won with suspicious regularity, but the real action—in cards, dice and "quick-buck" tricks—was around the big bases. There is always fresh money—as well as safety—in numbers for the crook.

For example, in one of the largest bases, two men were flipping a match the way you flip a coin. One side of the match was marked "50 cents" and the other "$1." The tosser collected whichever amount showed, and then the other player flipped.

"Tell you what," one of the pair said. "Bet I can make the match land on its side, instead of flat."

"Five dollars says you *can't*."

"It's a bet!"

As he tossed, he bent the match slightly into a very broad V, and it landed on its side. Try it for yourself.

Can you remember 2-6-10-14?

"Bet I can!"

"Bet you can't!"

The words were familiar, but the game being played off the base in Newfoundland was a new one on me. Fifteen matches were put in a circle and two players alternated in taking them out, removing one, two or three matches on each move, as elected.

The player who had to remove the last match lost.

For example, if 12 matches had been removed and only three remained, the player who then had the turn would win by removing two. His opponent would thus be stuck with the last match. If 11 had been removed, he would take out three; if 13 were already gone, he would pull one, in both cases leaving his opponent with the last one.

After watching the game for half an hour, I suspected something. One noncom won every game in which he had the first move and most of the others, too. There had to be a system! After a while, I worked it out.

If you have the first move, withdraw two matches. Depending whether your opponent draws one, two or three, you next pull enough so the total withdrawn is six. He pulls again and you then take out enough to make ten. Now you have him. If he withdraws one, you take out three; if he takes two, you take two; if he takes three, you take one —in all cases adding up to 14—and he loses.

However, if he has the first move and withdraws two, you may be stuck. You can win only if, along the line, he lets you get back onto the 6-10-14 progression.

Of course, you could also play a variation of the game in which the player who removes the fifteenth match *wins*. In this case, the "magic" progression becomes 3-7-11-15 rather than 2-6-10-14.

Fast and fatal

The essence of all flimflammery is speed and more speed.

"Bet you can't call it!"

"Heads."

"You lose. It's tails."

"How about you over there. Wanna bet, soldier?"

"Tails."

"Too bad. Guess this must be my lucky day. It's heads."

He was lucky, all right. Lucky to own a double-headed quarter and a double-tailed quarter.

"Bet I can put a bottle cap over this piece of match and turn the match around."

"Bet you can't!"

"Oh, oh, here we go again. But this time it looks as though the "gaff" man is being gaffed. Furtively, one of the bettors removes the match and more bets pour in because, if there's no match, obviously it can't be turned around.

The operator briskly taps the bottle cap and lifts it. There's the match! (Or, rather, another match that had been loosely affixed by wax to the inside top of the bottle cap.) And, of course, the bettor who stole the first match was the "shill," or confederate, of the operator.

Meanwhile, back at the card table

"Bet you $5 I can rip a pack of cards in two."

"Five dollars you can't!"

Whereupon, the five-foot-seven, 145-pound Charles Atlas bevels out the pack and, "no sweat," easily rips it apart because he is only tearing one or two cards at a time.

I could cite dozens more of these "fast-buck" tricks, but I hope the above samples document my point. *Never* get "suckered" into any kind of fast-betting proposition, especially one where the odds seemingly "favor" you! Now back to the slower but even surer card "gaffs."

Among GIs, the favorite games are blackjack, draw and stud poker and Banker and Broker. Unfortunately, these are also the most popular games among the cheats.

Let me give just one example in poker that I saw worked by a "tipsy" sergeant during a wild payday game outside one of our bases in Scotland. Dealing clumsily, he "accidentally" exposed part of his hand, showing three tens. I was kibitzing behind another player who was dealt four fours on the deal.

The drunk discarded two and drew two, presumably going for the fourth ten. My man, of course, discarded only one and settled back comfortably for the kill.

The drunk raised, my man doubled, the drunk doubled again. By now, everybody else had been driven out, and maybe my man had a little premonitory twinge. He called.

The drunk laid down—a royal flush.

Actually, the two cards in his original hand which he had *not* exposed were the jack and queen of spades. He held them, along with the ten of spades, discarding the tens of diamonds and clubs and drawing the ace and king of spades to complete the flush.

How did he accomplish it? The "drunken deal" is worked with an ordinary deck without switching or holdouts. I will describe it in detail in a later chapter, but I would like to pass on this bit of advice right now.

If ever you are sitting in a game that seems suspicious and draw four of a kind, your best bet is to discard one of them along with your fifth card and ask the dealer for *two* cards. This breaks up his "stack" and kills his chances of making the flush.

In a big payday poker game, the chances are excellent that you will be bucking at least two crooks working together who have mastered second or bottom dealing, the false shuffle and the false cut. Perhaps after finishing this book, you will be able to spot them. But probably the most prudent advice I can give is this:

Avoid games in which the same players win consistently, even if their winnings are modest, on the theory that "luck" is bound to turn against them. Chances are they are relying on more than luck to pay their way through their service hitch.

Some other divertissements . . .

Of blackjack, John Scarne says flatly that cheating "is more common than cheating at any other banking card game," and of Banker and Broker, "I guess, all things considered, sharks banking this game have rolled more chumps than ever were taken at three-card monte or the shell game."

I couldn't agree more!

Blackjack is an American cousin of baccarat, the favorite game in the elegant European gambling casinos. But it is so ideally suited to second, bottom and middle dealing that it's hard to believe the crooks didn't invent blackjack solely for their own convenience.

A number of the casinos have recently adopted a new precautionary rule for "Twenty-one" (the house form of blackjack) which I recommend for "friendly" games of blackjack. It is, simply, the use of *two* decks of cards.

Merely the doubled thickness makes it almost impossible for a "mechanic" to deal anything but the top card. Secondly, if a red-and-blue pack are used, and shuffled thoroughly together, the crooked dealer also runs a color risk. Whenever the top card is red and the second,

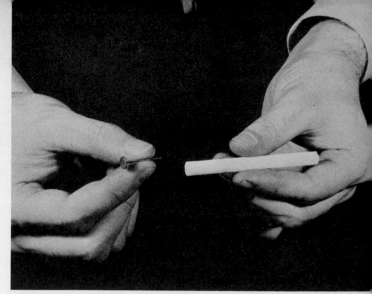

Figure 28. Any reasonably shiny object will reflect cards as they are dealt. This cigaret "shiner" is inserted into tip of cigaret. You can smoke while using it to peek.

middle and bottom cards blue, or vice-versa, the sudden color change is a dead giveaway of underdealing.

However, such other unethical techniques as peeking, shiners and marked cards also lend themselves to this fast, slapdash game in which any player's attention can be distracted without rousing suspicion. My advice is, *Never play blackjack with strangers—or with regularly "lucky" friends.*

Peeking, the use of shiners and introduction of cold decks of marked cards also greatly aid the "mechanic" in poker, red dog, *chemin de fer* ("shimmy"), bridge and rummy. If you know what you are looking for, you *may* be able to detect a peeker; almost invariably, he peeks when dealing. Almost any object (a ring, pipe bowl, cigar holder, even a tiny piece of a glass Christmas tree ornament slipped under the fingernail) may be used as a shiner. You have the right to be suspicious of them.

If a "mechanic" is dexterous, you will never catch him "switching in" his deck of marked cards, and if you studied the cards *individually,* you would not be able to spot the tiny markings. Usually, the cards are marked in the left- or right-hand corner for denomination rather than the suit, with the deuces left unmarked because they have such little value in most games.

Despite the misguided artistry that blends the marks into the decorative motif of the pack, there is one quick, simple method by which you often *can* recognize marked cards.

The method, known to gamblers as "watching the movies," is this:

Hold the suspect pack in either hand and run your fingers lightly over the top edges of the cards in a riffle motion. If the design seems to jump or move about, the deck is marked.

55

The cut that hurts

In Banker and Broker and particularly that payday variation of Russian roulette known as cutting for high or low card, winner-take-all, you will encounter "strippers"—and not the kind that the GIs like to whistle at. "Strippers" are cards that have been trimmed or shaved along the edges in a tapering effect. They are valuable in pinochle, gin rummy and bridge; *invaluable* in Banker and Broker and high-or-low cuts.

"Strippers" come in several interesting variations. For example, "side stripping" makes the deck wider at one end than at the other. Thus, you merely reverse favored cards—five cards to make a royal flush at poker, the four aces or four deuces for high-or-low or, if you are really greedy, all thirteen spades to make a grand slam at bridge.

"Side strippers" are thus inserted into the deck reversed so that, after a riffle shuffle, the "mechanic" can slide them out while cutting the pack and bring them to the bottom for the bottom deal.

In "end stripping," the cards are shaved at the ends, rather than the sides; in "belly strippers," also known as "humps," the favored cards protrude slightly at the middle of the sides. Properly prepared, they defy detection except by experts. Then there are the practically all-purpose "wedgies," in which one end of the deck is stripped differently from the other to provide different combinations of cards.

For as little as $2 to $4, you can buy such decks, prestripped, or the gambling supply houses will sell the cutting equipment to strip-it-yourself enthusiasts. However, to avoid carrying such damning evidence around in their duffel bags, the more skilled GI cheats resort to "latrine stripping."

Give them ten minutes alone in the head and they can fashion an ordinary deck into "strippers." I know; I've watched and timed them.

These cheats work on the theory that in practically any bathroom you will find a make-do cutting surface: a piece of jagged glass, the sharp end of a mirror, etc. Rubbing this edge gently against the pack, they shave down their favored cards.

Of snakeyes and boxcars

Later, I plan to spell out, *1-2-3,* the various steps in each of the "gaffs" I have been describing, plus many more cheating dodges.

Right now, I am trying to accomplish just one thing and, if I do, this one chapter is worth the effort that has gone into the entire book. I want to *rouse* the GI—and his family and sweetheart back home— to the cruel, consistent fleecing he takes.

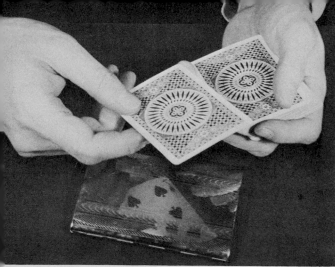

Figure 29. Ordinary cigaret case with high-polish surface makes excellent "shiner." The one shown here was seized in raid by New York police.

Figure 30. For "mechanics" who prefer pipe tobacco, there are pipe "shiners." This expensive French import has a mirror concealed in its bowl.

Figure 31. If you had been dealing the cards in Figure 30, here is what the pipe "shiner" would have showed you.

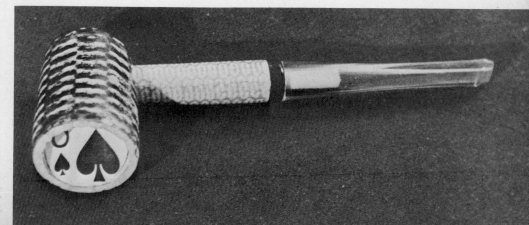

Figure 32. If you suspect a deck of cards is marked, study the backs carefully as you riffle pack. (Author has deepened original marks with indelible ink to make them show more clearly.)

Figure 33. Completion of riffle test, also known as "going to the movies" because the marks, otherwise invisible, will jump about in the course of a fast riffle.

Figure 34. When a player holds the pack in this position, he may be preparing to manipulate "end strippers." Cards are stripped at the ends and the desired ones reversed so "mechanic" can slide them out while cutting pack.

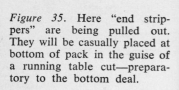

Figure 35. Here "end strippers" are being pulled out. They will be casually placed at bottom of pack in the guise of a running table cut—preparatory to the bottom deal.

Figure 36. Honest middle card is flanked by two "belly strippers" cut in exaggerated fashion by author. One on left is a "round"; one on right, a "hollow."

Figure 37. Of the six cards spread out before the author, five have been "gaffed" in different ways. Question: Which card is the honest one?

Nobody can even approximate the take of crooked gamblers from servicemen, but my own "educated guess"—and I think it is a conservative one—is that soldiers, sailors, Marines and airmen lose *at least* $10,000,000 annually to the crooks.

I base this figure on my firsthand observations, interviews with military brass who are doing their best to find and break the cheats, and countless talks with GIs here and abroad. Many of the latter like to ask my advice on some gambling "problem," *and it is obvious from the way they talk that they have no suspicions they are being cheated.*

Even worse, some have picked up a smattering of the cheating techniques; they are "wise guys" who can't be fooled. *Half*-wise, actually, and unless they learn one thing—crooked gambling is both a demanding and dead-end profession—I very much fear they will drift into a life of petty chiseling.

As an example, let's take that particularly popular form of pocketbook euthanasia known as dice. Among officers and men alike, dice are rolled for drinks, dinner, the month's pay. Servicemen play variations of the game with two, three, four and five dice; they roll exotic games of French and German origin; they are almost magnificent in the way they ignore correct odds and *in*correct cubes.

Yet everyone I talked to *thought* he was an experienced gamester and could only blame "luck" each time he was taken to the *laundromat*.

The invisible load

Fact is, dice playing is one of the black arts of gambling. Forget odds and percentages for the moment and let me, very briefly, capsule a few of the cheating methods that are all fully described in a later chapter on dice.

As I write this, I am looking at the catalogue of a supply house which devotes no less than ten pages to "gaffed" cubes and dice-"gaffing" equipment that costs as much as $1,000.

There are "edge work" dice in many styles which "favor" ace and 6, 1, 2 and 2, 5, and 6 or 4, 5 and 6, as you prefer to order. You can buy eight variations of capped dice for missing, passing or showing different combinations. There are prepared paste dice, transparencies, shaped percentage dice, flats, floats, special-filled white dice and misspots, also known as tees, tops and bottoms.

In most cases, the price per set ranges from $2.75 to $8.50, but "transparencies" will cost you more. Formerly, only solid-color cubes could be loaded, but now transparent dice also are "gaffed." I have seen specially made "transparencies" carrying delicate platinum loads that sell for $35 a pair—and win back their cost in the first few rolls.

However, this catalogue appeals more to the middle-income gambler and the pride of house, priced at only $32.50 per set, is a transparent three-dice combination set. One set "favors" ace, 2-6 and 2-4 while the second combination advertised favors 1-2, 1-5 and 3-5.

And a taste of honey

One of the most popular forms of "gaffed" dice are "tees," "tops" and "bottoms," in which each die has a duplicate set of numbers. It may be two 1s, two 5s, two 6s on one die; two 3s, two 4s and two 5s on the other.

These misspots are known as "no bust-outs" because they will roll only the numbers 4, 5, 6, 8, 9, 10 and 11, sparing the player the dreadful danger of crapping out by throwing a 3 or 12 or a 7. Offhand, you might think they would be as conspicuous as five aces in a poker hand; but, of course, when dice are tossed, the bottom side always is concealed. You can detect them only by double-checking that the top and bottom numbers add up to seven, no matter which way you turn the cube.

A more difficult swindle to detect is "honey dice," in which three sides of each die have been treated with a sticky substance resembling honey. (The preparation can be obtained for $7 a jar from the gaming supply houses.)

Being otherwise legitimate dice, the cubes seem to roll and bounce naturally. However, the coated sides (which are the numbers *not* wanted) retard the roll so that the favored numbers will come up 30 per cent of the time. The disadvantage in "honey dice"—to the hustler, that is—is that the substance will last for only three or four tosses.

How to get a load off your back

Because "transparencies" have become increasingly popular among the cheats who prey on servicemen, I feel I ought to get ahead of my story and tell you right now that there are three tests for detecting them.

First, hold the suspect die diagonally and lightly between the thumb and index finger of either hand. With the other hand, make the die revolve slowly. If loaded, it will revolve back in the opposite direction.

Second, take a tall glass of water and drop the die in it. A loaded cube will revolve to the favored number before it settles on the bottom of the glass. Repeat the process a few times to make sure.

Third, place the die in an ashtray and ignite it. The cube will burn rapidly because of its composition—but the load itself is not inflammable and will soon become apparent.

However, a cautionary note. As quickly as the members of my little profession detect and expose a new "gaff," the scientists who devise such equipment "for magic purposes only" come up with something new.

Thus, the catalogue of a gaming supply house advertises a set of loaded transparencies, which apparently defy Test No. 3.

I mention this, not to confuse, but to underscore the one bit of advice I hope every serviceman will take to heart for his own protection.

No matter how accomplished you may *think* you are at cards or craps, there is always a dedicated, 24-hour-a-day professional gambler waiting to take you with a new technique.

CHAPTER VII

♠
♥
♦
♣
♠
♥
♦

HOW TO WIN AT HONEST CARDS

♣
♠
♥
♦

WHILE I AM CALLED the gambling investigator, my work in a sense is like that of the diagnostician and surgeon. As in the 52-card pack we call the human body, the varieties of possible malfunctions at the card table are almost countless. Thus, I must first diagnose the particular cheating method that is being used in a rigged game. Then, with the drastic delicacy of the surgeon, I take curative action.

However, in gambling as in healing today, there is also something known as *preventive* therapy. If you play badly, you will lose to any reasonably experienced player whether he is a cheat or not, and all the advice in this book will be wasted on you.

So, before spelling out in detail how the cheat operates, let's discuss the built-in enemy of every mediocre player—*himself*—and see if we can't write out a winning R_x for him.

From Goren on bridge to Yardley on poker to Scarne on all the games, many books, good books, on the *how-to* of cards have been written by authorities on the various games. I am not going to try to compete with them. Rather, you will find the ones that I recommend listed in the bibliography at the end of this book.

However, drawing on such technical sources and my own observations and experiences in thousands upon thousands of games, I want to capsule our R_x in the form of ten *indispensable* DO'S and ten *indispensable* DON'TS. *If followed, they will help any player to win far more often at honest cards—and have more fun in the process.*

Undoubtedly, you already observe many of these 20 cardinal points in your play, but I submit that the only way you will improve your game is by faithfully practicing *all* of them. And if some seem rather obvious, they are included for a very good reason. A startlingly high percentage of average players violate them at consistent and considerable loss to themselves.

First, let's recap them briefly and then explain their importance.

Do! Do! Do!

1. Whatever the game, memorize the official (and local) rules.
2. Always be in top physical and psychological condition.
3. Adapt yourself to the particular tempo of the particular game.
4. Learn the odds against drawing different hands.
5. Memorize each card as it shows.
6. Bet more conservatively on good hands than on mediocre ones.
7. Lose deliberately on an occasional poor bluff or impossible call.
8. Ride with good luck and never try to buck bad luck.
9. Learn to shuffle.
10. Keep your mouth shut.

Don't! Don't! Don't!

1. Play cards with women.
2. Let wine, women or kibitzers distract you.
3. Plunge deeper to recoup.
4. Keep peeking at your hand.
5. Even feel emotion.
6. Dress up for the game.
7. Call a man a cheat.
8. Give anything away.
9. Vary your type of play from hand to hand.
10. Ever play with strangers!

Now to explain these golden rules of good cards.

Know what you're doing!

More than the biggest IBM computer could possibly calculate, pots (and tempers) have been lost simply because the players didn't operate according to Hoyle.

For some reason, a businessman who wouldn't sign the letter he just dictated without rereading it will cheerfully play cards on the *assumption* he knows all the rules. When a dispute breaks out, his clincher is, "But we always played it *this* way." Unfortunately, the pot goes to the player who can cite authoritative precedent.

Sometimes, it is saddening to add, the pot even goes to a cheat who brazenly cites a nonexistent rule and gets away with it because of his opponents' ignorance.

As a matter of fact, merely knowing the official rules will not protect you if you are playing in a gambling house casino or a strange town where there are special house regulations. The prudent player will insist on being briefed on any such variations before the first pack is cut.

Otherwise, he may find himself in the predicament of the traveling card cheat who collided with local poker in a town we will call You're-a-Sap, Arkansas. By some very expert dealing, the gambler generously gave himself a royal flush in draw poker and promoted the pot till there were several hundred dollars in it.

Then he showed his hand and started to rake in the money.

"Just a minute, stranger!" one of the local characters said. Triumphantly, he slapped down a deuce, five, seven, ten and queen of assorted suits. The cheat looked at the conglomeration of cards in amazement.

"This is what we call a Lalapalooza," the local explained, "and in You're-a-Sap, it beats a royal flush." He also put a Colt .38 on the table, so the traveler decided not to protest.

Instead, on his next deal, he dealt himself a Lalapalooza, raised, and again started to take the pot. And again, the same character stopped him, throwing down a pair of jacks.

"I guess you weren't paying attention the first time," he said reproachfully. "I distinctly told you that only one Lalapalooza is allowed during a night's play."

The story may be legend—in fact, it was first printed back in the nineteenth century!—but the moral is fresh and shining today.

Do you know, for example, that there are more than twenty *recognized* variations of draw poker, ranging from Spit in the Ocean to Hurricane? We are a creative race. The same applies to most any other game you may play.

Go for the throat!

Psychologically, every player should go into the game with a ruthless, killer spirit. Every other player is his enemy. When he has the cards, he will drive the others off the table. When he hasn't, he will fold quickly so they can't hurt him.

So far as he is concerned, friendship and sympathy are suspended for the duration of the play. He doesn't lend money to the losers to keep them in the game (and thus give them a second chance at winning). He insists on every fair advantage, demands penalties for misplays, constantly watches the pot to make sure no one is riding light.

Gambling is a severe, sustained strain on both body and mind and, properly, you should prepare ahead of time for it. Most experienced gamblers take a nap for an hour or two and then a cold shower before game time.

If something is nagging at your mind, you would be wiser not to play at all that night. And if, during the game, you find yourself tiring mentally or physically, drop out.

I realize that this advice sounds almost brutal, but then cardplaying is a bloodless form of dueling. You simply cannot play a relaxed, careless, friendly game if you have any hopes of winning.

Get in the groove!

Because they usually play the same game for the same stakes with the same number of friends, most cardplayers become "set" in the way they bid, raise and call. Subconsciously, they adapt their card judgment to these particular conditions—which won't obtain in a strange game.

Merely a different number of players around the table will change the odds when you are trying to improve a poker hand with a draw. So simple a variation as playing deuces wild means you are suddenly playing a *different* game. After all, now a royal flush can be beaten with three aces and two deuces.

Even the betting limits will change the nature of the game. For example, Herbert O. Yardley learned poker at the age of sixteen in frontier saloons in Indiana and thereafter, with amazing success, played the game all over the world. In *The Education of a Poker Player,* he lays down what you might call Yardley's Rule: "The smaller the stakes, the wilder the game, the easier to win."

On the 649,740th hand, bet confidently!

Players have gone far in poker by following the ancient admonition, "Never draw to an inside straight." However, a 52-card pack contains almost 2,600,000 possible poker hands (2,598,960, to be exact). So you should know considerably more than that about your probabilities.

Fortunately, there is a short formula in long division that tells the value of the hand you receive on the deal. By dividing the possible total of the different hands (four possible royal flushes, 36 straight flushes and so on down) into the figure 2,598,960, you find the odds against your receiving such a hand on the deal.

For example, with only four possible royal flushes among the 2,598,960 possible hands, four goes into 2,598,960 just 649,740 times. That is, once in 649,740 hands, you can bet *very* confidently.

At the other extreme, the pack contains 1,302,540 "busts," or no-pair hands, which is slightly more than half of the total. Thus, the formula shows, your chance of being dealt a "bust" is slightly more than even.

Between the two wild extremes of royal flush and "bust," here are your chances (rounded off without the decimals) of receiving various other hands on the deal. In each case, the first number is the possible total of such hands in the deck, while the second represents the odds against getting it on the deal.

Straight flush, 36 and 1 in 72,193; four of a kind, 624 and 1 in 4,165; full house, 3,744 and 1 in 694; flush, 5,108 and 1 in 509; straight, 10,200 and 1 in 255; three of a kind, 54,912 and 1 in 47; two pairs, 123,552 and 1 in 22; one pair, 1,098,240 and 1 in 2⅓.

Obviously, there is no need to memorize these statistics, so long as you have a clear concept of the *relative* probabilities. Certainly those incorrigible optimists who stay on a short pair should ponder that figure of 1 in 2⅓.

Now let's take our mathematics forward one table. What are the chances for you to better your hand on the draw?

About one hand in every five, you will be dealt a pair of jacks or better. Probably, you will discard the other three and draw to them (though some misguided players hold back a third card if it is high and draw only two).

Discarding three and drawing three, you face odds of 359 to 1 that you won't come up with a four-of-a-kind hand. Odds against a full house are 89 to 1, against three of a kind, almost 8 to 1 and against two pairs, almost 5 to 1. In fact, the odds are 7 to 3 (better than 2 to 1) that you won't improve your hand in the least.

Now, if you hold that high card "kicker" with your pair of jacks, discarding and drawing only two cards, the odds tilt to 14 to 5 against any betterment of the hand. They also are higher that you won't get four of a kind, a full house or three of a kind. There is only one advantage in holding a "kicker," and it's a mild one. You have a slightly better chance of winding up with two pairs.

Know them cards!

Crooked or honest, every successful gambler I've ever known has been blessed with (or painstakingly developed) a photographic memory for the pips. Once a card has been shown, he never forgets it, and recasts his strategy accordingly. I don't care how you do it—go to memory school, if necessary!—but improve your memory to the point where you can keep in mind every card that has shown on the table. The importance of this is too obvious for me to say any more.

The bet's the thing!

There's a curious similarity, or dissimilarity, between the bid in bridge and the bet in poker. In the former, you are trying to tell your partner something. In the latter, you are trying *not* to tell your opponents anything.

Thus, a strong opening bet on a strong hand will probably tell more than you intend. You may win the pot, but there won't be much money in it. On the other hand, if you have a so-so fist of cards, *and it is worth betting at all,* then bet it strongly. You may discourage some from staying in, giving you the opportunity to improve yourself on the draw. (Sometimes in such cases, holding a "kicker" reinforces the impression that you have a strong hand, though it's of little help mathematically, as we have seen.)

Till you get the "feel" of a game, bet prudently. This is good advice whether the game is honest or crooked. You need more than a few hands to study the personalities and idiosyncrasies of your opponents, and you can write off your early, modest losses under the heading of education. And if you build up a comfortable pile of chips, don't "go for broke" in your betting toward the shank end of the evening. If the game is crooked, you have been patiently nurtured along for a last-minute kill.

It should go without saying that you make sure at once whether raises are restricted, whether there is a freezer, what the limits are. A friend of mine (and he has been around a long, long time) recently had a frightening experience because of his carelessness about such things.

He got into a game where he merely signed with the banker for units and no money changed hands till all the play was over. He picked up 100 units (at 10 cents each, he thought), won handsomely and cashed in 800 units. Instead of $80, he was handed $800—each unit was worth $1.

"I was playing ten times over my head," he told me. "Supposing I had *lost!*"

You gotta pay to win!

Having talked so much about tight, prudent betting, I must seem to contradict myself when I now suggest that you occasionally lapse into deliberately careless betting.

For one thing, though you probably know that good poker players rarely, rarely bluff, I suggest you try it at least once during the evening's play. If you get away with it (which is doubtful), you know you're in a game with faint hearts—and you can try it again.

On the other hand, if you are called, which is especially probable when there is a tempting pot and a modest limit, don't bluff again— but don't regret your losses, either. For the rest of the evening, your opponents will never be quite sure whether you are bluffing or not. At least once—and even more often if you are a good enough actor to *look* as though you are bluffing—they will stay when you really do have the cards.

Similarly, sometimes, though your hand doesn't justify it, you should, purely as a matter of tactics, stay to the end and then call. It will cost a little money, but it's worth it, to determine what hands the other players think worthy of a ride.

Hot-and-cold—hit-and-run!

As happens even to the wiliest of pros, there are nights *and* nights. When you're "cold," you couldn't win a pot even from your mother-in-law. When you're "hot" (unless it's a rigged game and you are merely being sweetened), you simply can't lose. These peaks and valleys are the joy and despair of card gambling: the nights that all the laws of probabilities fly out the window and good luck (or bad luck) comes crashing down on your head.

There's only one thing you can do about it. Ride your luck for all it's worth when it is running with you. Cash your chips and get out of the game when it turns against you.

Can't everybody shuffle?

In a word, *no*.

Probably nine out of ten cardplayers take pride in their seemingly expert and graceful flourishes as they cut and shuffle the deck. Actually, the more motion they put into the operation, the greater the danger that they will expose the position of some of the cards to the other players. A man who knows one ace is at the bottom of the deck and then draws another on the deal can play rather confidently, can't he?

So I recommend that you master the Scarne shuffle. It isn't especially pretty to watch, but it has the workmanlike virtue of concealing all the cards all the time. As John Scarne would tell you, here is all you have to do:

Put the deck face down on the table. Using thumbs and middle fingers of both hands, pull out half the deck with the right hand. The other half remains in the left hand. Now put the halves end to end on a slight bias and run your thumbs up the sides in a riffle shuffle.

Next, *without lifting the cards,* gently push the shuffled pack together and square it. It is ready for a cut, an honest cut because nobody has been able to spot a card that he might want to cut to the top or bottom of the pack.

You lose a little showmanship with this kind of shuffle, but you won't lose pots to "locaters" in the game.

Shut up!

In a card game, talk isn't silver, it's just lead, and silence is more than golden. Many players think they can mislead or distract their opponents with bright patter, but unless they are master card conversationalists, they are only hurting themselves in two ways.

First, you simply can't keep your mind on the cards and chatter at the same time. Second, as your luck changes, you unconsciously give yourself away by your tone of voice. As Yardley points out, winners talk and losers remain silent.

Keep your mouth shut *all* the time and let your opponents worry about what's in your hand. Don't *tell* them!

Now let's run over our ten DON'TS which we can dispose of rather quickly because these are self-evident truths.

Women and cards don't mix

Considering all the bad jokes and good cartoons about the belligerency of husband-wife teams at bridge, I have mastered the courage to lay down Garcia's Law on Cards and Sex. It is simply this:

Never team with your wife in a card game. If possible, never team with any other woman, either. Best of all, if it is humanly possible, never play cards with women at all!

I realize this brash law will outrage the lovely half of the country, but I have my reasons.

First, *wives.* Admittedly, there are some champion married bridge teams, and some of the Reno casinos are so suspicious of expert marital collusion that they won't let husband and wife play at the same poker table. These are merely the exceptions that go to prove Garcia's Law.

If you team with your wife at any card game and win consistently, people will talk. If you lose consistently, you—or your wife—will talk. In either case, you see, you really can't win, and I offer my suggestion in behalf of harmony in the American home.

Second, *women in general*. When a man teams with or even plays at the same table with women, he must constantly remember his language and manners. He must put up graciously with strong perfume, jangling earrings, flashing finger rings and the inevitably spilled pocketbook. He must wait politely while the lady player makes up her mind, changes it, makes it up again and finally plays the card she started to play in the first place. There may also be time out while she does things with her lipstick.

I have never quite determined to my own satisfaction whether women *deliberately* do all these things, but that isn't the point. As distractors, the sex reigns supreme at the card table.

Too, men and women play entirely different, conflicting types of games. With most men, cards *is* a game; they play boldly, often rashly, sometimes intuitively, and when they lose, they take it philosophically, or try to pretend they are philosophical.

But women play with a certain *righteousness,* almost the same spirit with which they dispatch their civic and do-good responsibilities, and a man feels apologetic about beating them. I will freely concede that in cool, cautious play, in logic and grasp of the probabilities, women for the most part are far superior to the men players. Which makes it all the worse when you are teamed with one and drop a hand. *You've let her down.*

No, I say, let the ladies have their afternoon bridge clubs, let the men play poker Saturday nights at the firehouse. That's the way it was in Gramp's day, and there weren't nearly so many divorces.

Neither do whisky and cards

"Show me a drinking cardplayer," a veteran transatlantic gambler once told me fondly, "and I'll show you one I can take—honestly." Whisky is doubly dangerous: not only does it cloud judgment and memory, but it encourages recklessly heavy betting. Perhaps if you are regularly accustomed to drinking, one highball—no more!—will give you a lift in mid-game; otherwise, leave the stuff alone.

Similarly, if you are playing a hotel, convention or casino game where pretty girls usually are wandering about, forget them! I do not offer this as moral advice. Even when they aren't sitting at the table, women are distractors, and the professional gamblers often hire them for this purpose.

Try to ignore the kibitzers, too, unless you catch one looking at your hand. Tell him firmly to go away; he may be signaling one of the other players.

This takes will power

Whatever the limit of the game, bring a bankroll of forty times that amount (that is, $20 for a 50-cent limit, $40 for a $1 limit and so on) *that you are prepared to lose*. You need this comfortable amount of reserve to prevent your being washed out of the game altogether by an early run of bad luck. You need the fatalistic (but by no means defeatist) spirit to avoid the panicky feeling that often prompts losers to plunge ever more deeply.

If you are resigned that once your $20 or $40 has been lost you will quit the game, you are in a better frame of mind to make cool, prudent bets right to the end. Admittedly, it takes considerable strength to lift the seat of the pants from the chair. That's why I recommend that you go in fatalistically; it's easier to get out.

Stop peeking!

Memorize your hand, hold it close and don't look at it again until you are making a play. Gamblers who keep glancing at their cards are making two mistakes. First, there is the ever-present possibility that the fellow next to you will get a peek at them, too. Second, you will find that the poorer your hand, the more often you look at it. A man who has an ace in the hole *knows* what's there. So (unless you are pretending uncertainty or nervousness as part of a bluff), look at them once and leave them alone.

Don't even laugh!

This DON'T is beyond human attainment, but try to observe it as much as you can. Joy, sorrow and especially anger belong no more at the card table than they do in the tables of probabilities. Emotions can only backfire on you. Elation and despair lead to recklessness, anger can completely destroy judgment. And, of course, the more deeply your feelings affect you, the more difficult it is to avoid a telltale display of them.

Who cares if he's sloppy?

Unfortunately, much cardplaying is associated with social evenings, which means that we dress up for the game. The ladies, particularly, allow themselves to be distracted by tight girdles, neckless gowns that they keep hitching up and shoes that pinch.

But the men, too, often are guilty of what I would call sartorial self-distraction. A man accustomed to a sports shirt won't play as good cards when he has a collar and tie pinching his neck and, if he feels uncomfortable wearing a tuxedo, he will play an uncomfortable game. If you doubt that this bit of advice is important, think back to what you were wearing when you played your best and worst games.

If in doubt, go quietly!

After you have finished this book, you will (I hope) be able to spot some of the "gaffs" that card cheats employ. However, it's just as important to know how to use the information as to have it. When you suspect you are being taken, cut down the amount of your betting, but play on for a few more hands. It's well worth the money to watch a "mechanic" in actual operation—against a future day when you may be in a bigger game.

Once you are satisfied the game is crooked, make some plausible excuse and leave quietly. *Don't* accuse anyone! In the first place, you may be unable to back up the accusation which would be highly embarrassing. Even if you can, chances are there are at least two crooks in the game and possibly their "muscleman," too. You won't get your money back, and you may get beaten up.

Of course, if a club or organization is running the game, you should quietly report your suspicions to the responsible officers. From there on, it's their job (and maybe mine) to take any necessary action. In a hotel or pickup game, you can complain to the police, but you will have to sign the charges and, anyhow, the gang will probably have disappeared before the detectives arrive. Crooked gamblers move as fast as they deal.

Why be a samaritan?

If an opponent fails to call, don't let him see your winning hand. You're just giving away information that he is supposed to buy through his call bet. And, when all the hands are thrown in, don't let anyone poke through them or through the discards. In a way, card games are the sale and purchase of information, and you just don't give anything away.

As part of this necessarily uncharitable attitude, don't give away your hand by playing with cards that have become dirt-spotted to any extent. I have a little throwaway trick that dramatizes this point.

Someone from the audience picks half a dozen cards (*not* from a fresh deck, or I couldn't work it) and taps one. I am allowed to see only its back. I pick it up, the face still concealed, and hold it close to my nose to "smell" it. Then it is placed with the others, which are shuffled and then spread out, still face down.

One by one, I pick up the cards and "smell" the backs till I find the right card. Obviously, my scent isn't that keen. By pretending to smell, I have had the excuse to hold the card close to my *eyes* and examine it for some tiny, but telltale dirt spot, which I recognize the second time.

Another non-giveaway rule is to never allow play on a misdeal. If a player is dealt six cards, don't let him discard the one he doesn't like. It's too bad, but he's out of the hand altogether, and the players having the correct number of cards turn over. The one with the highest cards wins; if it is a draw, the pot is split.

Finally, as a selfish samaritan, don't let your arm be twisted to extend the game an extra hour or two. When you start the play, announce yourself. You will play to midnight or until you have dropped a specified amount.

Stick to it!

If you drop your bankroll by 11:00 P.M., get out *then* despite taunts or offers of credit.

If you are a heavy winner at the midnight deadline, say goodnight and go despite the anguished pleas of the heavy losers.

This is the only known rule for controlling losses and conserving winnings that I have ever heard of.

Lo wasn't such a poor Indian at that

When I think of the ideal cardplayer, I think of Lo, the Indian. He had an unreadable poker face. He grunted his bets. He never moved, smiled, frowned, flicked his eyelids, hitched his chair backward or forward, pulled his ear lobe, scratched his nose, laid down his cards and picked them up for another look or otherwise telegraphed his hand to sharp-eyed opponents. He was as inscrutable as a wooden cigar store Indian.

Last time I knew, Lo was the richest Indian in Oklahoma. And why not? All the other Indians just owned oil wells. Lo knew how to play perfect, impassive poker.

I have known only a handful of cardplayers who didn't somehow betray themselves by tone of voice or unconscious gesture. Sometimes, you have to sit in the game half a dozen times, but sooner or later you discover the weakness. A nervous cough before a bluff. . . . A scowl that is merely intended to conceal elation over a good hand but becomes just as obvious. . . . A twitch of the nose that means a high card in the hole. . . .

Now here is a time when a wife could be very helpful. Prepare a dozen hands, good and bad, and lay them face down on the table. Let her deal them to you without looking at them and ask her to guess, from your reaction, whether they are good or bad.

If she guesses right, *why?* How are you giving yourself away? You may have to repeat the performance several times, but eventually she will consciously see your telltale gesture that her subconscious spotted right away. Then it will be up to you to conquer the habit.

And now a word about our sponsor

I suppose I shouldn't detest cheats, because, after all, they indirectly provide me with an entertaining, exciting and profitable livelihood.

But I do despise them, and I can't possibly sign off our list of DON'TS without this warning. I say this so much that it must sound like nagging, so I will ask Mr. Printer to put my last word in italic type:

Don't get in a "friendly" game with strangers!

CHAPTER VIII

THIS IS HOW THEY DO IT TO YOU

BACK IN HIS POLITICAL SALAD DAYS, when he was only a U.S. Senator, a certain eminent personage hastened aboard a train in Washington, bound for New York and an important mission of state.

"Why, hello, governor!" exclaimed a well-dressed stranger in the club car. "It's nice to see you again."

Since the personage had once been lieutenant governor of Ohio, he assumed the stranger came from his home state and, obeying the first rule of practical politics, exclaimed with equal warmth, "It's nice to see *you* again! And how is the family?"

Well, one thing led to another, and soon the two Ohioans got into a bridge game with two other prosperous-looking passengers who also were traveling first class. Cutting for partners, the Senator and his friend found themselves playing against each other.

Though the Senator prided himself on his cool, conservative bridge game, it just wasn't his day. For almost four hours, till they reached Pennsylvania Station in New York, he lost and lost. So much so that, after emptying his wallet, he had to ask apologetically whether his fellow Ohioan would accept a check to cover the rest of his losses.

"Why, certainly, governor," his friend said. "Let me give you my New York address, and you can drop the check in the mails at your convenience. There's certainly no hurry about it."

In the way of bridge players, the eminent personage later conducted a mental post-mortem of the game, and the more he thought about it, the more suspicious he became.

When he returned to the capital in a day or so, he consulted the Senator from Kansas, who was generally acknowledged as Washington's leading authority on poker and bridge. This was no small honor because, traditionally, Congressmen, Cabinet members, not to mention most Presidents and practically all Washington correspondents, have played high, fast and hard games.

As the Senator from Ohio described it to the Senator from Kansas, the bidding of his opponents had been suspiciously high and successful. This was before Harold S. Vanderbilt's historic cruise from California to Havana aboard the *Finland* in 1925, during which contract bridge came into the world, and the Ohioan had been playing auction bridge.

The major distinction, of course, is that in auction you are credited with the tricks you take above your successful bid whereas, in contract, you get only what you "contract" to win. Thus, bidding at auction generally is much lower, and a grand-slam bid is almost unthinkable.

But the Senator's opponents had been blithely bidding fives, sixes, and even occasional slams, and the Senator from Kansas gave it as his opinion that apparently marked cards had been used. "Why not have the Secret Service check that New York address?" he suggested.

A day later, the Service reported back that the address was a cheap tenement used as a mail drop by gamblers. The Senator from Ohio tore up his check, and philosophically wrote off his cash losses as the premium you pay for playing cards with strangers.

The Senator who advised him was Charles Curtis, later Vice President under Herbert Hoover, and the victim was—Warren Gamaliel Harding, who was to become the 28th President of the United States. This footnote to history comes to us through the courtesy of my friend Francis Stephenson, veteran Washington correspondent now with *The News* in New York, who heard it directly from Curtis.

They took the Duke, too!

However, we pass it on for the two gambling lessons that it teaches—aside from the obvious ones that you never play with strangers and always suspect consistent, successful high bidding, whatever the game.

The interesting thing is that, at cards, Warren Harding was wise and experienced and yet he didn't suspect for hours afterward that, just possibly, he might have been taken. Secondly, what chance do we average Joes have when cheats will brazenly victimize even a Senator!

Matter of fact, Harding is only one among thousands of the rich, the famous, the powerful and the aristocratic who have thus been "suckered." By legend, even a ducal son of either George II or George

III lost £20,000 at a time when the English pound weighed a lot more than it does today in betting on a rigged whist hand which was then christened "the Duke of Cumberland's Hand."

In a subsequent chapter, I will explain the celebrated—or notorious —bridge derivative of this swindle, which is known as "the Mississippi Heart Hand."

From his approach, there is absolutely no way by which you can detect a card cheat. At one time, a common technique was to pick the victim's wallet, examine it for indications of his probable worth and then return it on the pretext that it had been "found." Waving aside the suggestion of a reward, the crook would then gently steer the "pigeon" into a game. However, so many travelers who had "lost" their wallets subsequently lost their shirts at the card table that the technique became notorious and is rarely used today.

Rather, because practically everybody has one, the crooked gambler will begin his prospecting by asking about your family. This is not only disarming but also helpful to him in gauging your standard of living and approximate worth. Probably, he won't even suggest a game but will maneuver the conversation so that *you* find yourself suggesting it.

Thus, Garcia's Law for those players with the death wish who still insist on gambling in pickup games is this, *The less suspicious the approach, the more suspicious the approacher.*

Actually, strange as it may seem, your chances for survival will be better if you stumble into a game with *two* cheats who have not previously played together. There is an Esperanto of words and signs by which they identify themselves to each other right in front of you and decide whether they will work as confederates to take you.

I now propose to reveal this universal code so you will know when to leave a game—fast!

Say hello to Mr. Hemingway

Mr. Hemingway sure gets around. Everywhere I go, in the circles in which I move, people are talking about him. Not long ago, while I was "card policing" a national sales convention to keep out the sharks, I heard his name mentioned in a New York hotel. A few weeks later, on a Southern cruise, I overheard another friend asking for him.

In Reno, out on the West Coast, east to Boston, people ask for Hemingway, and yet I've never seen him, never quite caught up with him. But I know Mr. Hemingway means trouble.

Usually, the dialogue goes like this:

"Have you seen Mr. Hemingway?"

"Oh, you mean Mr. Hemingway who is in the rabbit business?"

Or:

"Maybe you know my friend, Mr. Hemingway, who is in the rabbit business?"

"Of course! I hear business is very good, and he's looking for a partner."

Whereupon, Hemingway's friends shake hands and call for the cards.

As you may have surmised, there's no such person. "Hemingway" is the code word by which card cheats recognize each other. Once, apparently, a crook encountered an honest friend of the late author Ernest Hemingway (who would not have been overly charmed by this use of the family name) and had a confusing time trying to determine whether he was or wasn't a fellow thief.

So it is important to add the qualifying phrase "in the rabbit business"; rabbit representing "sucker," of course. And, judging from the number of times I've heard it, they can't have as many rabbits in all Australia as we have sitting at our card tables!

Anybody here seen Hennessy?

There are also underworld hand signals for mutual recognition which are more generally employed once the game has started. The chief ones (and remember they will be quickly, casually executed and acknowledged) are these:

Hand against chest, thumb spread out—When a stranger employs this gesture, almost as though he were going to stand up and make an old-fashioned bow, he is saying, "I'm out to take this game. Anybody want to partner with me?"

Right hand palm down on table, thumb out—"I'm with you, buddy boy, and we'll divvy afterward." (Or, sometimes, it is used instead of the hand-against-chest routine to ask the first question.)

Closed fist on chest—This is an antisocial reaction to the first question. The crook is answering, "I am working single-o, and I don't want you. I discovered these lambs first, so drop dead!"

Closed fist on table—The same surly response to the offer of co-operative cheating.

Oh, yes, one other thing. Not only the Hemingways but also the Hennessys have the unhappy distinction of being a code word for cheat. Occasionally, you will hear references to the Mr. Hennessy "who is in the rabbit business," but he isn't nearly as important a breeder as Mr. Hemingway.

Itch, hitch and twitch

Once a friendly relationship has been achieved through Hemingway, Hennessy or palm down on table, there are standard signs by which the new partners tell each other *exactly* the cards they hold, whether the game be bridge, draw or stud poker. This unethical ESP is achieved by finger signals, plus different ways of holding and laying down the hand.

Since these are universal, you can memorize them, but let me give a word of warning. They are not to be confused with *prearranged* signals which may be mechanical (use of electronic equipment), vocal (tone of voice, emphasis, phraseology) or what I like to call the *itch-twitch-hitch* technique, which is the employment of seemingly natural body movements to telegraph a crook's hand to his confederate.

We'll get to these three methods in a minute but, meanwhile, let's look at and memorize the standard signals.

In draw poker, extension of the right index finger on the table, almost as though it were pointing downward, indicates a pair. When the index and third finger are both extended, the crook holds two pairs. Three fingers extended signal three of a kind; four fingers flattened out, four of a kind; whole right hand on table, fingers spread out, a full house.

In this case, at least, the right hand *does* know what the left is doing, and the way the cards are held in the left hand provides supplementary signals.

For example, when the player's left index finger overlaps the pack he is holding in that hand, he is telling his confederate he holds aces (while the position of his right hand, as previously described, will signal whether it is one, two, three or four of a kind). Next, if the left index finger is retracted slightly, the code spells a king; if it lies atop the pack in the middle, a queen; if it is retracted still further to the end of the pack, a jack.

While the index finger alone overlapping the pack indicates an ace, index and middle fingers in this same position mean a ten. Two fingers, rather than one, in the king-signaling position, denote a nine; while two, in the jack-signaling location on the pack, spell a seven.

What's in the hole?

In *stud poker,* the cardsharper not only signals with his fingers but also with the apparently casual lay of his hand on the table. The aim, of course, is to tell his confederate what his turned-down "hole" card is.

Since the others are all dealt face up (except in games like seven-card stud), what more does a crook have to know!

Ace through nine in the hole can be wirelessed by the position of the first card dealt face up. If it lies almost squarely atop the hole card, the latter is an ace; if it is turned slightly, it indicates a king; if lying only two thirds atop the hole card, a queen; if only an edge rests on the hole card, a jack.

To wigwag a ten, the first face card dealt lies atop the hole card but pushed forward somewhat; pushed forward even more and also slightly to the left means the nine. Further moves in the same direction mean an eight, then a seven; after which the hole card is variously positioned *atop* the first face card to show lower denominations.

At the same time, fingers of the left hand are indicating the suit of the hole card. Clubs are shown by extending the forefinger, diamonds by two fingers, hearts by three fingers and spades by four.

In *bridge,* though many experts insist that cheating is practiced only occasionally, the sharps must think otherwise for there is a similar signal code. As the cheat holds his 13 cards in his left hand, he pulls one up slightly with his right hand. Across the table, his confederate counts the number of cards between the raised card and the cheat's palm. This indicates his strength in his strongest suit.

Which suit? The right hand resting on the raised card tells that. As in the stud poker signaling, one finger on the raised card means clubs, two, diamonds; three, hearts and four, spades.

Now let's signal a bit more. Which suit does the cheat want his ally to lead? Clubs? When it comes his turn to play, he places his card, whatever the suit, vertically atop the cards already played. Diamonds? He puts it diagonally to his left, for hearts, diagonally to his right, and for spades, horizontally.

Anyone for a rubber or two?

A loose board, a piece of string

Now let's talk about *mechanical* signaling, which must be almost as old as the sport of cards itself.

At least as far back as the middle 1500s, sharpers employed the "organum" or "organ," which was merely a loose floorboard to which a piece of string was tied. The cheat got signals on the sole of his foot as his ally gently tugged the string. The device is described in Girolamo Cardano's *Liber de Ludo Aleae* (Book on Games of Chance), translated from the Latin a few years ago by Sydney Henry Gould and published by Princeton University Press.

From this crude and possibly creaky technique, there developed a host of mechanical signals, some as simple as "kneeing" each other under the table or communicating by a bit of thread tied at one end to the pants leg of a crook and held by his confederate at the other. Some are as complicated as scientific progress in electronics and miniaturization will permit. These devices, about the size of a pack of cigarettes or cards, are known to the trade as "radio cue prompters" or, more simply, as "peek joints."

His master's voice

As with holdout machines, mechanical signals are used for the most part only by inferior "mechanics" who cannot master the more complicated forms of skullduggery and by superb "mechanics" who feel supremely confident that they won't be detected.

But for the great run of prudent cheats, mechanical signals pose the same danger as a Kepplinger or Martin holdout. The evidence is damning if discovered. So they prefer signaling that can never *quite* be proved against them, though they may find themselves eventually barred from polite cardplaying circles.

One of the oldest and simplest systems (similar to that employed by blindfolded stage "mind readers" as they identify articles held before them) involves phraseology. In the English whist clubs of Vic-

Figure 38. Herewith, Congressional confirmation of what I've been telling you about luminous readers. The surprised solon is U. S. Senator Karl E. Mundt, the senior Senator from South Dakota. If you were wearing those glasses, you'd look surprised, too!

torian days, a cheat would tell his partner which suit to lead by casual conversation seemingly directed to one of the other players or the bearded and elegantly dressed kibitzers.

"Have you seen old Jones the past fortnight?" he might ask.

The first letter of the first word—in this case, "H" for Hearts—indicated what suit he wanted.

In an amusing story, "My Lady Love, My Dove," by Roald Dahl that appeared some time ago in *The New Yorker,* an enterprising fictional couple developed this primitive code into an enormously complicated combination of phrases, vocal tones and finger positions to cheat at bridge.

Bidding "a *club*" meant that the cheat held one combination of cards, "*one* club" signaled a different combination, "I'll say *one* club," yet a third—and so on for some 500 signals!

And so to itch and twitch again

Ingenious as this system seems, it poses two serious drawbacks. First, it is almost impossible in the tension of play to remember all 500 combinations; in fact, the crux of the story is that the lady cheat *did* forget, thus losing a considerable sum for herself and husband. Secondly, of course, in shrewd bridge games, anything except unvaryingly toneless bids will quickly become suspect.

Thus, the smoothest operators consider *silent* systems best of all, and I agree that they are the most difficult to detect. By the way a crook smokes or holds his cigarette, by the almost imperceptible flicker of an eyelid, by the movement of his hands, by the way he strikes a match or lays a pack on the table, he telegraphs his partner.

Perhaps he scratches his nose or hitches his chair forward or twitches his nostrils or does any of a hundred other *natural* movements—and the shrewdest honest player will suspect nothing.

Thackeray, the great English novelist, was fascinated by professional gamblers, and in "Barry Lyndon" his hero thus describes how, masquerading as his uncle's valet, he signaled that conscienceless gentleman at games of écarté:

"Everything successful is simple. If, for instance, I wiped the dust off the chair with my napkin, it was to show that the enemy was strong in diamonds; if I pushed it, he had ace, king; if I said "Punch or wine, my lord?" hearts was meant; if "Wine or punch?" clubs. If I blew my nose, it was to indicate that there was another confederate employed by the adversary; and then, I warrant you, some pretty trials of skill would take place."

I thoroughly agree that, in card signaling, "everything successful is simple." However, as a gambling authority (certainly not as a literary critic), I have one strong reservation about Barry Lyndon.

I can't imagine I would require more than three hands of play before I began suspecting a kibitzing butler! Maybe they were more trusting back in Victorian days.

What can an honest guy do?

Unhappily, the detection of signaling is chiefly a job for the experts, and often we can offer only our professional judgment rather than concrete evidence that such techniques are being used. However, I can offer the following fundamental precautions:

Never play with your back to the wall. That picture or mirror may conceal a peephole through which a confederate in the adjoining room is signaling *your* hand. Even a seemingly blank wall can contain such a device.

Never trust two players who seem to be "enemies" in the game, bitterly quarreling over each hand. Probably they are confederates who are faking animosity to mislead you and perhaps even using their exchange of insults as signals.

As more constructive advice, I urge that you memorize the universal signals previously described, *but don't relax once you find they are not being used.* Remain alert for suspicious changes in tone, phrasing or movement. (Obviously, without a physical search, you won't be able to detect electronic signalers.)

Sometimes, merely by closing your eyes to avoid sight distractions, you can more easily spot tone or phrase signaling. On other hands, try to close your ears to the conversation and concentrate on watching body movements.

And don't be discreet about it! Even if you don't smell out the signaling, your actions may make the crooks *think* you have tumbled to them. After that, they will play a worried, near-honest game or maybe allow you to break even to avoid trouble.

And now—the "honest" cheats

Finally, there is a form of confederacy in which no signals are exchanged, no cards marked, no "coolers" slipped into the play. And yet, in my opinion, it is the lowest, most unethical form of cheating of all the hundreds of ways that you can cheat.

It is simply when three good players agree in advance to "gang" the fourth man at the table and split the take afterward. Immediately, the odds favor the cheats by 3 to 1, and by simple, uninspired play, they almost have to win.

Or, by resorting to the technique known as "crossfiring," they can practically insure quick victory. They merely keep raising till they force the luckless fourth man out. Even if he is game and tries to stay, his wallet cannot compete indefinitely with the other three wallets (which are really one).

Parenthetically, I might add here that the same "wolfpack" approach holds true in dice. In one New York game I monitored recently, no less than 11 "mechanics" were observed preying on *one* "sucker"!

By and large, however, I suspect that "ganging" is chiefly practiced by the quasi-amateur cheats who have jobs and play regularly in the same good clubs, fraternities and lodge halls. There is no way to detect them except through "guilt by association." That is, that the same three are *always* in the same game at the same time.

If you suspect such collusion in your own circles, you must take steps to break up the combination, though you must be careful not to make public charges. Some six decades ago, in *The Expert at the Card Table,* E. S. Andrews (writing under the name of S. W. Erdnase) laid down Erdnase's Law which still covers this situation today:

"No single player can defeat a combination, even when the cards are not manipulated."

CHAPTER IX

♠
♥
♦
♣
♠
♥
♦

THEY READ 'EM, YOU WEEP

♠
♥
♦
♣

ONCE UPON A TIME, there were two Irishmen named Bianco and Laforcade. Señor Bianco, I regret to say, came from Spain, which is my father's birthplace. Monsieur Laforcade was from France, and they met in Havana. At that time (as always in Cuba between revolutions), gambling was the chief diversion, almost the obsession of the populace, and yet this unholy señor and monsieur were able to perpetrate upon the game-wise Cubans the biggest, most successful swindle in the long, spotted history of marked cards.

Though there are two or three versions, I rely on Maskelyne, the careful Victorian chronicler of crooked gambling, and I relate the story to dramatize the danger of marked cards, *which is far greater today* than back in the time of Señor Bianco and M. Laforcade.

As I visualize them, both were voluble, gracious, charming, elegant in manners and attire and utterly worthless. Possibly, Señor Bianco was a feather's weight more admirable because he possessed patience and imagination, but when either grasped a pack in his stubby fingers—only in novels do gamblers have long, tapering fingers—the cards each became instruments of larceny.

Back home in Spain, Señor Bianco had industriously marked hundreds upon hundreds of packs of cards and resealed them in their original wrappers. It was an enormous task. True, he probably doctored the shorter Spanish deck which contained only 48 cards, but they probably were handpainted, engraved or woodcut decks, rather than printed playing cards, and he would have worked with the painstakingly

86

delicate brush strokes (though not the conscience) of a medieval illuminist.

Bianco then exported his wholesale artistry to Havana and arranged that the marked decks be sold at such ridiculously low prices that no private club or public gambling casino could resist stocking them. Not long afterward, he followed his cards to the New World and had a joyful, profitable reunion with them.

Thanks to his Continental manners, he gained entree everywhere, and everywhere he went, of course, he played with cards whose backs he knew like the back of his own hand. Without ever a lapse into such vulgar practices as cold-decking, piking, crimping or false-cutting, he won and won at cards *he* had not introduced into the play.

Typical shadework on the ace. Note how the tip of the fan rib is flattened slightly. Try riffling these pages. With practice you should be able to follow the marks across the fan. This is known as "watching the movies."

The unethical intruder

However, to mislead his victims, Señor Blanco adopted the melancholy hauteur of a grandee, carelessly complaining of his heavy "losses." Thus, the word got around in Havana that the señor from Spain must indeed be a very wealthy man to sustain such runs of bad luck at the table, and the future looked very bright to Bianco.

Enter M. Laforcade.

By what ruse we do not know, this Parisian sharper of much more limited talents and vision managed to insinuate himself into the most exclusive Havana club that was, without its knowledge, currently supporting the señor. M. Laforcade stole a quantity of its cards, intending to mark them and slip them back into play.

Naturally, he discovered they were already marked.

Once you recognize a marked deck, the spots seem to leap at you, and it is difficult to believe the other players can be so blind. Thus, everywhere M. Laforcade ventured, he detected the same doctored packs and realized that some mastermind was quietly working a colossal swindle on the gamblers of Havana.

But who?

87

Investigating much as I would investigate such a challenging problem (but for purely selfish reasons of his own), M. Laforcade night after night observed the play at the club and in the various casinos. Finally, a somewhat peculiar pattern of betting, plus lamentations over nonexistent losses, led him to Señor Bianco.

A prisoner of his own game

When the Spaniard politely invited the Frenchman to a game of écarté, M. Laforcade obligingly accepted and lost. According to the etiquette of the club, Señor Bianco asked whether he wanted a second game. With equal courtesy, M. Laforcade declined and said he would prefer to tell the señor *how* he had won.

This he did and with a deferential bow added that he was now cutting himself in for half of Bianco's profits, the alternative being exposure and probable arrest. Mustering as much grace as he could under the unfortunate circumstances, Bianco agreed.

Thereafter, a slave to his own scheme, he played and played, day and night, while M. Laforcade did *nothing* except to spend his unearned loot on the wine and beauty of Havana. Eventually, the injustice of the situation became insupportable. Señor Bianco did all the work, took all the risks, kept only half of the money. He made as big a killing as he could and vanished.

Now M. Laforcade was in trouble. The supply of Bianco decks was running low. There was increasing danger that honest cards might slip into the play and yet, so long as any chance of making a dishonest peso remained, M. Laforcade could not bring himself to discard the scheme. He began sitting in the games himself.

And the game still goes on

Eventually, lacking the talent of his vanished partner, M. Laforcade was suspected of being what he was and suffered the indignity of arrest as a common cheat. But this whole surprising story has one more surprise.

The public prosecutor could not prove that the Frenchman had either marked the cards or arranged their import into Cuba because, after all, he hadn't done either of these things. Nor could frustrated justice legally establish that M. Laforcade *knew* the cards were marked.

The one witness who would have been delighted to establish this point had long since left the country.

So M. Laforcade had to be acquitted and, like his slave partner, he promptly disappeared. Later, perhaps, in some squalid gambling den on the pirate-haunted Isle of Pines or in the smelly bazaars on the African side of the Mediterranean, they met again. Unfortunately, the record is incomplete, but I have a strong suspicion where they must be *now*.

Down below, for eternity, Señor Bianco and Monsieur Laforcade are seated across from each other on uncomfortably hot chairs, doomed to eternal play with their own marked cards. They are unable to cheat each other since both can read the backs, unable even to enjoy the thrill of honest playing since the moment the cards are cut, shuffled and dealt, they know instantly which one will win and the other is powerless to stop it.

Thus they must go in tedious, endless play that is neither honest nor dishonest, only monumentally boring. . . .

The marked card murder

Surprisingly, though there have since been many refinements in techniques, Señor Bianco had mastered the three fundamentals upon which today's flourishing marked card industry exists. Naturally, in this shadowy profession, there is no trade association to collect and publish statistics, but I have heard estimates by those who *should* know that some 100,000 doctored decks are sold yearly and the cheats reap perhaps $20,000,000 annually—or more—from them.

First, there must be wholesale manufacture which now is accomplished by assembly lines of artists who specialize in shading, linework and the several other forms of marking. Numerous factories (*not* to be confused with the legitimate playing card manufacturers) turn out marked decks.

Second, as Bianco did it, the phony decks must be widely and innocently distributed, and this is often accomplished by offering them to hotel cigar stands, neighborhood shops, private clubs and lodges at tempting bargain prices. By Broadway legend, Arnold Rothstein, the shrewd professional gambler, lost $100,000 at marked cards that had previously been deposited at a hotel lobby stand. When he discovered the trick, the story goes, he balked at paying, and instead of losing the $100,000, lost his life.

The same caper on a grander scale was reportedly worked all over Europe shortly before World War I with "DeLands," the marked product of an American engraver named Theodore DeLand. The packs were identified by an ace of spades fearsomely decorated with scimitar, crossbones and skull, inspiring a lurid but dubious story about them.

When the fraud was finally exposed, those "in the know" whispered that an international underworld terrorist society had masterminded the coup. I consider this highly doubtful, for the underworld has always indicated a preference for fixed horse and dog betting, slot machines, policy and similar wholesale frauds that sacrifice finesse in favor of huge turnover and cruelly unfair odds.

As you will remember, Bianco resealed his cards in their *original* wrappings. This is the third—and most important—element, for if a player tears the government tax stamp off a deck of familiar Bee backs, how could he possibly suspect they had been tampered with!

Matter of fact, while some experts complain that the legitimate manufacturers could thwart marked card artists by changing their designs, *I* blame the government. Let me explain.

In a highly competitive business, the honest manufacturers must offer the decks the public will buy; and gamblers are curiously conservative in one respect. They like the old, familiar backs. *Anyhow, any deck of cards ever made, including those with perfectly plain backs, can be successfully marked.* Thus, the manufacturers cannot prevent misuse of their product any more than Smith & Wesson can avert murderous misuse of one of its guns.

As I have warned, the deck that comes so innocently from behind the bar in a private club or upstairs from a hotel lobby stand may be marked. But, of course, "paper work," as gamblers describe it, can also be introduced during play and, in the cheating profession, there is a curious specialist known as the "switchman" who concentrates solely on this lightning maneuver.

Once a crook with mediocre talents smells out and insinuates himself into a big, honest game, he retains a "switchman" on a commission basis, usually 10 per cent of what he can steal during the evening's play. The "switchman" sits in on the game, waits patiently for the right opportunity and then slips in the marked deck. He signals his partner who immediately begins to bet with great perception.

However, in one lamentable instance that I know of, the "switchman" was disgruntled because his associate had bargained him down into accepting a 5 per cent commission. He went through with the deal, but he introduced cards that he had glued together.

Picking up the deck, the dealer found he couldn't shuffle. "I've heard of cold decks," he said slowly, "but this is the first time that one ever froze in my hand."

Like the ads say, 57 varieties

As I write this, I am leafing through the liberally illustrated catalogue of a supply house which devotes almost a *dozen* pages to a bewildering variety of "readers," as marked cards are politely called.

It is rather depressing. Many experienced players can recognize marked cards, they think. Perhaps they know one or two forms of markings, but there are literally dozens of ways in which the same deck can be doctored. I recommend reading this catalogue as a money-saving antidote to false pride!

For example, in recent years, plastic backs have been especially popular with clubs because they can be washed and used longer. There also is a touching popular belief that plastics are "mark proof." This catalogue offers a variety of the most popular plastic backs marked aces down to 2s for $12.50 per set (and $2 extra for suit markings). The same decks, unmarked, are $8.

Among amateur cheats, there is an equally false belief that "luminous readers" are the greatest advance in card manufacturing since printed decks were first introduced to the gambling world in 1832. Luminous readers bear huge markings on their red backs which can be detected only with the aid of red tinted luminous glasses or visors.

The same helpful supply house offers them in any design (but only in red) for $3.50 a pack, or $40 per dozen, while the luminous glasses, luminous clip-ons to go over your own glasses or luminous visor, are only $3.50.

It's a hoax

Among sophisticated gamblers, "luminous readers" are pretty much of a joke today. Obviously, if a player is wearing tinted glasses or visors, he immediately gives himself away to the rest of the table.

If you are ever in a game where you suspect someone is pulling this rather boyish cheating device, there is a very simple way to expose him. Just ask politely, "Mind if I try on your glasses (or visor) for a minute? I've been thinking my eyes get overstrained in long games."

Even simpler, just get a fresh deck. But *you* get it, and not at the lobby stand downstairs. To make doubly sure, get a blue, yellow, green or brown back, anything except a red-back deck.

But they never give up

To get around such obvious giveaways as tinted glasses or visors, sensitive gamblers—sensitive enough, that is, to recognize a tweak on the nose as their luminous glasses are yanked off their faces—pursued their research into ophthalmology somewhat further. Contact lenses might be inconspicuously tinted, they decided, and one supply house, ever alert to aid science, put its technicians on a 28-hour day to crack the problem.

The contact lenses developed as a result described as "new improved triple curve contact lenses," requires a special ophthalmometer reading by your eye doctor, plus your regular spectacle prescription, *and* cost over $150 per pair. But, if you can believe the description (and who would suspect the purveyors of so much fine dishonest equipment), the lenses are worth every stolen penny that they cost.

Spotting the cheater's cheaters

Other supply house catalogues present a glowing picture of the possibilities in contact lenses for undetected thievery, but, while I hate to disillusion the innocent crooks they service the fact is that, like luminous readers, contact lenses *can* be detected.

True, the glass is slipped over only the pupil ˌand the iris, so that the white of the eye is not reddened. But if the light is good and you know what you are looking for, you will see a ruby tint around the pupils. Again, by catching the suspect in profile, you may detect a slight but suspicious bulge in the center of the eye.

Finally, a research specialist for a contact lens laboratory suggests still another approach which he calls the "blink test." Normally, we blink about 14 times a minute and, if your suspect is going at that rate, he probably is not wearing the lenses. But if he blinks at the rate of 20 or more times per minute, beware!

As with luminous readers, the Rx to stop the fraud is simple. Bring in a new deck with backs of any color except red.

Aside from these two shaky new advances in the field—the plastic cards that are not mark-proof, as honest people think; the luminous readers and contact lenses that are not detection-proof, as the cheats think—there is a long list of staple designs in marked cards. Maybe I'm just a conservative, but if *I* were going to play with "paper work," I would much prefer to rely on the time-tested frauds.

The range is bewildering. Bee decks may have enlarged red or blue diamonds or reduced white diamonds; single line work; tapered single line work; double line work; one side of a diamond reduced (neostyle), or two sides widened.

SYNDICATED
GAMBLING
IN NEW YORK STATE

A REPORT OF THE NEW YORK STATE COMMISSION OF INVESTIGATION FEBRUARY, 1961

Figure 39. The intensive investigation by the State of New York put on official record many of the practices that I reveal in this book. This is the cover of the 136 page report.

Figure 40. Read it and weep. Page 68 of the New York State report.

SCHEDULE 13

ADVERTISEMENT FOR SPECIAL CONTACT LENS AND MARKED PLAYING CARDS*

 K·C CARD CO.   / CHICAGO / WEbster 9-3515

40

NEW IMPROVED TRIPLE CURVE CONTACT LENSES

Contact Lenses, developed by K. C. Card Co. to read red backed playing cards, have been unsuccessfully copied by many others, but we offer the only practical lenses for reading our Contact Lens Cards.

So small they are invisible. Cannot be seen even under the very closest inspection. Guaranteed.

We have done tremendous research in color and in inks, and we can assure you that our Contact Lenses and our Contact Lens Cards are truly the only combination which complement each other.

Now you can be sure of getting the only TRIPLE CURVE CONTACT LENSES thru special machinery techniques available only to us.

This guarantees you IMPROVED VISIBILITY, MORE COMFORT, the ability to WEAR THEM LONGER, in fact all the time if you wish.

These NEW, IMPROVED, TRIPLE CURVE Contact Lenses are medically approved, and we FULLY GUARANTEE the fit.

SPECIAL NOTICE: In the event you desire a *second* pair of Contact Lenses, or another single lens, using your original prescription, you will not be charged full price, since we will have your original prescription on file and can save you money. We are the only firm able to offer you this money saving value.

No. CL-1. Triple Curve Contact Lenses ....Per Pair **$160.00**

Notice: Full amount must be sent with orders for above.

SEE INSTRUCTIONS FOR ORDERING ON OPPOSITE PAGE

CONTACT LENS CARDS
CONTACT LENS CARDS CANNOT BE SEEN WITH NAKED EYE

NOW: LOWER PRICES

Contact Lens Cards are the newest card work on the market. ORDER YOURS TODAY.

This work cannot be seen with the naked eye, but with our Contact Lens described above, the work is seen as plainly as the Ace shown here as A. The King is shown as K, and on down to the Deuce, shown as 2.

THIS IS GUARANTEED TO BE ALL WE SAY! Contact Lens Cards are tedious to make, but well worth the price.

No. CL-8. Contact Lens Cards

Sample Deck ....$ 8.00

6 decks 45.00

12 decks 85.00

SUIT MARKINGS: ADD $2.00 per deck to above prices.

PLASTIC CONTACT LENS CARDS

Improved techniques in marking and special inks make it possible for us to offer you red back plastic cards for use with our Contact Lenses. Available in Club or Windsor red back cards only. Work is perfect and each set contains two decks, both red. Specify back desired in your order.

No. CL-6. Plastic Contact Lens Cards ....Set of 2 decks **$35.00**

Suit markings: add $2.00 per deck to above prices.

*Exhibit 12 at the public hearing.

There's a formula *to marking*

For only $3 per deck, you can purchase either the popular Rider or New Fan back, each marked in any one of six ways that you may prefer. You will examine them for the fine blockout on the flower at end, the perfect shade work on the Fan, or the clever work on the dots at the end of the card, etc.

What on earth does it all mean!

To know where to look for what markings, remember that there are certain inescapable principles of this deplorable art:

So they can always be seen, the markings should be within about an inch of the top of the card and repeated in the same position at the bottom diagonally across. Thus, no matter which way they are held, the mark is visible both in the deal and in the victim's hands.

10

While they must merge inconspicuously into the color and design of the particular back being doctored, they have to stand out sufficiently to be recognizable during fast play.

Thus, in one of the marked decks described above, you would know that within about an *inch* of the top or bottom, there is a mark of *almost* the same color or design as the rest of the back. Nonetheless, improbable as this may seem, I would wager that you still wouldn't spot it unless you know at least the five general styles of marking (and maybe not even then).

These styles are:

Shading—a tiny bit of the design is darkened almost imperceptibly in the same color.

Line work (and double line work)—Thin single or double lines are added to the design in positions where they seem to be part of the design.

Bracing—Addition of extra bars (as to the bicycle in the Bicycle decks or to the fan ribs in a Fan deck).

95

Blockouts—Parts of the design which are supposed to be in white (such as white diamonds) are "blocked out" in red, blue, green or whichever other color is predominant in the particular design.

Border work—On cards with white margins, the outer or inner border lines are fattened in various spots to bulge.

The mark that fooled Houdin

I might add an early variation that, for several weeks, completely stumped Houdin, the great French authority. A number of decks that had been confiscated from a known cheat were given to Houdin for examination. Apparently, they were plain white-back club cards of the period without any design in which markings might be concealed.

In view of their source, the Frenchman *knew* they must be marked and yet the closest inspection revealed nothing. Finally, in frustration, he hurled them across the table.

As they scattered and the sunlight struck them from a different angle, Houdin found his answer. Tiny bits of the glaze were missing from different cards in different positions to indicate both value and suit.

(Ordinarily, I should point out here, only value is indicated today and often only on aces through jacks, on the theory that if you know where they are, you control most games. However, a very prudent

Figure 40a. Notice "humped" edges along left and right borders, the key to this marked deck series. In figure 40b, the flowering pattern is broken by an irregular arrangement.

crook can have suit markings added at a nominal cost of about $2 per pack. Usually, 2s are left unmarked since they have little importance except in something like deuces-wild poker.)

By today's standards, the Houdin pack was rather primitive, but the principle of optical illusion that fooled him fooled me in a variation I will tell you about in a moment.

Primitive but sometimes good

Originally, "paper workers" merely spilled water on the backs of the high cards, let it stand a few minutes and then wiped it off. This left a blotted area that stood out somewhat like "shade work," but a bit too conspicuously. This technique (or the use of a sharp knife to remove the glaze) was employed by the sharper whom Houdin detected.

Other primitive methods of which you should beware, since they are sometimes used today, include the following:

Steam ironing the high cards to dull their polish.

"Sunning the deck," which is merely putting the high cards on a windowsill in strong sunlight for a few hours. This gives them a yellowish tinge which is visible only if you know what you are looking for.

Pressing the backs with some rounded instrument. Back when penholders were fashionable, crooks used them, but any similar device will serve. This technique produces a tiny concave mark recognizable by touch to the crook as he deals.

Probably, since these methods tamper with the glaze, you are thinking that *unglazed* cards might beat the cheats. At one time, "steamboat," or unglazed, cards were in wide use—whereupon, the crooks glazed on their marks, using paraffin wax and not too much of it, so their lines were visible only at a certain angle.

In this simple code, aces were left unmarked, kings had a diagonal line running from left top to right bottom; queens, a straight line down the center; jacks, a diagonal line running from right top to left bottom; tens, a lateral line in the center; nines, a vertical and lateral line that crossed in the center; eights, a combination of the king and ten markings; sevens, a combination of the jack and ten mark; sixes, the combined king and jack; fives, two lateral lines; fours, two lines like the king; threes, two lines like the queen; twos, two lines like the jack.

And suits, too

In many games, like poker, merely knowing or controlling the disposition of a few high cards gives all the advantage that a shrewd player needs. But there are also systems, necessarily more complicated, that mark for both value and suit.

One such method quarters the top and bottom section of the cards; in descending order, the location of the mark or tiny pincture indicates clubs, diamonds, hearts or spades. Simultaneously, value is indicated in descending order by its location crosswise on the card. Extreme left is the ace, extreme right, the seven, and if the smaller cards also must be indicated, double marks are made over king, queen, jack, ten, nine to indicate the six, five, four, three or two.

Another more ingenious method has been applied to packs which have some radiating design like a fan. If there are 13 lines, ribs, wheels or spokes, each denotes a different value. Thus, a dot on the second line from the left would indicate a king, and the spacing of the dot down from the top of the design would tell the suit. Where the design does not offer 13 convenient lines, the shape of the mark must be changed. If there are only four lines, they can be dotted to indicate the face cards; for the other values, curlicues, crosses, etc., can be employed.

In general then, the position of the mark, either vertically or horizontally or in combination, represents value or suit or both. In such a small area as the back of a playing card—and only an inch of its top and bottom, at that—the marks, of necessity, must be crowded close together. That is, the dot indicating an ace is very close to the position which would indicate a ten, and a "paper worker" must know the intricacies of his design the way an Indian knows his forest.

And this mark fooled me

For a time, manufactured marked cards enjoyed a vogue, though it is difficult to see how they could have been profitable, for the gamblers kept the supply as limited and secret as possible. First of the type was a scroll back in which the shape of just one scroll, and the direction in which it pointed, was the mark.

When eventually this pioneer work became too popularly known, plaid backs came into vogue. The spaces in various sets of parallel lines that ran right to the tops of the cards were widened to indicate value, while a band of lines that ended on the left side of the cards was similarly widened to show diamond, heart, club or spade in descending order from the top.

Still later came a remarkably ingenious floral back in which two tiny sprays in the left-hand corner were altered. The lower spray curved up, down or ended in a shape vaguely suggestive of heart or spade, thus indicating suit. The upper spray had dots and wavy lines resembling hieroglyphics which gave value.

However, manufactured marked cards gradually fell into disuse and the individual artistry of shading, tinting and line work, first with pen, more recently with brush, became the accepted technique and is so today.

Plain-back cards readily adapted themselves to delicate, over-all tinting, while, with ornamental backs, only parts of the design are subjected to a subtle wash of the different-colored aniline dyes. It was a combination of these two techniques that kept me fooled for a week. Finally, I discovered that the *entire* ornamental back had been shaded except for the mark itself.

I felt rather proud of this bit of Sherlock Holmes detection—until I happened to reread Maskelyne's excellent *Sharps and Flats,* published in London more than 60 years ago. There, to my chagrin, I found the technique fully explained!

Now you *read 'em!*

Having progressed this far, let's re-examine some of the most popular backs which we mentioned earlier and see precisely how they are marked. We can't describe every variety of marking because they run into the hundreds, but we can thumbnail the ones that are being most widely used, or rather misused, today.

As you no doubt know, the Bee back consists of a combination of white diamonds with either red or blue diamonds. One technique is to enlarge the diamonds, preferably all on the left side but also along the top or on the right, if the customer so prefers. A second technique reduces the over-all size of the white diamond, while in "neostyle," only one side of the white diamond is reduced.

In a triumph of artistic miniaturization, a fourth variety manages to concentrate tapered single line work on four lines of the upper left corner, and yet indicates every card from ace down to deuce. Still another packs in all "the work," as the cheats call it, in just three diamonds on the upper right corner by variously reducing parts of the diamond to show A-2 values.

The Rider back, you may recall, is a design brimming over with pastoral innocence: two angels in circles are surrounded by flowers, birds, grass and cherubs in each of the four corners. And never has innocence concealed quite so much deviltry!

Sometimes, "the work" is in the scroll design above the top left cherub . . . or the birds are blocked out . . . or the flowers . . . or the markings are concealed in the grass.

Similarly, the New Fan back, in which a bicycle is superimposed upon an opened fan, seems a quaint, fussy Victorian anachronism in today's harsh world, but, according to one supplier, it offers seven different possibilities for doctoring.

Similarly, I should add, whether the back be Racer, Bulldog, Tally Ho, Angel Back, Circle, Club, Aviator or any other standard design, marked sets are available. Matter of fact, for the modest fee of only $1 above catalogue price, the houses will put your private markings on a deck, or if you won't trust them with your secret code, they will supply the tools so you can do your own marking.

For $10, you can obtain a complete "card marking kit," which includes two bottles of French type card ink, in red and blue; plus two brushes and two glass palettes, 24 cellophane wrappers and the same number of red tear-off strips and a bottle of cellophane cement.

Blockout ink and blender in any color costs $8 per bottle, regular blockout ink is only half that price, while a camel's-hair brush and French pen (both imported, naturally) cost merely $1 and 50 cents, respectively.

Though the trick is laughably obvious, I think I should warn you about "one-way" packs or "single-enders," as they also are called, because particularly impudent crooks still try to use them. These are cards in which the design in some manner looks different when the card is turned upside down.

For example, several years ago, as you may remember, there was a fad for collecting "artistic" backs which carried paintings by many famous artists. While most praiseworthy from the aesthetic point of view, the cards offered irresistible temptation to anyone with a larcenous mind.

Honest, marked unmarked cards

I am sure that many naive players were regularly cheated out of their pants by sharpers who reversed the aces in the pack so they could second-deal them or held key cards upside down in their hands to signal partners. Any deck in which the design is not *exactly* the same, no matter how you hold the cards, is dangerous!

And now for the most frustrating form of marked cards—a deck that has been legitimately printed by an honest manufacturer taking every precaution, a deck that has not been deliberately tampered with or accidentally doctored with telltale dirt spots and yet is flagrantly marked!

How can this be?

The manufacturers check and recheck their engravings against the possibility of the slightest nick or flaw and print their cards in big sheets, a full deck or more at a time. They stamp, rather than cut, the separate cards from the sheets; then their staffs of inspectors examine and re-examine the cards so that every pack is absolutely uniform, top, bottom, sides and rounded corners.

But here is what happens. There are separate large printings, and while all the tens upon tens of thousands of cards in any one printing

Figure 41. Starting at the lower right hand corner, note five arrows up the side, across the top and down the left hand side of card. These are five places where Bee back cards can be most effectively marked.

Figure 42. These are known as "sorts." If you will look very closely, you will see edges have been cut so that some of the diamonds are smaller than the others. This indicates value.

are uniform, they may differ, ever so slightly, from the cards in other printing runs. That is, in one run, a tiny bit of the design may be "bitten" off closer at the end. It could be anything, scrollwork, floral pattern, diamond or whatnot—but it is enough.

By patiently sorting through thousands of decks, the supply houses reconstruct *new* decks from the different runs, and the tiny variation in the size of the design *is* the mark. Quite logically, such packs are known to the profession as "sorts."

It was worth the $200

Since the supply houses *do* carry much equipment that is primarily used by entertainers, their declarations that they offer their wares for demonstration of magic or for exposé purposes only has a seeming plausibility. However, they give themselves away in their catalogues by recommending certain marked decks as primarily for poker and others for blackjack and even advertising special pinochle "readers." Poker, blackjack, pinochle, I can assure you, are not magicians' games —not the games of honest magicians, anyhow.

Unlike the movies or television, where the right guy wins out eventually, victory in real-life gambling goes almost always to the cheat. Thus, whenever I hear stories of a cheater cheated, I like to remember them, and here is the best one I know about marked cards.

A "paper worker," who prided himself on the secret value markings he had personally applied with the best imported French ink and the most expensive camel's-hair brush, was sitting in a poker game with several less talented thieves. One of the heavy losers suspected the cards were marked but could detect nothing on them.

So, in the course of gathering up the discards, he managed to get a fast peek at and memorize the top ten cards. This is not difficult for an accomplished peeker, and anyone can train himself to memorize up to 26 cards by remembering in blocks of two, as you would memorize a phone number. CR-aps 7-71-12, for example.

Then he slammed his fist on the table. "I say these cards are marked," he shouted, "and to prove it, I'll read the backs of some of the top cards on the discard pile. Jack of *spades,* nine of *hearts,* six of *diamonds,* ace of *spades.* . . ."

After the game had ended in mutual suspicions and exchange of insults, the "paper worker" quietly took the accuser to one side.

"How much did you lose?" he asked.

"Two hundred dollars—and I'd like to know which guy rung in that lousy deck!"

"That was *my* deck," the "paper worker" said. "Here's your $200.

"Now tell me just one thing. I know how you spotted the values, but how in heaven's name did you tell the *suits!"*

CHAPTER X

♠
♥
♦
♣
♠
♥
♦

THESE BELLY STRIPPERS ARE
DANGEROUS

♠
♥
♦
♣

IN MY TRAVELS through the U.S. and abroad, I constantly see strippers in action as they take susceptible men for everything they have. However, these are not the curvaceous strippers who remove their clothes. They are the doctored cards known lovingly to the crooked gamblers as "strippers," and they remove men's wallets far more effectively than a mere woman could.

Once, for example, I was casually kibitzing a poker game at a plush summer resort hotel in the Catskills an hour's easy drive by parkway out of New York City.

You know the kind of place: patios and swimming pools, tennis courts and a fairly good 18-hole golf course for those guests able to bestir themselves under the sun. Nights, name bands for dancing, three oval bars that were always more popular than the bands—and, day or night, pickup card games all over the place.

That was why I was there. The way some men follow the horses, I follow the cards, both as my business and as my hobby.

Today's game was pretty stiff and, I suspected, might just be getting out of hand. According to awed reports from the other kibitzers, one player, a tall, slim, well-dressed "executive from the garment district," as he vaguely described himself, had won more than $1,000 the day before.

In my line, of course, you instinctively distrust such runs of "luck," and I decided the game merited more than casual kibitzing.

The opening "wedgie"

I thought of all the possibilities: cards that had been premarked or were being marked during play, switching in of a "cooler," peeking, signaling, the use of "strippers," sometimes also called (among many other aliases) "wedgies."

However, since the game was now in its second day with the same players, I had no excuse to get into it and study the cards.

Instead, half-stretched out in an oversized chair, as though I were just killing time, I lazily watched the play. Presumably, I was another vacationing Joe, and I wanted to keep it that way.

I concentrated on the "garment executive." He was, I decided, an honest player—or a superb "mechanic."

Closely as I watched, I couldn't spot the slightest irregularity in the way he dealt and handled the cards. He did not use the "mechanic's grip" to hold them, and his cuts and shuffles seemed above reproach. Matter of fact, I noticed that on his own deals he usually lost or at best raked in very modest pots.

Probably, I told myself, I was beginning to contract the occupational disease of all investigators—*over*suspicion. And then it happened.

A short, stocky player who constantly needled the garment man was dealing. I noticed the faintest flicker of triumph as my man studied the cards dealt him. Then he closed his hand over them and made a stiff opening bet.

A bluff? The other players didn't know, and it was amusing to see how cautiously they reacted.

One dropped out right away and the dealer, drawing two cards, just stayed.

Funny, Funny poker

The third hesitated, then stayed, too. He was the big loser in the game and beginning to play with more stubbornness than intelligence.

Now the garment man raised again. Grumbling, the dealer folded, and the third player called.

My man from West 32d Street slapped down a full house, kings high, and took the pot.

This was funny poker, I thought. Normally, a man dealt such a strong opener bets modestly to keep the other players contributing to the pot. Instead, my boy had wasted his full house on a small pot.

Why? Was it possibly a setup for a kill later in the game?

For almost an hour, the play droned on without incident. I was beginning to think that I had been overly suspicious, after all, and that the garment executive was just another mediocre player riding a lucky streak.

Then the short, unpleasant character dealt again. He grumbled impatiently as the garment man studied his hand hesitatingly and finally discarded one card.

As the betting started, this "executive" pushed forward the minimum amount of chips. Promptly, everybody else began raising, and the pot went up, up, up.

I didn't need the services of a swami from the mysterious East to read their minds.

Obviously, they thought, since he had bet heavily on a full house before and now was just staying, he probably had two pairs. Or, just possibly, three of a kind which he held along with a "kicker," having hoped to fill out a full house. Or maybe he had rashly drawn toward a straight or flush—and didn't have anything.

Aces, anyone?

Anyhow, his cautious manner inspired the heavy losers in the game to keep raising (why do amateur losers always plunge!) and there was several hundred dollars in the pot before someone called. This time, my boy put down—four aces!

Now I was convinced that the game was "gaffed." The full-house had been throwaway bait for the kill. It was more than coincidence that both times the cards had been dealt by the unpleasant stocky little man, and his hostility toward the garment executive was intended to conceal the fact that they were working together.

If my hunch was right, there would be another long stretch of honest, innocuous play, and then again the little man would deal a winning hand to his confederate. In a lively game that went for most of the day, they only needed four or five such hands, well spaced out, to make their $1,000-a-day quota.

I had to get into the game, discover how the cheats were operating and disrupt their pattern to protect the other players. Fortunately (for my plan, that is), the heaviest loser threw down his cards in disgust. "I'm cleaned out," he said. "Six hundred in two days is too steep for me."

I took his chair and, as soon as I got my hands on the cards, gave them a riffle shuffle to "watch the movies." I didn't see any dots, shade or line work dance back and forth, so tentatively I ruled out marked cards.

Then, on the pretext of stacking the deck, I ran my fingers lightly along both sides and both top and bottom edges. This was it! I felt almost imperceptible bulges on the sides. The cards were belly "strippers," as plainly marked by scissors as any artist could have marked the backs with camel's-hair brush and French ink.

My hand is forced

However, for very practical reasons, I could not immediately challenge the crooks and break up the game.

First, I needed a little time alone with the deck, or some of the cards from it, to confirm what my touch told me. When confronted with "strippers," I follow the prudent advice handed down by John Philip Quinn, one of the great crooked gamblers of the last century, who later in life turned over a new, honest deck and reformed.

"Strippers," Quinn postulated, "cannot be detected without a delicate touch and close scrutiny, implying suspicion and inviting a quarrel if the rogue be vicious, as none is so jealous of his honor as a thief."

I didn't especially mind blocking a punch to the nose, but I couldn't risk the possibility of a suit for slander in case I happened to be wrong.

So, I decided, I would palm out three or four of the unimportant cards, which wouldn't be missed in a fast poker game. Then, on some pretext, I would excuse myself and by calipering the samples or simply comparing them with an honest, unscissored deck, make sure that they were "strippers."

If the thieves followed pattern, I would have an hour's breather before their next big pot. This would be ample time to complete my research and alert the hotel management to what was going on.

Then, unexpectedly, the heaviest loser who was still surviving in the game disrupted my plan.

"I want to begin getting my money back!" he shouted. "From here on in, we double the stakes."

The others quickly agreed, and I had to go along or get out of the game. At least, it was my deal. I thought momentarily of palming the suspect deck and bringing in an honest one.

I'd better be right!

But, if I did it right on my first deal in the game while they were still sizing *me* up, I'd give everything away. So, praying that I was right, stocking the "strippers" in the pile in two different combinations, I dealt the garment man a full house—and the heavy loser four aces.

At least, I thought that was what I was doing. When the pot had reached $500 and the loser displayed his four aces to take it, I didn't have to act. Dabbing my forehead with a handkerchief, I said, "I'm sorry, gentlemen, but this game is much too rough for me." I got out with the deck and showed the startled manager how the game had been "gaffed."

"I don't care if it is bad publicity for the hotel," he said angrily. "I'm going to have those cheats arrested as a warning to others to keep away from this hotel."

"You'd better act fast," I advised. "I'm afraid I was in a spot where I couldn't help tipping them off."

Sure enough, the minute I left the game, they had checked out. "But the doorman remembers their license number," the manager said triumphantly.

"You'll find they registered here under phony names and addresses, and the car was rented," I told him.

All of which also checked out.

But I have a good memory for associating faces with a particular *modus operandi,* and someday, somewhere, on a vacation ship, at a hotel convention, in a private club, I will catch up with that pair.

I especially want to because I despise "stripper" gamblers more than I do any of the other breeds of card crooks.

History in your palm

To anyone who really loves cardplaying, there is a fascination in the history, the romance, the artistry contained in a deck of cards—and it is a profanation to mutilate them with a pair of scissors. If you were a book collector, you would similarly despise those barbarians who strip off old bindings, and there are rose growers who cannot abide cut flowers.

I don't propose to don black robe and mortarboard and, as Professor Garcia, lecture my students on card history.

However, let me tell you just briefly that recently, at the Peabody Museum in Baltimore, I had the opportunity to browse for hours through a $150,000 collection of more than 200 decks that cover almost seven centuries.

Among them were concave, convex, oval and round cards and, rarity of rarities, a 78-card deck hand painted for Charles VI of France back in 1392. Cards are first recorded as being used in Europe in 1299, and the Charles VI deck is the earliest known pack that is still in existence.

And I could tell you the names of dozens of "mutilators" who would cheerfully strip the sides, ends or both if they could lay hands on that pack and use it in a game!

Though we take it for granted that a deck consists of 52 cards, this is only the Anglo-American and French deck. Actually, during the Middle Ages, there were no less than four other sizes that have survived down to the present: the 78-card Tarot deck of the Mediterranean, the Italian deck of 40 cards, the Spanish deck of 48 and the 32-card German deck.

And, every time you pick up a card, you hold in your hand the symbolism of a class struggle that dates back to Renaissance Italy.

Modest Jeff Davis

For example, our word "spade" is derived from the Italian for sword and, originally, the suit of swords signified nobility. The clergy was represented by chalices which became hearts, the merchants by coins which changed into tiles and then into diamonds. Poor low men on the Renaissance totem pole, the peasants were depicted by clubs.

Always, there have been political associations with cards. About the time of the American Revolution, an English deck declared the kings to be "the four present powerful and flourishing monarchies of Europe, viz.: Great Britain, France, Spain and Prussia."

Alas! Within a few years, the French Revolution "dethroned" royalty and put commoners' heads in their places on the kings, queens, and jacks of French cards. Similarly, some 40 years ago, the Soviet used cards as a sacrilegious propaganda device. A capitalist in silk represented the joker and nuns who were shown embracing monks became the queens.

During our own War Between the States, a special Union deck made in New York issued to the Boys in Blue pictured various victorious Northern generals. The Confederates also distributed packs to the Boys in Gray (which were likewise manufactured in New York and smuggled into Confederate territory). This deck represented both generals and statesmen of the Gray, and Jefferson Davis took modest billing as only the nine of spades.

But you'd better stop me here because I could go on and on. Actually, I just wanted to make my point about the "mutilators" who so callously mangle cards into "strippers" and then manipulate them to win at poker, gin rummy, seven-up, coon can, high-low cut, banker and broker, you name it.

Handy little things

According to some authorities, "strippers" first made their appearance on the baize in the eighteenth century. However, it was the popularization in America of such games as faro and poker that made them practically indispensable to the crooked gamblers in stovepipe hats and their illegitimate great-grandsons of today.

When faro was the most widely played game in America, the locale of the action was heralded by a poster depicting a tiger. Hence, the phrase you still occasionally hear today—"bucking the tiger"—and the poor faro player certainly had a tiger by the tail! In his excellent book, *Fools of Fortune* (published in 1892 in Chicago by an outfit that sternly called itself "The Anti-Gambling Association"), the reformed Quinn says matter-of-factly:

"The 'skin' gambler never deals a game of faro without making use of cards known as 'strippers' or 'humps.'"

In "humps," which are commonly called "hollows," "rounds" or "belly strippers," all the cards are shaved $\frac{1}{32}$ of an inch, but the sides of the desired cards have a concave or convex cut in the middle. It requires a fine touch to find the spot, but the beautiful part of them is that they do not have to be turned any one way in the pack.

On the other hand, ordinary "side strippers" are the normal width at one end and then shaved in a tapering effect. Thus, when certain cards are desired, they are merely *reversed* in the deck and their wide ends then protrude. This makes it comparatively simple for the "mechanic" to locate them, pull them and misdeal as he desires.

There are other varieties and names such as "end strippers," in which the ends, rather than sides, are stripped, and I possess an interesting, 60-year-old deck in which one *corner* is stripped. Do such cards *really* work?

This is practically unbeatable

Let's take this "stripper gaff" which I once saw in cruel, profitable operation.

It was the shank end of the evening. Everyone had dropped out of the poker game except the "mechanic" and the victim he had been patiently nurturing along all night.

By now, the victim thought he should be giving poker lessons himself, and when he was dealt a full house (two aces, three kings), he went for broke, and was promptly punished for breaking two of the most fundamental rules of self-protection.

First, you should *never* be inveigled into a two-handed game because it is almost childishly simple for a clever crook to control it. And, second, you should *never* bet heavily on the last hands of the evening's play. That is when you are being set up for the kill.

And, of course, it happened. When the victim put down his full house, the "mechanic" showed four fives and an ace to take the pot.

How had he accomplished it? This is the old, reliable "ten-card deal," in which the whole deck are "strippers" and the desired cards (all the fives, three aces and three kings, in this case) turned the opposite way in the pack so they can be controlled.

By "stacking" (which I will later explain in detail), the crook gets all ten together at the top of the deck and holds them there by false cuts and shuffles.

Now, even supposing that he can't control the *exact* disposition of these ten cards between his hand and the victim's, what does happen? By looking at his own hand, he apparently enjoys the powers of a mind reader and accurately reads his victim's cards.

Thus, *he knows,* that if he holds—

1 A and 4 5s, the victim has 2 As and 3 Ks—and loses.

2 As and 3 5s, the victim has 1 A, 3 Ks, 1 5—and loses.

3 As and 2 5s, the victim has 3 Ks and 2 5s—and loses.

3 As, 1 K and 1 5, the victim has 2 Ks and 3 5s—and wins (hurray!).

3 As and 2 Ks, the victim has 4 5s and 1 K—and wins (hurray again!).

I don't want to take up your time completing the cycle, but if you are interested, you can lay out the 4 5s, 3 As and 3 Ks and work out the infinite combinations for yourself. However, remember one thing. When the "mechanic" fails to give himself the right cards, he still knows the exact cards the victim holds and bets as lightly as he can without arousing suspicion.

Now let me carry this "gaff" forward two more sad steps.

First of all, progressive-minded cheats would probably use "belly strippers" rather than "side strippers," thus making it unnecessary to turn the desired cards in the pack. Any technique that saves a motion makes a "gaff" harder to detect.

Finally, to show how the black art of card manipulation has developed since the days of Quinn and his friends, good "mechanics" today employ a variation known as the "nine-card stack," *using an ordinary deck* with no "strippers" in it.

Only the 3 As, 3 Ks and 3 5s, rather than all four 5s, are stacked. (Or, of course, the stack can be any other nine-card combination that the cheat prefers.) His goal is to manipulate the play so that the victim draws the tenth, "oddball" card, which can be any of the 43 cards remaining in the pack, and then the victim will always lose.

If it is the victim's deal, the "mechanic" makes sure that the stack of nine is on top of the pack. Then—

However he distributes the stack, the victim unfailingly kills himself with the tenth card.

On the other hand, if the operator is dealing, he needs the "oddball" card atop the stack, or *he* will wind up with it as the last card dealt. Problem? Not at all!

Usually, he can maneuver it without effort to the top of the deck. If, for some reason, he fails to get it in that position, he can fall back on another strategy. The first card is dealt to the victim from the bottom and then the next nine, the stack, all from the top.

To be completely accurate, I should emphasize that there is no set pattern for such cheating. Depending on his own skill, the crook manipulates "strippers" the way that comes easiest to him. There is only one general rule. Very rarely today are royal flush or four ace hands stacked. They would be *too* suspicious, even in rank amateur play!

Most often, "strippers" are used to set up full house or three ace hands, and if you encounter a "lucky" player who usually seems to have them on the big pots, I would advise you to leave the game quietly.

I hope that you maintain a healthy respect for these "strippers"; they are more deadly than the female.

"The benefit of these cards can be estimated only in one way: How much money has your opponent got? For you are certain to get it, whether it is $10 or $10,000; the heavier the stakes, the sooner you will break him and he never knows what hurt him.

"For Poker, they are a sure thing, for what could be better than to hold the *best hand* which you certainly can do with these cards?

"Or, for playing Seven Up, what better thing would you want than to have your opponent deal you three aces every time he deals, with a chance of the fourth; or in playing Euchre to force your opponent to give you or your partner three bowers every time he deals, in spite of himself. These cards will do it."

(Euchre isn't played much today, so perhaps I should explain that the jack of trumps is called "the right bower" and is the highest-ranking trump. The other jack in the same color is "the left bower" and second highest trump—and *three* bowers! I'm confident that "strippers" must have inspired that woeful slang phrase you still hear at the card table, "I was euchred!")

The above fulsome testimonial to "strippers" (and certainly not an exaggerated one, in my opinion) is contained in the yellowed catalogue of a New York dealer in "sporting goods" way back in the early Nineties. I happen to have it in my library of crooked gambling literature.

Now any product must be good to survive, and a *current* gambling supply catalogue of the 1960's offers more than a dozen varieties of "strippers" at $3 to $4.50 per deck ($33.50 to $47.50 per dozen).

There are special "combination strippers" in which one set of cards can be stripped from the side of the pack and another from the end. There are "stakeouts" (usually short on the sides or ends and ideal to cut to) which can be furnished in *any* combination.

In concave "side strippers," as the name would indicate, the sides are somewhat hollowed so, by pressing his fingers along them, the "mechanic" will easily cut just above this concave "marker." In the reverse, convex cut, which are "humps" or "belly strippers," he can cut precisely at the doctored card.

However, when manipulating "rakes," which are also known as "end strippers," the cheat holds the pack at both ends. He presses his fingers lightly against them and, lifting up the unevened end, cuts. He knows that the cut will come at the next card on top of the "rake."

Similarly, he can use just one "side stripper" in an otherwise untampered deck (which card is known as "a brief") to cut to. And if a hand has been preprepared, the "brief" lies atop it so a confederate can feel how deep to make the cut.

Finally, for the cheat who wants everything, there are available "strippers" and "readers" combined into one deck of king-sized larceny. Of course, for such added insurance, you pay more. This sight-*and*-touch swindle retails for $5 per pack, $55 per dozen of the doubly doctored cards.

Doing the belly dance

Actually, if I were playing crooked, I think I'd stay with the "belly strippers." John Scarne calls them "one of the most highly prized—and high-priced secrets—of fast-money winners," and out of my own experience in confiscating and calipering them, I must agree.

In such decks, all except the desired key cards, which may be various different combinations for poker, gin rummy, skin, coon can, etc., are first shaved down on both sides by about $\frac{1}{32}$ of an inch. When they have also been recornered, you have an "honest" deck, give or take $\frac{1}{32}$ of an inch.

Now the "mutilator" goes to work on the key cards. If he wants a full house combo, he selects two sets of three of a kind denomination, plus four smaller cards of a kind; if he wants to deal out flushes, he needs ten of the desired suit. With his shears, he doctors the cards at both ends till they are somewhat narrower than the rest of the deck, but in the middle he leaves a bulge or "belly" that sticks out imperceptibly.

The result is that when he squares and taps the deck and runs his right hand fingers along the sides, the "belly strippers" practically leap into his dealing hand. While shuffling, he works the wider cards to the top of the pack. Thereafter, having brought, say, the four aces together, he is limited only by his dexterity—certainly not his conscience!—as to what happens next.

A spot of bottom dealing, perhaps, until he can pass three or all four aces to himself or a confederate? Matter of fact, even if he is too clumsy-handed for adroit fake shuffling and dealing, "belly strippers" always give him that precious little "advantage." At least, by touch, he knows who *does* get the high cards and refuses to bet against him in a two-handed game.

You cut—your throat

By now, I am sure you will agree, "strippers" can be perfectly murderous in games like Banker and Broker or cut-for-high card where the cut has special importance. If the pack is stripped so the high cards are convex, the low cards concave, the cheat can manipulate the piles so that he always turns over a face card to the opponents' low cards.

Even when it isn't his deal, he can stack the piles on the blind of "helping" the banker set up the various piles. Therefore, I suggest as a rule for this game that *no one except the banker* be allowed to cut the deck into piles. Of course, *he* may be a cheat, too, but you will prevent him handling the cards except when he banks and, if he wins too often, you are justified in becoming suspicious.

In high-low cutting, the victim will almost invariably cut on a low, convex card, but this is such a witless, suicidal form of gaming to begin with that you should automatically suspect anyone who suggests it!

In earlier chapters, you may remember, we discussed various methods for marking cards during play. Somewhat similar in "stripping," there is an in-play mutilation technique known as "crimping." This is the device of slightly bending the corners of key cards so they later can be felt or seen. At one time, an old gambler once said, every crook first looked at the aces dealt him to see whether the other crooks in the game had already crimped them—and if not, he bent the corners himself.

If someone attempts this whiskery fraud, and now and then cheap crooks do, here is how you can have some fun. Unobtrusively, uncrimp the high cards—and bend the corners of the twos and threes instead!

And now—a mystery

During my career, I have spent many thousands of dollars on a collection of modern and historical "gaffs" used in crooked cards. These include both the commercial offerings I have just described and many do-it-yourself creations.

In "strippers," the latter are made by secretive or fussy gamblers using special tools that are by no means cheap. For example, a pair of steel shears attached to a brass cutting block and regulated by a micrometer that refines the cut "to the fineness of a hair" costs from $125 to $175. For corner rounding, a smaller device of the same materials and somewhat similar design is priced at $75.

But the prize of my collection—and my biggest exasperation!— couldn't possibly have been fashioned in this manner. Unlike any other "stripper" I have ever seen or heard of, this mystery card is *wider* by about $\frac{1}{64}$ of an inch than the ordinary card.

Seemingly, it is just another Bee Back king of hearts, and the width is imperceptible to the touch unless you know what you are feeling for. (And even wise gamblers aren't prepared for this!) Once you do know, however, my "biggie" is ideal as a place card to cut to.

What I can't understand is *how* it was made bigger, and yet so perfect. I know something about doctoring cards, and I am sure that parts of two cards were not peeled apart and then pasted together. If that had been done, one edge of my "biggie" would be thicker. It isn't. It feels and snaps like a perfect card.

I obtained the card from a friend who doesn't recall how he came into possession of it, so I can't backtrack on its history. Nor are my technical sources of information helpful.

Can anybody help me?

Matter of fact, I visited one of the biggest and best-equipped gambling supply houses in New York City. Without showing the "biggie," I described it to the proprietor and asked him to make up a few for me.

"No such animal," he said flatly. "Can't be done."

I took out the mystery card and silently handed it to him. He examined it, measured it, looked suspiciously at me. Then he took it in into his back room to show to his rogue artists who mark and strip cards in every conceivable way.

Ten minutes later, he came back and handed me the card.

"Nobody makes this," he said shortly.

"But here it is," I objected plaintively. He shrugged.

And here it is!

I don't know who made it, or how it was made, or why no other "biggies" are ever known to have existed. If *you* have any information or suggestions, please get in touch with me.

Maybe this is the latest top-secret "gaff"!

CHAPTER XI

♠
♥
♦
♣
♠
♥
♦

AH, THOSE LOVELY, LARCENOUS LADIES I HAVE KNOWN!

♣
♠
♥
♦

COURTESY OF THE WORRIED PROPRIETOR, I was enjoying an evening of sure-thing cards at one of those hospitable poker houses that dot the West Coast. That is, any losses would be refunded, any winnings (within reason) would be mine, and there would also be a sizable retainer. Obviously, the proprietor *was* worried!

Though the dealers in gambling houses are wise to most forms of cheating and the spotters who oversee them are vigilant, the houses can be taken. Even though they don't spot the precise "gaff," the proprietors know when this is happening. From the amount of the play and the law of probabilities, they can estimate their expected "take" within a few dollars—and when it falls suspiciously short, they call in a gambling investigator like me.

"Any particular character I should watch?" I asked the proprietor.

"That's what worries me! There doesn't seem to be any pattern to it. Once or twice a week, different tables are hit for $2,000 to $3,000 by different men. I'm sure of only one thing. I've double-checked my dealers. And it's not a crossroader." (An outsider who conspires with an employee to take the house.)

Well, that certainly left it wide open for me, so I sauntered from table to table as though I were looking for a friend. The play seemed normal, and then in a corner of the large, soft-carpeted room, I spotted an erect, well-groomed woman in her late fifties.

She was wearing a smart, conservatively tailored cotton dress and a small dark hat to match. She wore her waved, silver-tinted hair high

118

on her head, she had on a minimum of makeup, and her only jewelry was a string of pearls.

Apologies to the real Grandma Moses

Engrossed in the play, this eminently respectable looking lady apparently didn't see me. Hastily, I retreated to the proprietor's office. I described her to him and asked what he knew about her.

"The dowager!" he laughed. "Come off it, Frank. She's just a rich old bag who plays a smart, tight game. She wins a little, loses a little, that's all."

"And, by any chance, is she usually at the table where the big hits are made?"

Now he was getting uneasy.

"Come to think of it, she was on two or three occasions. But she didn't even know the winners. And you certainly aren't trying to tell me—"

"I've got news. 'The dowager,' as you call her, is a daub worker. She daubs the high cards and then signals those men she apparently 'doesn't know.' They make the hit, and there is no suspicion on her."

He nodded thoughtfully.

"But that's an awfully fast gaff, Frank. I don't believe she could pull it."

"I've got one more bit of news," I told him. "You see, out here, you call her 'the dowager,' and she seems *so* respectable that you aren't even watching her. But back home in the East, we call her 'Grandma Moses'—the best woman daub worker in the business.

"We'd better talk to her."

But those sharp old eyes had spotted me, after all. By the time we returned to the table, "Grandma Moses," alias "The Dowager," had vanished.

A $55,000,000 swindle!

Today, women gamble at cards *everywhere*. Not only in the traditional "friendly little games" at the weekly bridge club and the Friday night at home, but increasingly in the public casinos and even at laundromats. Many of the coin-operated "washeries" now obligingly provide card tables and chairs so that women can enjoy a spot of bridge— and often poker—while the family laundry is being done.

Just in New York City, there have been estimates that some 15,000 women's *poker* games are held regularly, many of them the rough, night-long ordeal you would normally associate with the men addicts. And, in a given year, some 600 women may be arrested in the metropolis on various charges connected with cardplaying.

As clergymen and police authorities have told me, the problem of feminine gambling and its inevitable corollary, *cheating,* has become one of the great social problems of our society. It is still largely a whispered problem because most husbands of such addicts are ashamed to admit their wives gamble away their household money.

However, from my own observations, plus interviews with pastors and gambling authorities, I can give you some indication of the seriousness of the situation. *Conservatively,* there are:

Some 30,000 "amateur" women cheats, mostly middle-class housewives, office workers and professional women.

Some 5,000 professional women gamblers who live off the proceeds of crooked cards, working either "single-o" or as accomplices of men "mechanics."

Together, the amateurs and pros yearly gross $55,000,000, most of it stolen from other women cardplayers.

The amateur talent

Let me break down my estimate. There are some 3,000 counties scattered throughout the country. If you balance off the sparsely populated ones against those of medium or large size, it is the height of prudence to calculate that, in each, at least ten women "amateur" cheats are operating.

These are "respectable" women, at least to all outward appearances, who are motivated by greed, excitement or some strange, dark compulsion to cheat *consistently,* week after week, one way or another. Their regular "take" may be as little as $5, and often averages $25. But if these 30,000 are each credited with stealing only $10 weekly, it totals $300,000.

Yearly, that comes to the sizable total of $15,000,000! On a 50-week year, that is, because many of them take two-week vacations financed by their steady, small thefts from the table.

Now consider the professionals, by whom I mean those ladies earning all or most of their livelihood at crooked cards. Some of them like "Grandma" are talented "mechanics" in their own right, but most work in teams with men. They help to inveigle innocents into a rigged game, they serve as "distractors" and, very often, innocently kibitzing, they signal the victims' hands to their partners.

Considering that their living expenses are unusually high—they must live in good hotels, travel first class, spend considerable money on hairdos and clothes—I make the rock-bottom estimate that they earn $150 weekly, plus expenses. If I pegged the amount any lower, the poor things would be actually starving!

Even at my minimum figure, however, they gross $750,000 weekly —or $37,500,000 yearly. Now I have to add only the absurdly low amount of $10 weekly for expenses; that comes to $50,000 weekly or another $2,500,000 a year. The total, added to the amateurs' take of $15,000,000, makes a grand ladies' night total of $55,000,000.

Nothing new, really

I can appreciate that defenders of our womanhood will react with shock or disbelief. Actually, the feminine passion for gambling, honest or crooked, is a matter of indisputable historical record.

Before Louis XIV, French ladies known to gamble lost their reputations, but *with* Louis (not after) came the deluge of tolerated, wide-open gambling by both sexes, and the ladies now lost livres, virtue and beauty sleep. Says one writer:

"Under the infatuation of the play, they would remain up all night in company of their male fellow gamesters and would give up their honor to pay their losings, or to secure a loan with which to continue the indulgences of their passion for play."

Intermittently, there were whispered stories that they even sold their daughters' virtue, which may or may not have been true. However, it is record that the beautiful Countess of Schwiechelt of the Napoleonic era lost 50,000 livres gambling in Paris—whereupon, at a ball given by one Madame Demidoff, the Countess stole the Madame's magnificent emerald coronet, using it as collateral to raise more money. She was convicted and, despite her beauty, the susceptible Napoleon I refused to pardon her.

In this country, women began dealing in the San Francisco gambling halls almost from the time they opened, the first one being Mme. Simon Jules, an attractive French brunette who presided at a roulette table in the Bella Union. Though the *Alta,* only paper of the time, thundered against the saucy innovation, the other houses quickly adopted the practice—and today in Reno and elsewhere, you will find women not only presiding at roulette but also at chuck-a-luck, poker, faro, and dice.

The woman addict

However, the important thing is not that self-indulgent ladies of the upper class and professional hustlers in petticoats happen to cheat at cards. Rather, it is the spread of the vice among the great middle class

—the young mothers in suburbia, the bachelor girls who share small city apartments, the women in their forties and fifties who have too much time on their hands—that is shocking today.

Personally, I think the corruption began with Prohibition when our moral standards were lowered and, much as in the time of Louis XIV, women were tolerated at all-night drinking and cardplaying sessions. Unfortunately, when a woman becomes addicted to drugs, whisky *or* gambling, medical authorities will tell you, she becomes more hopelessly "hooked" than most men.

Admittedly, the following is written in that tearful school of writing you might call *Mother-dear-Mother-come-home-with-me-now,* but it describes the compulsive woman gambler I have so often seen in Miami, Las Vegas, New York and Los Angeles:

"Yonder stands a tall, thin lady who seeks the table on which small sums can be played. See how anxiously she glances over the table, and how cautiously she deposits her little sum. Once or twice, she wins, and her pale cheeks become flushed, and her eyes kindle. But in a short time it is all gone, and then, leaving the place, she retires to one of those garden chairs, sitting apart from the rest of the people, her cheeks more wasted, her eyes duller, apparently broken-hearted, as if the thought of her confiding husband and little ones far away oppressed her spirit . . ."

What drives them to addiction? Usually, they have told me, they just wanted a little excitement, and the habit got away from them the way drinking can. To women of certain temperaments, "social cardplaying" presents the same insidious hazards as "social drinking."

Instead of sex?

In many cases, there are curious sexual connotations, psychiatrist friends have explained to me. Sometimes, the women are motivated by masochistic feelings and subconsciously derive gratification in losing more than they can afford. Again, in the tensions of gambling, repressed women may find substitutes for their unsatisfied sexual needs.

Whatever the motivation, once "hooked," compulsive women gamblers almost invariably resort to cheating. They *have* to in order to feed the monkey on their backs. But, by and large, they are less dexterous than men, less coordinated and they also suffer the disadvantage of size. That is, their hands are too small to palm successfully or to grasp the deck firmly for other manipulations.

Thus, except for the pros, they resort to the simplest "gaffs," relying more on the trusting nature of their friends than their own finesse to remain undetected. And, surprisingly, year after year, thousands of them do get away with it!

Let me give you the case history of one respectable suburbanite who is typical of the "amateur" cheat. She is in her middle thirties, wife of an ambitious junior executive, mother of two grade-school children. As yet, her husband doesn't make too much money, but they have their own comfortable home and a station wagon.

Mary, as we shall call her, got into the habit of playing bridge one or two afternoons a week with more well-to-do neighborhood women. At $\frac{1}{10}$ of a cent a point, the game was reasonably modest and when she lost, it was only $5 or so.

Then one of the other women suggested there would be more "action" in poker. Mary only knew what her husband had told her about the game, but by now she was a confirmed cardplayer. She went along with the suggestion.

The lady's downfall

Though the stakes were kept low, this definitely wasn't Mary's game. Instead of winning occasionally as at bridge, she lost consistently. Besides, every so often, she had to hire a babysitter so she could play, and her "little relaxation," as she called her vice, soon was costing her $15 weekly.

For a while, she juggled the household funds to keep going but, after a couple of months, she was $50 behind. Tearfully blaming "inflation" in food prices, she got the $50 from her husband. But even she realized that she couldn't go on like that and, in desperation, she became that lowest form of card cheat, "a check copper." That is, every so often, on the pretext of shoving the pot toward the winner, she managed to slide a few of the chips into her own lap.

Maybe, as she later insisted to me, it all started "accidentally" when a chip stuck to her sweaty palm. But I doubt it. Too many thousands of women practice this form of petty larceny, which can be mastered with a minimum of practice, for me to believe they all began "accidentally."

As a matter of fact, the gambling supply houses boldly peddle "check cop" concoctions in strip or invisible liquid at only $3 per packet or bottle. Applied to the palms, the substance picks up the chips which are then surreptitiously deposited in lap or pocket.

Once Mary became "a check copper," her financial problem was solved but, under the naggings of her conscience, she became so tense and irritable at home that her husband finally consulted the family pastor.

What do you tell a husband?

Though Mary refused to unburden herself to the clergyman, he shrewdly surmised after a talk with her that gambling was the cause of her unhappiness. Through a mutual friend, her husband appealed to me to investigate the game. Mary probably was being cheated, he said in all good faith, and if he could prove that to her, she might stop playing.

To avoid rousing any suspicions, he introduced me to Mary as an old college friend, and the day before a game was scheduled for Mary's home, I was their overnight house guest. Thus, during the afternoon, when the "girls" arrived for their poker, I was naturally on hand.

Within 15 minutes, I spotted Mary's rather obvious "gaff" and now *I* suddenly had an uncomfortable problem. From talking to her husband, I had taken it for granted that she was being cheated. How was I going to tell him his wife was the cheat!

Waiting for the game to end, I mapped out my strategy. The moment her guests had left, I braced her.

"Mary, your husband will be home within half an hour. There's something we have to get settled between us before then. I am really Frank Garcia, The Gambling Investigator. And I know that you're a cheat."

"How dare you talk to me like that!"

"Look, Mary, we don't have time to spar. I'll demonstrate."

Quickly, I spread some chips on the card table and pushed them toward her as though I were shoving the pot to the winner. I drew back my hand and turned up my palm, exposing three chips.

"That's how you do it. An old and not very good 'gaff.' "

Her eyes widened, then filled with tears.

"But your husband, who loves and trusts you, thinks *you* have been the victim," I went on. "What am I going to tell him? We've got 15 minutes now before he arrives."

Coffee and cold decks

It was then that she spilled out the whole story to me.

"But you *can't* tell Joe," she pleaded. "It would break his heart! I'll do anything you say."

Ethically, my job is to expose cheats, large or small, and not to attempt to reform them. But, like most men, I'm a sucker for a tearful, pleading woman.

"I'll make a bargain," I said slowly. "I'll lie to him. I'll tell him the game is entirely honest—if you promise him that you'll *never* play cards again for money."

"Oh, thank you! And I promise, I promise."

So far as I know, Mary is keeping her word, but I am sure you can understand why I avoid as much as possible exposing the amateur lady cheats. It's a sticky, embarrassing business. Almost always, it is the same tearful story, though the pathetic little "gaffs" may vary from time to time.

In a limited way, some women can switch in "a cold deck" when they happen to be hostesses for the game. On the reasonable excuse of getting a tray of sandwiches or drinks, they obtain their prepared deck and hold it under the tray. As they place the tray on the table over the legitimate deck, they pick up the latter, simultaneously depositing the marked cards. Then they remove the tray and the honest deck, and return a few minutes later for the kill.

Done expertly, this maneuver escapes detection because the eyes of the other players are on the sandwiches or coffee—and, anyhow, who would dream that this charming, gracious hostess is a cheat!

Cognac and a lady's compact

In my own opinion, most of the women amateurs are what the gambling underworld would call "glim workers." At poker, canasta and even bridge, they peek or glimpse at the corners of the cards when they are dealing or drawing. This requires keen eyesight, of course, and they probably miss three out of five. But if they "peek" the disposition of even one high card during a round, they enjoy a distinct, unfair advantage over the other players.

The more enterprising also resort to "shiners," which are tiny mirrors or highly polished objects that will reflect the faces of the cards. Historically, the first "shiner" was merely a little water or cognac which the cheat "accidentally" spilled on the table alongside him. The first known mechanical "shiner" was an instrument that would horrify our genteel lady cheats—a straight razor.

According to legend, the gambler who introduced it brazenly placed the razor on the table alongside him and disguised its real use by announcing, "I hate cheats! The first one I catch will get this razor smiling—meaning from ear to ear." The blade was so highly polished that the reflections of the card pips danced on the ceiling overhead, and another cheat in the game complained plaintively, "I don't mind the razor, but those butterflies up there are making me seasick."

Today, from the gambling supply houses, you can purchase "shiners" at prices ranging from $4 to $12.50, concealed in finger rings, bill clips, matchboxes and other ordinary-seeming objects. However, few of the lady amateurs have access to such professional sources and they use what comes most naturally—their own compacts, cigarette cases and cigarette lighters or one of their hostess' ashtrays, the bigger and shinier the better. Unfortunately, it wouldn't be polite for them to use one of the best in the business—a bone toothpick in which one end is hollowed to conceal a tiny mirror.

And a Merry Christmas, too!

However, I must admit, one ingenious lady had me fooled for almost two days. From the way her eyes remained glued on the pack as she dealt, I felt sure that she must be using some kind of "shiner." Yet she wore no rings and there were no objects on the table nearby that might reflect the cards.

Finally, I thought I caught a glint of light from the middle finger of her left hand. I stopped the game and told the outraged ladies that I suspected someone was employing a ring "shiner." When I asked if I could examine their fingers, all indignantly thrust their hands forward, including the suspect.

On the pretext of waving her aside since she wore no ring, I managed to bump her left hand hard. A tiny sliver that had come from a broken glass Christmas tree ball dropped out from under her fingernail. It was the smallest "shiner" I had ever seen.

Because long fingernails arouse no suspicions, many women crooks also resort to "nail-nicking" the sides or edges of the cards, the location of the nick indicating value, suit or both. Sometimes, the marks can't be seen, but they always can be felt. Others "wave" the high cards by bending them slightly around their fingers. Either in the pack or in an opponent's hand, "waved" cards stand out conspicuously if you know what you are looking for.

To frustrate the "amateur" cheats, I suggest five precautionary rules for every ladies' game—and I don't care how small or "friendly" it is! Frankly, next to love, most women make the biggest fools of themselves in trusting games of cards.

Here are the rules and no one except a cheat should take exception to their strict enforcement:

No, no, ladies!

1. Each game starts with a brand-new deck taken from its cellophane wrapping right at the table. After every five hands, the cards are routinely inspected for "waving" or "nail-nicking." As soon as a pack becomes stained or dirtied in the least, it is discarded.

2. By common agreement, pocketbooks, compacts, cigar cases, cigarette lighters and any other highly polished objects are kept *off* the card table. If possible (but I realize many women protest that they can't remove them), finger rings should not be worn during play.

3. Especially at bridge, consistently "lucky" teams should be broken up. Chances are that the partners have devised a signaling system.

4. Rules against "peeking" or "glimpsing" are to be strictly enforced and violators penalized without argument.

5. *Only* the winner rakes in the pot and no other player is permitted to touch a chip, no matter how "helpful" she means to be.

I can sympathize with the lady who first dares suggest such precautions in *her* "friendly little game"! However, to still the outraged cries of her friends, I suggest that she quote the following dictum handed down by one of the most famous and experienced gamblers of another era:

"It has often been remarked that with the so-called respectable, there has been less honor among women gamesters than among men, many of them, indeed, not hesitating to claim unfair advantage, and even to engage in downright lying and cheating."

Remember, ladies, it was not I, Frank Garcia, who said that but, out of my own experiences, I must reluctantly add, Amen. The best way to enjoy honest cards is by impartial enforcement of rules that avert temptation in the first place.

10 ladies' rules for winning

However, I don't want to conclude this ladies-only chapter on a sour note. In the process of detecting women cheats, I also have observed thousands of honest women players and the mistakes they make.

So, assuming that your game *is* honest, I would like to offer some suggestions on how you can improve your play and win more frequently, whether you prefer bridge, gin, canasta, poker or any other game.

Here, especially tailored to the requirements of the ladies, are my ten rules for better cardplaying:

1. At most, have one cocktail during the game, but you would be wiser to stay with tea or coffee.

2. Avoid distracting chatter, comment about the other players' dresses or hairdo and gossip. If there is some irresistible item to be discussed, stop the game till it is talked out and then resume play.

3. Control your temper! Just as many men gamblers are accomplished "needling" artists, women cardplayers often are deliberately

catty in the hopes of angering their opponents. If you try to retaliate with an equally catty remark, then you are taking your mind from the cards. If you allow yourself to become angered, you will play more rashly.

4. Don't try to fool the other players with squeals of delight and moans of despair about the cards you are holding. Only a trained actress can squeal or moan convincingly when her hand doesn't merit such ecstasy or sadness. Make bids and calls as tonelessly as possible.

5. Beware such mannerisms as tapping the cards with your nails, toying with your bracelet or fiddling with compact or pocketbook (which, of course, shouldn't be on the table in the first place). These unconscious gestures are a giveaway to alert opponents.

6. Set yourself a weekly "card budget." This amount, $4, $5 or $10, is what you can afford to lose comfortably without dipping into the house money. Then, if you have disastrous luck, don't get panicky and plunge in an effort to recoup—which is the surest way to lose more money. Say to yourself, "Well, I just won't be able to play next week," and continue to play a cool, conservative game.

7. If you have a deadline—you have to be home by 5:00 P.M. to start dinner—*stick* to it, whether you are winning or losing at 5:00 o'clock. If you yield to the pleas of "just one more round," you will play hurriedly and distractedly and almost inevitably lose. Worse, you may get arrested for speeding as you race home. My friend, Police Chief Joseph W. Kinsella, of suburban Stamford, Conn., tells me that it's between 5:00 and 6:00 P.M. when most women speeders are ticketed.

8. Don't play cards "just for fun." The game becomes so sloppy and gossipy that you will ruin yourself for sharp play. Rather, insist on a modest stake that can't hurt anyone but makes the game "for real."

9. Don't adhere rigidly to either systems, rules, logic or hunch. Vary your play as much as possible to confuse your opponents and take advantage of the breaks. For example, memorize your hand before tossing it into the discard. If the dealer is careless, the hand may remain unshuffled in the pack. If you happen to draw one of the cards, you will know the location of the others that you had held. This is sharp but not exactly unethical play. The moral, of course, is to insist that every deal be thoroughly shuffled and cut.

10. In an earlier chapter, I recommended that husbands never play cards with their wives or with any other women, if possible. To show my impartiality in the battle of the sexes, I now make the same recommendation to the ladies. Don't play cards with your husbands or other men if you can politely get out of it.

I base this suggestion on the broad generalization that men tend to play intuitively and often rashly, whereas the ladies, who pride themselves on their "feminine intuition," actually play *logically* and conservatively. Either attack has certain strategic merits, but they don't mix in harmonious team play, and when husbands and wives are involved, the results can be literally homicidal.

The most famous example I can think of offhand is the tragedy that befell John Bennett, a wealthy perfume executive in Kansas City some three decades ago, who daringly overbid a spade hand in bridge and went set. Whereupon Myrtle, his wife of 11 years, shot him dead with the family automatic. Subsequently, Myrtle was acquitted and bridge authorities Sidney S. Lenz and Ely Culbertson agreed that her criticism of her husband's play had been technically correct, if somewhat harsh.

The point is, I think, that if ladies *will* persist in playing cards with men and yet want to remain ladies, they must resign themselves as they do in the dance—that, for better or for worse, the men will lead and they will follow.

CHAPTER XII

♠
♥
♦
♣
♠
♥
♦

THE CROOK'S FALSIES—CUTS AND SHUFFLES

♠
♥
♦
♣

JUST RECENTLY, on a slow southern cruise, I was idly passing the time of day with an eminently sedate and respectable looking middle-aged gentleman who still wears rather high collars and pincenez glasses and usually has *The New York Times* under his arm. Actually, he is one of the most accomplished crooked dealers in the profession.

As a master of the false cut and false shuffle in their many, bewildering varieties, he deplores such uncouth "gaffs" as marked cards, nicking, crimping or daubing. Relying primarily on the lightning speed of his practiced fingers, he looks down on mechanical aids to cheating much as a pianist looks down on the player piano.

"What would *you* do if, say tonight in the salon, you spotted somebody at a nearby table pulling some of these gaffs?" I couldn't resist asking him. I thought his sense of artistry would be offended, but a look of happy anticipation came over his face. "Back him, of course," he said genially.

Later, I discovered that this worldly wisecrack was first uttered by the urbane Richard Brinsley Sheridan, the Irish-born playwright, back in the eighteenth century. However, this didn't lessen my respect for my friend, for he has considerably more knowledge of "gaffs" than the late Mr. Sheridan and undoubtedly hit upon the same thought independently.

In this chapter, in large part due to the paternal interest of this friend who feels he should remain anonymous, I intend to describe false cuts and shuffles. Some that have never before been published,

130

to my knowledge, are the most successful. At least, I learned them from this friend, and I can report that he is still alive, unscarred, and in his late fifties, testimony enough to their success.

The more they move, the less they move

The false shuffle is an intricate dance of the cards in which either nothing takes place or a previously prepared stack is guided back to its original position for the deal. It is accomplished *con fortissimo,* the cards seeming to flutter haphazardly through the pack, but actually, as someone once said of a slow writer, right before your eyes, nothing is happening.

Professors may frown, but I have a weakness for the colorful vocabulary of the gambling cheat. These shuffles carry such delightful names as the "6, 3, 4, 1 stack shuffle," the "table, noisy and butt shuffles," the "chop shuffle," also known as the "barnyard" and "haymaker" and "haymow" shuffle. Then there are those that more austerely bear their creators' names.

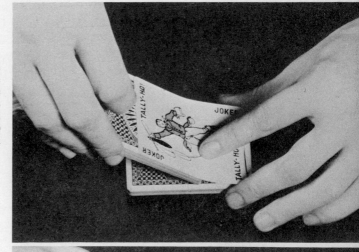

Figure 43. Here is the beginning of the false "slip" cut in which the "mechanic" keeps his prepared stack intact, losing one card (the top card turned face up in the photo).

Figure 44. The "slip" cut being completed. Sometimes, this maneuver is called the "spinge" cut or "spinging the deck."

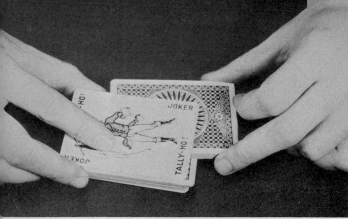

Figure 45. First move in a variation of "spinging the deck."

Figure 46. Completing this variation of the "spinge" cut.

Like the false shuffle, the false cut is designed to keep the stack in its same position after a *seeming* cut or is an extra move to nullify an honest cut that has just been made. It is, of course, less spectacular than the shuffle, but an interesting technical problem is involved.

Since the dealer doesn't perform the cut, he must force the victim to cut where he wants him to, or so arrange the cards that his confederate will know where to perform it. Only rarely, and the move must be superbly executed, does the dealer himself tamper with the cut.

And again, the delightful names! There are the table cut for the entire deck, the pivot cut, "table hop," the "Las Vegas running cut," three-packet cut and the "riffle hop," also called the "pass," "jump" or "transfer" cut.

Don't get discouraged. With the help of the photographs, taking the important ones separately, you will be able to understand them better.

Some trade terms

First, though, here are a few terms you should know. A *riffle*, obviously, is the form of shuffle in which the deck is divided into two packets on the table, and the latter are interlaced into one another. The riffle is a perfectly proper way to shuffle, *but can be easily manipulated by the cheat*.

A *jog* is a card which protrudes slightly from the deck, thus marking the position of desired cards. When the *jog* sticks out slightly over the left pinkie, it is an *in-jog*. Over the first finger of the left hand, an *out-jog*. (Assuming, naturally, that the dealer is right-handed.) A *step* is a block of cards that similarly protrudes.

The desired cards that are thus marked constitute the *stock,* and all false shuffles and cuts are consecrated to building the stock or holding it together once it has been made. When you withdraw a packet from the bottom of the deck, you *undercut*.

To make the break in the deck where you want the victim or a confederate to cut to, you *crimp* the card; that is, wave or bend it slightly. If you *crimp* it both sidewise and endwise, you *debone* it, and it thus becomes in effect a crimped, uncrimped card. You can't help finding it again by a *riffle*.

A *crimp* also is sometimes called a *bridge,* and thus clumsy cheats who *overcrimp* are accused of "building a bridge you could sail a battleship under." However, an expert *crimp* is almost undetectable and, nine times out of ten, a victim will unconsciously and obligingly make the cut there.

Even better, when the cheat sits to the right of the dealer, he can cut to his own crimp and have the stock dealt to him. If he is a "single-o" (playing without a confederate) and has the deal, he works his crimp to the bottom of the deck. Then, on conclusion of the deal, he places his dealt hand near the deck. Now watch!

Block that pull-through!

As the other players are examining their hands, he subtracts the crimped cards from the bottom with his left hand and drops the deck atop the hand he had originally dealt himself. He's in business.

Now let's assume that the crook has arranged a tasty stock for himself, consisting of a full house, aces high. Problem, how can he shuffle the deck and keep these cards in position? One of the surest methods is the "intricate" or "pull-through" false shuffle.

First, there is an honest riffle during which, remember, the cards are not yet actually mixed together in one pack. The sharper then pushes the packet containing his stock through the middle of the deck and, in cutting, brings the deck right back to its original position. (If you study the photographs, some of these moves will become much clearer.)

There is one way by which you might detect the pull-through and one way by which you might frustrate its purpose. Properly, immediately after the riffle, the shuffler should square the two packets into one unit. If he doesn't, he probably is pulling through, though the maneuver itself may be too swift to be seen.

If you suspect him and you have the cut, *don't* cut about the middle of the pack like most players. The crimp will be about there. And don't cut high or low because, if you do, he may pull a "pass" or "table hop" to get the cards right back where he wants them.

No, pull out a packet right from the *middle* of the deck and then follow with a regular cut.

Another tried-and-true method (and the name itself will tell you it is a well-tested oldie) is the "faro shuffle." For two-handed poker or any similar two-handed game, every other card is stacked.

Shuffle as directed

Now let's deal ourselves another full house, aces high, with this "interlace riffle stack," as it is also called. Here, in 1-2-3 order, is how we go about it:

First, probably from the discard which has been carelessly left unmixed, the sharp scoops up two aces and three queens and drops them atop the deck. Second, he makes with an impressive false shuffle which disturbs nothing. Then, cutting the deck evenly, he puts the ends of the two packets together at a slight angle.

As he shoves them together and riffles once, the cards become interlaced, every other one being stacked for his hand. (At this point, we are assuming a two-handed game, which means one shuffle.) If it is four-handed, he shuffles twice or—for a big Saturday night game of eight players—three times, and the full house is still distributed to fall to him.

Of course, accidents can always happen, especially on the cut, but if the sharper fails to get his full house combo, he knows it is falling to another player, and he quietly drops out of the betting.

In a neat gin rummy variation of this same shuffle, the crook puts runs from previous hands atop the deck and covers them with a card which he crimps or otherwise marks. Now he administers the "faro" or "interlace" so the cards in the runs are every other card. (Or he can riffle two times, as above, for four-handed gin.)

If he survives the cut successfully, the runs will drop into his hand but, in any event, once he spots the marked card, he knows the run is beginning—and who has it. This stack, known as "the key card

Figure 47. Beginning of the push-through for a stacked deck.

Figure 48. Here the packets are being pushed through.

Figure 49. Set-up of the deck prior to the push-through.

Figure 50. "Work" being put into maneuver so the two packets will not intermix as they are pushed.

Figure 51. Author is apparently cutting deck. Actually, he is pulling out the bottom stack intact.

Figure 52. Completion of push-through. Right hand places bottom stock in front of him, comes back for packet in left hand and throws it atop bottom packet. This seemingly mixes the cards— but we know better!

gaff," is neat but dangerous. If the crook disrupts just one card, the whole stack is disrupted. Nonetheless, don't think I'm a nag if again I say, beware particularly of two-handed games!

Compliments of a friend

Now I'd like to describe a very pretty stack which was witnessed by a friend of mine, Jay Ose, in some fast West Coast company. Jay, I want to emphasize, is *not* the anonymous friend whom I mentioned at the beginning of this chapter. He is a card-wise, thoroughly honest gentleman whom I call my "West Coast correspondent." You see, in my business, I can't be all over the country at the same time. In the spots where gambling is particularly heavy, I have a number of friends who keep me posted on new capers and new "gaffs."

The way Jay describes it, the game was a rough, five-handed betting duel of seven-card stud. On the payoff hand, the dealer (whom Jay later discovered was a cheat working in concert with a confederate) overbid to open. "What's the limit" he exclaimed, shoving a big pile of chips into the center of the table.

As Jay subsequently reconstructed the little scenario, the dealer was trying to divert suspicion from himself (indicating that he thought he had a winning hand) and from his confederate (who actually did have it but, thanks to his partner's heavy opener, could seem to ride along).

The victim stayed, the confederate saw and raised him. The dealer reopened, pushing up the bets. But, after the victim saw his confederate, the dealer dropped out. Now the victim put down two kings—and the confederate showed two aces to take the pot.

Here is how the "gaff" was worked. First, from the deadwood, the dealer scooped up the four key cards; that is, the two aces and two kings. With a natural, casual gesture, he used three other deadwood cards as his scoop and laid them on top of the pack over the two sets of A-K-K-A.

Just simple mathematics

Now, using a "chop" shuffle, he chopped the five cards off the pack. This reversed the stack but kept it on top. Then, after a false shuffle to mislead the victim, they still remained on top and when he dealt, his partner caught the two aces and the victim the two kings.

By a simple mathematical formula, you can adapt this stock to a game of three, four, six or seven hands, just as easily as to a five-handed game. To determine the number of cards you take from the dead wood as your "scoop," you subtract the number two from the number of players. Thus, you scoop with one card in a three-handed game, two in a four-handed game, four for six players, five for a seven-handed bout. Then you "chop" the same number of cards as there are players.

Admittedly, the chop shuffle is difficult for amateurs, but the beauty of the gaff is that the dealer, holding an even worse hand than the victim, diverts suspicion from himself and the stack can be used over and over during the course of the play.

Now here is another, known as the "6, 3, 4, 1" shuffle, which also is a mathematical beauty. Get out a pack of cards and we will do it together.

First, put the four aces together atop the deck (face up, so that you can follow the operation). Now crimp the bottom card. If it is a nice, crisp, fresh pack, as should always be used in these finger exercises, just use a joker as your marker instead of crimping and you won't damage the cards.

Next, undercut; that is, take out the bottom packet with the right hand. With the right hand ready for the overhand shuffle, you now shuffle six cards from the bottom packet atop the four aces.

Round and round again

Now, apparently, you casually throw the remaining packet of cards in the right hand atop the left-hand packet. But, actually, two fingers hold the left packet and switch it so as to throw it over the right-hand packet. This brings the packet right back to its original position.

I know this may sound slightly confusing, so let's stop right here and take our bearings. If you have come this far correctly, six cards will be atop the four aces and the bottom card is still the crimped card (or joker).

Next, shuffle off three cards from the top, leaving only three atop the aces. Now four, then one to the bottom. Here you have just completed the cycle for stacking two aces for a four-handed game of poker.

But if you want to prove the theory, you now have to cut the crimped card (joker) to the bottom. Notice that every fourth card is an ace. In four hands, the aces will fall to the dealer.

Remember, the whole operation is executed once for a four-handed game and a stock of only two aces; twice for a four-handed game and a stock of four aces.

In all these "gaffs," you must first understand the mathematical principles of the necessary moves. Therefore, I suggest that, without trying to execute them quickly or expertly, you merely run through them a dozen times as though they were new dance steps.

Then, with the progression firmly in mind, you can work on the execution. I advise this *not* to encourage you in learning cheating methods. Frankly, to become accomplished would take more hours of patient practice than nine out of ten people would care to give. But, by actually working out the moves yourself, you will be better able to detect them —and thus protect yourself.

Chop, chop, chop

I am proud (not vain, I hope) that I can execute every technique I describe to you. I can deal four aces, full houses or a 13-spade bridge hand, and I have sufficient manual dexterity to riffle-shuffle with one hand or second deal while holding the cards in one hand. I know moves not described in this book.

But, except in emergencies and for good and sufficient cause, I wouldn't dream of pulling such "gaffs" in a game. Forgetting ethics for the moment, the risks are just too great and the best "mechanics," almost without exception, sooner or later are detected and disgraced.

There was, for example, the elegant Lord de Ros, many years ago one of the greatest whist players of all England, who could not resist giving himself the ace of trumps on his deal by planting an ace at the bottom of the pack. Most times, he probably would have won, anyhow, but he just couldn't play honestly, and eventually he left England in disgrace and died in exile.

His name survives because a cruel wit of the day thought up this epitaph for him: "Here lies Lord De Ros—in confident expectation of the last trump." Which reminds me of a somewhat similar epitaph for one of our own unfortunate American gamblers: "Played Five Aces, Now Playing a Harp."

Now back to our lessons.

You remember I mentioned the "chop" shuffle, alias the "barnyard" or "haymaker" shuffle? Let's do it together because the "chop" is a particularly dangerous maneuver by which the "mechanic" can deal himself *any hand* that he wants.

It is four-handed poker, and the crook has the deal. . . .

From the discard, he quickly, chooses the desired cards and casually slides them to the bottom of the deck. Problem, how to get them to the top in deck positions 4-8-12-16-20 so all five will drop into his hand?

Reading from top to bottom

With his left-hand fingers, he "chops" from the deck which is being held in his right hand.

When he starts stacking, he then pulls off top and bottom cards simultaneously. The bottom (desired) card is covered by the card from the top of the pack. He shuffles off two cards on top of that.

If you stop and think a moment, you can see that he is stacking a full house for a four-handed game of poker. The desired card is now in No. 4 position.

Four more times, he does the same thing, thus maneuvering the other four desired cards at the bottom into positions 8-12-16-and-20 in the pack. To keep his stack intact, he in-jogs the 21st card as a marker and shuffles above it.

For the sake of convenience, I have called the stack 4-8-12-16-and-20, but its actual position at the moment in the left hand is at the *bottom* of the deck. But one more maneuver quickly brings the stack to the top. The "mechanic" can complete the shuffle by shuffling to the break. Or he can offer the deck for a cut and his partner will bring up the stack, cutting at the jog card.

(And, of course, as in the other stacks, the number of cards spaced between each desired card varies according to the number of hands to be dealt.)

Since the days of Quinn and Erdnase, innumerable systems have been devised for locating, selecting and stacking cards. These are somewhat portentously known as "runup systems," and the quick-buck purveyors of dishonest gambling equipment sell "booklets" purporting to describe the latest systems.

Objectionable literature

If you purchased *all* such booklets, you would spend several hundred dollars and, I assure you, learn far less in the end than you should learn from this book.

Now, after this warning (and modest self-advertisement), I would like to submit an interesting study in contrasts.

First, an elaborate "gaff" which requires no less than three cheats working in collusion. Second, a deplorably obvious "gaff" which is dangerous only because neophyte cheats practice it on neophyte players. (But, of course, neophytes, cheats *and* players alike, constitute the biggest segment of the cardplaying public!)

Let's take a look at the complicated swindle. Cheat No. 1 is the dealer. He "bottoms" the three or four desired cards and, after a few preliminary shuffles that, of course, do not reach down to these particular cards, cuts the deck.

Then he transfers 14 cards from right to left hand, inserting them at the bottom of the packet *under* the desired cards he had previously bottomed.

Next, he passes the deck to confederate No. 1 on his right, who cuts lightly and falsely so as not to disturb the bottom stock.

This will take your breath away

Now the deal. I forgot to tell you (underscoring just how rarefied and complicated this "gaff" is!) that the game is *seven*-handed poker and it must be draw poker, at that. In seven-card draw, of course, a total of 35 cards is dealt around the board, which gets us down to the three or four desired cards lying atop the 13 or 14 that he had previously transferred under them, from right to left hand.

Now confederate No. 2, who fortuitously sits to the left of the dealer, comes into the act. He discards three or four and draws the desired cards which now are sitting at the top of the deck.

Frankly, though different experts have described this gaff approvingly to me and Floyd Moss quotes it in his excellent little book, *Card Cheats —How They Operate* (The William-Frederick Press, New York, 1950), I have some skeptical reservations.

The essence of a superior "gaff" is a classical simplicity, and here is a caper that requires three little cheats sitting all in a row! In a word, it's cumbersome. Certainly after one winning hand, I would suspect a setup in which the same man dealt, the same man cut and the same man won in such apple-pie, 1-2-3 order.

Now the other extreme. The "faro" or "interlace" shuffle (also occasionally known as the "butt" shuffle) interlaces the cards, as you will recall. Now reducing this not to classical simplicity but almost absurd simplicity, neophyte crooks sometimes rummage through the discard, interlace desired cards with unneeded ones and place this stack right on top of the deck.

It is so brashly unconcealed that it presupposes a two-handed game, because there wouldn't be the time or cover to construct a more complicated interlacing. And even two-handed, it presupposes a childlike trust or serious astigmatism on the part of the victim.

But, take my word for it, I have seen it accomplished!

Three riffles, and away we go

Honestly performed, the riffle shuffle mixes the cards far more thoroughly than the showy, old-fashioned overhand shuffle, but there is a nasty, invisible technique for controlling it. The crook slows down or speeds up the riffle of the packet in either his left or right hand. Thus, instead of meshing cards from the two packets in 1-2, 1-2 order, a block of several cards can be held together and meshed intact.

Let me illustrate. It is four-handed draw, the dealer wants to award himself three aces, and he does so with only three riffles and a false cut!

Having picked the three aces out of the discard, he drops them atop the deck, which he now divides for the riffle shuffle.

Riffle No. 1—He executes this in what you might call 3-2 time. That is, when the packet being riffled in the right hand is all shuffled except for the last three cards, he *holds* them with his thumb. Similarly, he riffles the left-hand packet (which has the three aces on top) and *holds* the last two. Now he slides the three right-hand cards atop the riffled pack and the two remaining aces over them. Do you see what

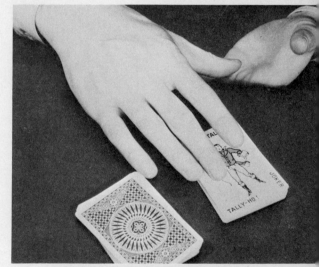

Figure 53. The deck has just been offered for the cut. (Joker is turned up so you can follow the table hop.)

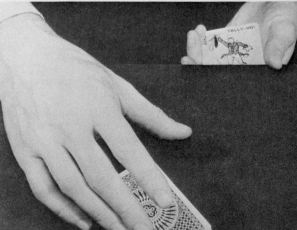

Figure 54. Author has pushed the top stack into his left hand, which is slightly off the table.

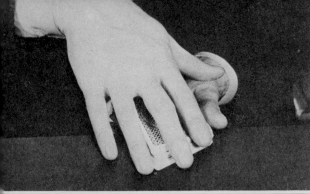

Figure 55. Right hand slips bottom stack on top of top stack in left hand. But wait—

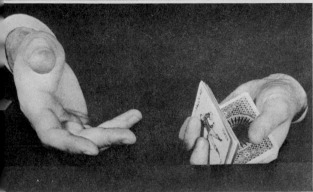

Figure 56. The left hand *reverses* the deck, so the pack is now as it originally was!

has happened thus far? Two of the aces are atop the pack, the third below, separated from them by three intervening cards.

Riffle No. 2—He repeats the same ritual, except that he holds back only one card in the left-hand pack. Now he has one ace at the top, three mediocre cards under it, then the second ace, then three more mediocre cards and finally the third ace.

Riffle No. 3—This time, he holds back three from the right packet until all the left packet is riffled, then drops the three on top.

Actually, I know a method in which you can do the same thing in only *two* table riffles.

Cut, uncut and deal

Voilà! The cards are now stacked so that all the aces will come to the dealer as he passes out the four hands.

But haven't we forgotten something? What about the cut that presumably puts his top stock of aces down to the bottom of the deck?

In spots like this, a confederate is particularly helpful to come through with a false cut. However, even working "single-o," a crook can undo the cut, bringing the stacked packet back to the top.

It's tricky and it requires a strong amount of distraction which he himself supplies, by conversation, a fit of coughing or an "accidentally" spilled drink to cover his movements. But he can do it.

Possibly, casually resting his right arm on the table to provide a screen, he will pick up the deck in his left hand and, with his left thumb, press the top part of the deck upward. Simultaneously, with his left fingers, he raises the bottom part toward the vertical, then releases his thumb so the top half drops underneath it.

This is the one-handed shift, a variation of which is the two-handed shift. In completing the cut, putting the bottom packet on top, the crook leaves a step at the juncture. As both hands close over the slightly separated pack, he quickly reverses the order of the two packets, so the deck is right back where it was in the beginning.

Even better, but it requires a prestidigitator's speed, is the table shift. Ostensibly placing the bottom packet on top, the manipulator slides it under the packet lying on the table, again negating the cut.

Now I want to tell you about an outrageously brazen false cut that often works because it is practically an optical illusion.

It looks so natural!

You have often seen players cut by grasping the deck with the thumb and third finger of both hands, in effect pulling it apart. The natural movement is to grasp the top packet with the left hand, and the bottom packet with the right, then putting the latter atop the left packet.

However, the crook will *reverse* this procedure, pulling out the bottom packet very quickly with his left hand, shoving it toward the dealer and slapping the top packet on it—right where it was in the first place. Done with quick, careless-seeming confidence, the maneuver is rarely detected because it so closely simulates the honest cut of this type.

Then there are the conscientious players who cut up the deck into several small packets, and this more elaborate cut can also be closely simulated without actually disturbing the top stock. Watch it in slow motion.

Left thumb and second finger draw off the top stock into one packet. . . . Right hand drops right packet on top of it, but as the pack is evened, the right thumb keeps a break between the packets. . . . The deck is now held up in the right hand as the left hand draws off three or four small packets, one atop the other, till the break is reached. . . . Then the rest of the cards in the right hand (with the stock, of course, uppermost) are casually slapped atop the pile of smaller packets.

With very little variation, the same technique of cutting to small packets can be utilized without disturbing stock at the bottom, rather than the top of the pack.

Now, for pure pyrotechnics at the card table, let me tell you about probably the fanciest false cut I have ever witnessed.

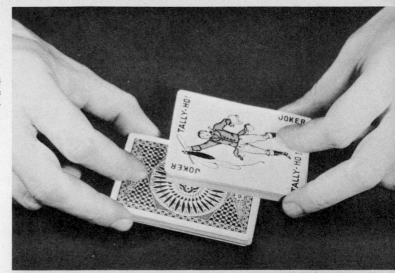

Figure 57. Author begins fancy, but effective false cut for entire deck. Follow the exposed top card.

Figure 58. Author takes cards from bottom of deck, throwing them atop exposed Joker. (In actual cut, stepping of packets would be less exaggerated than shown here.)

Figure 59. Author has not released his grip on this packet, and here he is pulling it out again—still intact—with a portion of bottom of the original top stack.

Figure 60. Now he has "cut" the deck into three packets, but actually, nothing has happened. Left hand holds original top stack, middle packet is original middle stack, and packet nearest you is original bottom stack.

Figure 61. Author puts packet with exposed card atop middle packet so it is back in same position as in Figure 57.

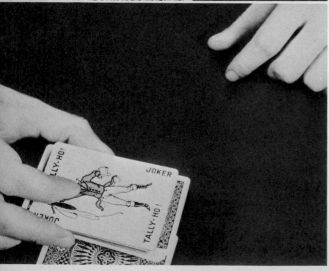

Figure 62. Cut "completed" by putting top and middle packets back on top of bottom packet —and deck is just as it was in the beginning.

So beautiful and yet so dangerous

The manipulator holds the deck near the ends with the thumb, second and third fingers of the left hand, and the thumb and second finger of the right hand. Remember this grip and if the following maneuvers also occur, don't bet. Despite the elaborate cut, not a card in the deck will have been moved from its original position.

With the right hand, the cheat extracts about a quarter of the deck off the bottom, placing it on top. However, he doesn't let it fall free but, keeping his hold, maintains a slight break from the rest of the pack.

Next, with his left hand, he raises a third of the remaining under packet and then with his right hand, grasps half of what is left of the under packet. Finally, with his left hand, he holds the very bottom packet.

Thus, two packets (top and third down) are controlled by the right hand, and the other two (second and fourth down) by the left hand. Now he whips them apart and begins to let them drop. First, the upper packet from the right hand, then the lower packet from the left hand, then the right, then the left.

Seems impossible, doesn't it? But just take a pack, arrange the four suits in order and go through the motions. At the end, your four suits will be intact and in their original order. I don't mind spelling this one out in some detail because there's a catch to it. You need hours *and* hours of patient finger exercises to cut true and manipulate two packets in each hand. But certainly you can remember how it is worked —and beware the showoff who works it.

I've by no means exhausted the almost infinite variety of false cuts and shuffles, but at least I am sure that you have learned the following general laws of self-protection against them:

Seven safety regulations

1. When hands are thrown into the discard, make sure that they are properly separated so that pairs, straights, runs and other winning combinations do not remain bunched together.

2. Beware the dealer who ever so casually picks out key cards and slaps them on the top or bottom of the pack.

3. Be on the alert for crimps. If a crook overcrimps, the break may be visible in the pack, and if he doesn't have the opportunity to uncrimp while dealing, you may be able to detect the waved card in the deck or in someone's hands. *Without* accusing the dealer, point it out and call for a misdeal and a fresh deck. He will get the message.

4. In cutting, cut high or low, rather than to the middle. And don't just trustingly tap the pack to waive a cut! If there happens to be a crook sitting to your left, you are signaling him that next time he can place any simple stock atop the deck and you probably won't disturb it.

5. If, for any reason, you suspect another player, also observe the player sitting to his right. That would be the convenient seat so the confederate could cut for his ally's deals.

6. When *you* are dealing, make sure that the hands from the previous play are thoroughly shuffled through the deck. Otherwise, you may be an unwitting crooked dealer yourself, accidentally dealing out interlaced pairs.

7. As you shuffle, make sure that no peeker can get a glimpse of the cards. If he does peek one and it's part of an "undigested" hand from the previous play, he pretty well knows who holds four or five cards, and if one or two of them are high cards that is valuable information.

Now, a bit of good clean fun

You have been a good pupil. So I am going to give you a little throwaway trick which will impress your friends with your mastery of shuffling. Fortunately, though, it requires no skill at all.

Tell a friend to think of a card. Then have him shuffle the pack thoroughly. Ask him what card he has in mind. (Let's assume it is the ace of diamonds.)

Now say something like this. "I am going to locate your card in a highly unusual manner."

Take the pack from him and shuffle it yourself, making a production out of it.

"Yes, I'm going to do something much more difficult than merely locating the ace of diamonds. I am going to make an ace of *another* suit come up next to a diamond. In other words, I am going to manipulate *two* cards so that the suit and denomination of the one you picked will pop up side by side."

Shuffle again. Sure enough, someplace in the pack, the ace of spades, hearts or clubs will show alongside one of the diamonds.

Other than the laws of probabilities, there is no trick to it. It's just the way the cards fall and, in the thousands of times that I have tried it, I've known it to fail only once or twice. And an initial failure makes it all the more convincing, as a matter of fact.

Sure, it's just a throwaway but an *honest* one. I thought that you might like a breath of fresh air before we get back to the crooks in our next chapter.

Figure 63. Notorious "mechanic's grip." Notice pack is firmly locked in hand by last three fingers of hand, with forefinger curled around top edge of deck.

Figure 64. Another tell-tale clue to "mechanic's grip." Deck is held in a bevelled position under thumb.

Figure 65. "Poor man's" or grifter's variation of "mechanic's grip." Position of pinkie is dead give-away.

Figure 66. Newest, best, least obvious, most relaxed form of "mechanic's grip." Study it carefully.

Figure 67. Start of the second deal. Notice that as right thumb strikes the top card, left forefinger is pushing forward second card.

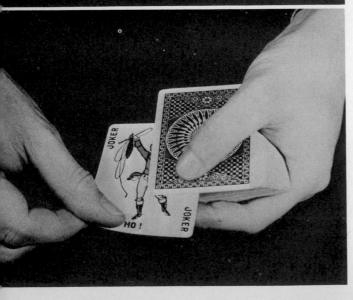

Figure 68. Now right thumb has slid off the top card, which is retracted by the left thumb and instead grasps the protruding second card (turned face upward in the photo so you can follow the action).

CHAPTER **XIII**

♠

♥

♦

♣

♠

♥

♦

THEY NEVER DEAL <u>YOU</u> THE TOP CARD

♣

♠

♥

♦

LIKE MOST MEN who live dangerously and by their wits, crooked gamblers have a wonderful, lemony sense of humor. Even while you are deploring their morals, you can't help laughing at their stories— at least I can't—but one thing rather puzzles me.

The most stories, and the best ones, concern crooked dealing. Yet, as you are fully aware by now, second, middle or bottom dealing is only one weapon in the card cheat's big arsenal of tricks.

Probably they like these particular anecdotes because the deal is the crook's great hazardous moment of glory when he cheats and wins.

Anyhow, here are a few of the stories I like best.

A Frenchman, kibitzing a two-handed game in which a friend was playing, observed that the other player frequently second-dealt and alerted his friend. The latter merely shrugged, explaining with Gallic logic, "I realize it, but it is agreed that every time I catch him at it, I score an extra point."

Transposed to a Mississippi riverboat and the American gambler's brand of logic, which can be pretty strange, too, the story goes like this. When the observant friend warned a player against the cheat, the player retorted almost indignantly, "What of it! It's his deal, isn't it?"

Finally, I like another yarn related by John Philip Quinn, the repentant nineteenth century gambler whom I have previously mentioned. Quinn once encountered a physician who, having gone to the dogs because of gambling, wanted to earn his living at it as a bottom dealer for Quinn.

Figure 69. Author has reversed Ace of Spades on bottom of deck to show what the bottom or "cellar" deal looks like. Left hand holds pack in "mechanic's grip." As right hand approaches deck, he "rips" Ace of Spades off bottom.

Figure 70. Look closely. Here the Ace is being "ripped."

Quinn's worst cut

The gambler granted the rogue doctor an audition, *listening* very carefully because, as we shall see, there is a sound as well as sight hazard in bottom dealing.

You can judge the poor physician's proficiency from what Quinn told him immediately afterward:

"Well, doctor, I have a horse pistol right here in my pocket. I've noticed your skill as a bottom dealer, and I believe if you will only give me a signal when you intend to draw a card from the bottom of the pack, I'll fire off my gun at the same time, and so fully attract the attention of every man in the room that nobody will notice what you are doing. At all events, nobody will hear that *horrible* noise that you make in practicing your little game."

152

Figure 71. For the legendary middle deal, the favored cards first must be controlled to bottom of deck. In replacing after cut, author shows four Aces face up on bottom of deck to clarify the move.

Figure 72. Again, the deck is held in the "mechanic's grip." Notice the break by the index finger. Normally, thumb would apply enough pressure to close the break at front, keeping the break in rear of the deck with the pinkie.

Figure 73. Now, from the middle of the deck, the author deals Ace.

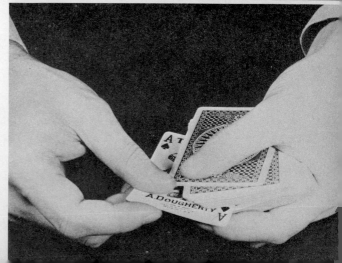

Today, I regret to warn you, there are many thousands of bottom dealers who are successfully silent. There is an even greater number of expert second dealers and a few (*very* few) accomplished middle dealers. The latter, I suspect, were scarcely even known by the "black-legs" in Quinn's era of cruder cheating. At least, in his compendium of crooked gambling, *Fools of Fortune,* Quinn fails to mention middle dealing at all. So does E. S. Andrews who, under the *nom de table* of "S. W. Erdnase," wrote *The Expert at the Card Table,* a classic of chicanery, shortly after the turn of the century.

Before taking pack in hand—in the mechanic's grip, naturally—for a few rounds of shady dealing, let's distinguish between the three techniques.

The *second dealer,* usually known to his friends as a "No. 2 Man," deals "seconds," that is, the second cards from the top of the deck, retaining the top card for himself or a confederate.

As dangerous as they come

Almost always, he must rely on cards that have been premarked or are nicked or punched during the game. Thus, by sight or touch, he knows when a valuable card has reached the top and he then second deals to hold it there.

The *bottom dealer,* alias "base," "subway" or "cellar" dealer, requires much more proficiency, but the way things usually work out in this world, his rewards are greater, too. He does not have to rely on markings, nor in many cases need he go through the intricate evolutions which we have just described in the preceding chapter on false cuts and shuffles.

Rather, he deposits his desired cards at the bottom of the deck and can shuffle almost the whole pack without fear of disturbing them. If the cards are then cut, he must get the original bottom packet to the bottom again by one false cut to nullify the honest one. But thereafter, it is laughably simple—for him, that is. He deals "bottoms" to his friends and himself, "tops" to the rest of the company, and a good time is had by all, except the rest of the company.

But the artist of artists is the *middle dealer*. He not only ignores marked cards, but he doesn't give much of a damn about the cut, either. He places his aces or what-have-you at the bottom of the pack and, in offering it for the cut, crimps the top. The rest of the cut is honest and why not? The victim obligingly arranges it so the bottom half, containing the aces, will rest atop the crimp, and then the artist deals from there.

John Scarne, who himself can perform this difficult feat, calls the middle dealer "about as dangerous as a man can get with a deck of cards in his hand." Check, John. I can do it—for friends, that is—but I wouldn't dare try to pull it off in a real action game.

Anyone want seconds?

Since the deal is so critically important in *any* card game, I think the class should study these three unethical techniques in some detail.

Let's take seconds first.

Grasping the deck in the mechanic's grip, the dealer uses his left thumb to force the two top cards to protrude slightly over the right side of the deck near the top, the second card sticking out just a shade further than the top card.

Now the dealer "strikes" with his right hand, thumb first. Apparently, the thumb is grasping the top card, but actually it slides over it to make contact with the edge of the second card.

Thus, as the left thumb is retracting the top card, the right thumb finds the second card and, with the second finger which is underneath, locks it for the throw. Sometimes, in a variation of the move, after the two top cards have been made to protrude, the left thumb lies "dead" atop the pack. In its descent, the right hand then hits the left thumb out of its way to the left, during which movement the thumb also retracts the top card.

In the hands of an adept practitioner, the top card will shuttle back and forth like a bobbin until the dealer is ready to release it to himself or a confederate. Yet you won't suspect that it is being held back

Figure 74. Author holds out number of cards from bottom as he offers deck for cut. Left thumb on edge of table is red flag.

because the retraction move is so swift and the cards are being dealt with such an authoritative-sounding snap.

However, there are several ways that you may spot a second dealer and curiously, as in bottom dealing, *sound* is one of them.

This is hard to describe in writing, but if you practice a little second dealing yourself, however fumblingly, you will notice the slight difference in sound from an honest, top-card deal. And, during a game, if your ears know what to listen for, you can also detect the difference.

Of course, your first tipoff is the mechanic's grip which gives the cheat the opportunity to bevel out the underlying cards slightly. Another thing you can do if you have any suspicions is to watch the upper left corner of the top card for back-and-forth movement. Finally, keep an eye on the dealer's left thumb. If he is dealing honestly, it will lift a bit as he moves it back to the left preparatory to pushing out the next card to be dealt. If it doesn't lift, he obviously is moving back the top card preparatory to pushing it out again.

I don't like to seem discouraging, but I should add that some second dealers can operate without the mechanic's grip. As a matter of fact, they can even second deal *with the left hand alone,* and I suggest you be on guard against the following casual-seeming one-hand deal.

Holding the deck a little above the table in the left hand, the dealer drops the cards, one at a time, to each player. There is a disarming clumsiness to the move, plus a few gestures of the wrist which cover up what is actually happening.

The dealer pushes two cards downward at the same time, but the left thumb holds back the top card while gravity deposits the second card, face up, for blackjack.

Considering that a one-hand deal is unnatural and involves the exertion of reaching out the left hand toward each player in turn, I recommend that you watch such a dealer. Maybe he is just showing off his big, strong hand, but more probably he is a cheat.

Guarding against bottoms

Thanks to large hands and long practice, I can deal "bottoms" from a full, 52-card pack, but I defer to the prudent advice of all veteran crooked gamblers.

Because the "gaff" is difficult to execute, they say, bottom dealing should almost never be attempted till the deck has been partially depleted. (The reason will be obvious when we explain the moves.) Additionally, as a matter of psychological timing, you will find, thinking bottom dealers rarely "cellar deal" as they are distributing the first cards of a hand. That is because the eyes of all the players are, naturally, on the dealer.

Most often, they throw bottoms on the next round as the other players are studying their first cards. They may or may not "cellar deal" the third and fourth cards, but the fifth round (assuming a five-card deal) is almost always honest. Again the players are watching the dealer as they impatiently wait to fill out their hands.

Thus, your first precaution against bottom dealers is to watch the way they manipulate the second, third and fourth cards in any deal. But what, precisely, are you watching for?

First, of course, the reliable old mechanic's grip on which almost all bottom dealers rely. Second, the faint slap as the bottom card hits the table the moment before it is dealt. Third, a telltale movement of the left thumb as it shuttlecocks the undealt top card (as in the second deal technique). Fourth, any movement of the second finger of the left hand with which most bottom dealers slide out the "cellar" card.

Let's run through a bottom deal in 1-2-3 order.

Look, Ma, one hand!

Most of "the work" is performed by the left thumb and second finger. As in second dealing, the thumb pushes out the top card, presumably so the right hand can grasp it. But as the right hand is descending, the second finger of the left hand starts to feed out the bottom card (which is concealed by the protruding top card). Now both top and bottom cards are equally extended from the pack.

The right thumb hits the pack just as the left thumb retracts the top card and continues downward to grasp the bottom card with the first finger of the right hand. As you can see, because the manipulation is at the bottom rather than the top, there is a danger that the whole pack will shift its position in the left hand. That is why bottom dealers prefer to work with fewer cards, which gives them a firmer grip on the deck.

Most deceptive—and it can be done—is the *one-hand* bottom deal. Till he reaches his confederate or himself, the dealer pushes off the top cards honestly with his left thumb. But, to bottom, he pushes forward on the top card and simultaneously pulls back the bottom with his third fingertip. With a natural gesture, he waves his wrist toward the player receiving the card. The motion covers up his sudden, simultaneous retraction of the top card with his thumb and forward push of the bottom with the third fingertip. This can be either done face up or face down.

A nice variation is to top deal with one hand until the crook comes to his confederate. Then he casually switches to a two-handed deal, giving his man the bottom card and finishing out the deal with both hands. This has the advantage of misdirection.

That is, by moving his right hand to grasp the deck, the cheat attracts the attention of the other players to *that* hand—and distracts them from "the work" being performed by the left hand.

Dai Vernon's long search

In the telling, the middle deal is probably the easiest to describe— and in practice, the most difficult to pull off.

As we have seen, the middle dealer puts a slight crimp at the top of the deck before the cut. Thus, when the bottom packet (which contains his desired cards) is slapped on top to complete the cut, the crimp serves as his marker. (Matter of fact, even without a crimp, there is a tiny break at the cut which sharp-eyed middle dealers can detect.)

As he picks up the deck, the dealer holds this break point with his left fourth finger. As in any deal, honest or crooked, the left thumb pushes the top card forward and the right hand descends to grasp it. Now comes the difficult part.

The left hand must squeeze the lower. portion of the deck below the break, but not so obviously that a gap shows. Then the left second finger comes up under the desired card just above the break and feeds it out. The right thumb passes the top card which, of course, is withdrawn by the left thumb and catches the middle card with the right first finger.

Among card manipulators, this feat is so prized that Dai Vernon, one of the greatest experts in the country on card sleight-of-hand, once spent more than six months tracking down a legendary middle dealer. He traveled from New York to Chicago, St. Louis, Kansas City and a number of small Midwest towns before he finally found his man. Even then, much of a card master as he is, Dai required three days to master the basic moves under the tutelage of the old gambler and many, many more months after that to perfect his middle deal.

I don't want to seem like a topper, but I would like to pay a moment's tribute to an artist even greater than Dai's master of the middle deal.

The honest crook who couldn't lose

The goal of all successful cheating is unhurried, unvaried movements that will avoid rousing any possible suspicions, but this is almost impossible in practice. Thus, unlike the versatile magician who masters many tricks, almost all crooks have to specialize in either the second or bottom deal, and even Dai Vernon's friend knew only the middle deal.

The point is that switching from top to bottom or middle during the course of play entails different movements which the crooks don't dare risk. However, my friend (whom I obviously can't identify) has perfected a top, second, bottom *and* middle deal—all of which he executes with absolutely *no* deviation of the position of the pack in his hands!

The only character who comes close to matching him probably is fictitious, though I've often heard his story and know that it has been printed once or twice. This Runyonesque individual perfected a middle deal which he *never* used in actual play.

Instead, he displayed it in private to certain hard-eyed gentlemen, thereby persuading them to bankroll him in a series of no-limit poker games. The deal was that he would split his winnings with them fifty-fifty, and he entered into play with a light heart. Why not? Any losses would be fully subsidized, and even split winnings would be far greater than he could dare to try for on his own slender stake.

Best of all, he ran no risk of detection. You see, being basically an honest man, he did not employ his middle deal but depended on his skill alone to win. And, as the story goes, anyhow, he thus enjoyed a long, carefree, profitable season at his favorite sport before his honesty was exposed. He won, but not quite enough to satisfy his backers, and they fired him.

Rx for sticky fingers

I would like to believe this inspirational little fable but, for one reason, I find it difficult to do so.

In the underworld, job severance in such cases is rather strenuous and if the story were true, there would be a record in some hospital emergency room—or obituary column.

Curiously, though card cheats have no consciences, they cannot completely control their emotions. Often, in the excitement (and fear) which accompanies crooked dealing especially, their fingers get either dry or sweaty. This raises a serious technical obstacle to split-second manipulations of seconds and bottoms.

The gambling supply houses recognize this problem and helpfully offer a glycerine-like substance which has no smell or feeling, but will keep the fingers properly moist. One of the largest purveyors of "gaffs" claims that its "No Miss" concoction gives the perfect "feel" at all times, and never a miss.

Purely for magic or exposé purposes, you understand!

Actually, there are two top-secret concoctions which, in my own opinion, are far superior for second and bottom dealing. Either the gambling supply houses haven't heard of them, which is very possible, or are keeping quiet because you can buy them in stationery stores and pharmacies at a much cheaper price. They are intended for clerical and banking employees who must handle papers and count money and can be bought for as little as 50 cents per packet.

However, I am not suggesting that you buy them!

I just want to alert you against any player who may occasionally dab his fingertips in a "snuffbox" or a similar innocent-seeming container during play. In a "hard" game with experienced gamblers, no crook would dream of doing this, but sometimes they get contemptuously careless when they are fleecing "the laity," as they sometimes call the general public.

Much smoother is the "nervous" player who rubs the sides of his nose, pokes a finger under the corner of one eye near the nose, plucks at his ear lobe or the ear itself, or rubs the corners of his temples. Sometimes, he absentmindedly runs his fingers through his hair or sticks his thumb into his mouth.

Presumably, these are unconscious gestures by a man trying to make up his mind about the next play. Actually, all of us have waxy deposits near the nose, eyes, ears and temples, and he may be moistening his fingertips preparatory to a second or bottom deal.

In like manner, when he runs his hands through his hair, he may be getting a little vaseline on them, while thumb in mouth, of course, is the most primitive of all the moistening techniques.

Bucking such a player, you have a decision to make. Is he really nervous? If so, his gestures can be a profitable giveaway about the kind of hand he is holding. But if the nose-rubbing, ear-plucking, etc. usually precede a winning hand for him or one other particular player, you can rightly become suspicious.

The Garcia Locked Grip

We have talked so much about the "mechanic's grip" that one question naturally arises. Is there *any* completely honest grip that can be used for the deal?

I have done a lot of research into this problem and I can recommend two grips. Unfortunately, both of them are somewhat slow and clumsy. So you have another decision to make. Do you prefer speed and aesthetics (during which you may be cheated) or a deal that really gives you the cards that were intended for your hand by the gods of luck?

In the "mechanic's grip," you will recall, the deck is held deep in the palm and the fingers curl around the pack. Thus, the manipulator has firm control of the cards for his dirty work. Let's reverse that and see what happens.

Hold the deck at the lower left-hand corner by the fingertips and at a 20 per cent downward angle. In that position, I defy the best "mechanic" in the country to slip you a second or bottom! I call it the Garcia Locked Grip or Frank's Honest Deal.

Secondly, you can insist that the deal be made off the table *with one hand*. Using both hands, I am sorry to report, even a poor second dealer will be able to fool you. But never with one hand.

Admittedly, the dealing will take longer and the fellows who are clamoring for "fast action" may protest (especially if they are second or bottom dealers!).

But these are the only two crook-proof grips that have ever been devised, so far as I know.

Back in Chapter VI (What Every GI *Must* Know), I promised that I would describe how the "drunken deal" is worked. Certainly this is the chapter for it.

Do you recall the scene?

How did it happen!

A "drunk" hustles a two-handed game of poker with a barroom victim. The pack, as he holds it, is a mess; some of the cards are face down, others face up. As he shuffles, more of them are exposed. Then, swaying, he deals out the two hands. To the victim, it seems perfectly natural when the "drunk" deals himself three of the face-up cards, and he notices that they are all tens.

Thus, when the "drunk" later discards and draws two cards, his opponent figures that he must be going for the fourth ten. The opponent, who has been given four fours on the deal, naturally stands pat. That is, he will if he is a good poker player. The "drunk," he reasons, will guess he has a full house or possible straight, but not four of a kind.

Happily, he raises *and* raises, and finally the "drunk" lays down not three tens or four tens—but a royal flush. What happened!

This swindle, which I like to call "Four Fours, Anyone?," is what the crooks term a "one-pop deal." They mean that it can be worked only once. Further, it requires a deck that is already stacked and then switched into the game just before the deal. After that, all the "drunk" must do is keep his ten-card stack intact with false shuffles, which we have already discussed.

Reading down from the top card (which, of course, goes to the victim), here is the order of the stack as it lies atop the deck—all the cards face down except for the three tens:

Four, ten, four, jack of spades, four, ten, four, queen of spades, an indifferent card, ten, ace of spades, king of spades.

On the deal, as you can see, the victim catches the four fours and the indifferent card. The "drunk" gets the three tens, including the spade ten, along with the queen and jack of spades. With all his apparent clumsiness, he does not expose the latter two cards.

A gentle observation

And, you may be sure, while he seems to be all thumbs as he discards and draws from the pack, he does not let the victim see that he is throwing away two tens and getting the ace and king of spades to complete his flush.

Occasionally, in my lectures, I demonstrate this "Four Fours, Anyone?" routine to drive home one important point. Beware of the "sloppy" player, drunk or sober, who fumbles with the pack, drops cards and generally makes like Mr. Tassle from Corntown! More often than not, he is deliberately concealing his deadly expertness.

Of course, even in the most polished cheating circles, accidents will occasionally happen, and when second or bottom dealers are caught plying their trade, harsh words or worse usually follow. (Do you blame them for needing "No Miss" for nervous fingers?)

However, among my acquaintances is undoubtedly the world's most courteous crook. What he said one night, when he suspected that a "subway" or bottom dealer was taking him, goes on the record as the mildest reproach in the history of hustling.

"I wouldn't want to say flatly that you are dealing off the bottom," he sadly told his fellow "mechanic."

"But the top of the deck *is* a little dusty."

♠
♥
♦
♣
♠
♥
♦

HIT ME! BUST OUT! BLACKJACK!

♣
♠
♥
♦

TO ANYONE WHO CAN COUNT to twenty-one without serious difficulty, there is a certain deceptive attraction to the game variously called twenty-one, blackjack, pontoon or vanjohn (which sounds like an American corruption of the French vingt-et-un).

In this country, it is the one game that you will find in practically every gambling casino and, according to a recent report of the New York State Commission of Investigation, ranks right with poker as our favorite gambling card game.

In principle, blackjack derives from baccarat, the staple of the European casinos, and thus the game, in its ancestry as well as professional and amateur acceptance, stands way up on the Card Hit Parade.

I say this not to plug Local 1 of the Blackjack Dealers Union but to warn you against a very common fallacy shared by millions of cardplayers. All of them *think* that they know the game; very few of them do. In its rules, possible cheating methods and proper odds, blackjack is a simple game full of booby traps.

First off, though the names are often confused, twenty-one has different rules from blackjack. The first is the game you play in your best bib and tucker as you buck a professional dealer in a casino. The latter is the slap-'em-down game you enjoy at home when you are just sitting in the kitchen, your tie and shoes off, a can of beer at your elbow.

You can find the rules in any standard card book and you will save yourself a lot of arguments if you learn the distinctions.

Cheaters' paradise

More important, from our point of view, twenty-one and/or black-jack is, both psychologically and technically, the world's finest game for cheating with the exception of high-low cutting, and the latter, as I have said before, isn't so much a game as an expression of the death wish.

Visualize a typical blackjack game: the extremely rapid play, the tension, the players' absorption in their own hands, the complete control of the cards exercised by the dealer. But most of all, that mile-a-minute play that doesn't give a man time to get suspicious. Speedwise, blackjack compared to poker is like basketball compared to a leisurely nine innings of baseball.

Think back now over the various "gaffs" I have been describing. Don't practically *all* of them give aid and comfort to any crooked dealer?

Such contrasted authorities as Albert H. Morehead in *The Pocket Book of Games* and John Scarne in *Scarne on Cards* concur in my feelings. "Very easy to cheat at," warns Morehead and Scarne goes further. Hustling at blackjack, he says, is more common than in any other banking card game.

In the casinos, the houses enjoy both a cut on the game and a very comfortable advantage. Take a game with six players as an example. If two beat the dealer, the house pays them out of the losses of two of the other players, and still pockets the chips of the last two plus its regular cut.

There are many other little refinements that work only for the house, such as "bonus" prizes that tempt the player to "bust out" and maximum bets that hold down his winnings in case he really gets hot.

Just a peek or two

Thus, with so much running for them, the honest houses conduct honest twenty-one. Why shouldn't they! But we certainly can't accuse all the casinos of honesty, and we are also justified in suspecting almost all non-casino games played in public or semi-public places.

I will go so far as to doubt *your* "friendly little game" unless you can assure me that you've known these friends for years and have been winning on more Saturday nights than they. In which case, I might suspect—Oh, let's politely drop the matter.

The essence of the game is to reach twenty-one points or as close thereto as possible without "busting out" above twenty-one. (The cards have their pip value with face cards counting ten and aces either one or 11 as the player elects.)

Hence, a crooked dealer has several very fruitful possibilities. If he merely knows what card he is about to receive, he can signal a shill to take it for him, thus avoiding a "bust out." This insurance requires only the art of peeking or the employment of marked cards.

Despite the speed of the game, peeking can be easily accomplished, and so can the reading of marked cards—if you know how to read them. Usually, blackjack is played with a Bee deck but, to simplify, let's say numerical value in a marked deck is indicated by "shade work" on the various spokes of a bicycle wheel. Does the dealer begin with the lowest, "ace spoke" and laboriously count up to the spoke that is shaded to find the numerical value? Much too slow!

Instead, he starts with the middle spoke, which represents an eight. From there, for example, he may count two to his left to the shaded spoke, which means a six is coming up. Or if the shaded spoke is the third to the right of the middle spoke, a jack is indicated. With proper practice, such "speed reading" can be easily pulled in blackjack or twenty-one.

It's the house's game all the way

Obviously, the player is peculiarly vulnerable to house shenanigans. He plays with cards furnished by the house which are shuffled and dealt by a houseman, and his only contribution to the possibility of honesty in the game is that he can cut (unless the houseman hands the deck to a shill for the cut).

So the honest casinos, knowing even better than you and I how many rotten apples they have in their barrel, try to alleviate suspicion with an iron-clad rule to the dealers: "Stand on 17, hit 16." If by chance you wander into a casino which dispenses with this rule, mentally substitute another sign, "We use crooked dealers and marked cards." Ransom your hat from the checkroom and go home.

Now suppose the dealer can do more than just peek or read marked cards. (Admittedly, he should be a free-lance "mechanic" in business for himself but, for the sake of argument, say that he is putting a son through college and needs steady work.) What can he do with a twenty-one deck?

He can second deal to the "square John" players, reserving good cards for himself or the house shill.

He can use the old, simple but highly effective "gaff" of nail nicking which is also sometimes called "rim jagging," "creasing," "nail pricking" or simply "punctuation." In the crude old days, the gamblers filed their left thumbnail to a point, but today a thumb prick of soft gold is favored because it impresses the cards without puncturing them so the marks become conspicuous.

Worst of all, he can false-shuffle a prestack of one deck (usually for a slow game) that will be 95 per cent accurate—in favor of the house. These stacks are so mathematically devised that even in case of that rare event, an honest cut which goes unnullified, the house is still favored though the percentage may decrease.

A secret I shouldn't tell

I myself know two of these closely guarded systems for stacking. By repute, one was worked out by a twenty-one dealer who made five mimeographed copies which he sold for $1,000 each. That's a considerable bit of money for a smudgy piece of paper which contains only 52 symbols in a certain order for the 52 cards in the deck. But worth it, I assure you.

Because of the manner in which I obtained these systems, I feel that I would be breaking a confidence to publish them. Besides, I have no intention of *spreading* knowledge about cheating methods. At the same time, I can appreciate that the more skeptical reader may say to himself, "This Garcia makes with the mysterious big talk, but could he really deliver?"

So, to prove my point which is that blackjack decks *can* be easily stacked, why don't I do this? I will give you a third system which I worked out for myself, thus breaking no confidences and not causing much damage because this system is only about 65 per cent accurate.

I'm somewhat mathematically inclined and I think that if I spent the time on it, I could refine it to a much greater degree of accuracy. But why bother? I have no ambitions to go around the countryside slipping in "coolers" of stacked twenty-one decks. Maybe if you are also interested in numbers games, you will try to improve it—for "magic or exposé purposes only," I implore you!

Here it is, a 13-card stack for one deck, repeated four times. Reading from the top down the "magic numbers" are: ten, ten, eight, ten, ten, nine, four, ace, five, two, three, six and seven.

You know who loses

With six players, the stack favors the second, fourth and sixth hands (which, of course, would be held by confederates of the crook). Thus, the game would have three winners and three losers, the latter all representing "fresh money."

Actually, however, the stack is most lethal in a two-handed game of twenty-one.

I have recently heard of a reverse switch whereby the player uses a "system" to beat the house. This was worked out by a young mathematician with the aid of a computer, and I will discuss it later in a chapter discussing "systems."

Meanwhile, may I add a word of corollary caution?

Inasmuch as we know that twenty-one can be stacked, I must assume that somewhat similar games like *chemin de fer,* red dog and skin are being "gaffed" in the same manner in private games. Certainly, you should be on the alert for such a possibility.

Red card, red face

How can you protect yourself in this game?

Unless you are reasonably expert in the detection of "gaffs," you will for the most part just have to rely on the house's reputation for honesty. In my book, that means playing twenty-one *only* in the casinos that are legitimately licensed. The other houses are almost forced to cheat because they must pay so much "ice" or "sugar"—graft, by any name—to stay in business.

In private games, beware the dealer who often hits himself on a 17 without "busting out." Blackjack players are a gallant lot, and many will take a hit on 17—but the honest ones rarely survive to win. And beware the apparent "loser" at a long poker session who suggests a hand or two of blackjack at the end of the evening. This is often a setup for the introduction of a prestacked deck and a quick kill.

Playing with two decks rather than one is an excellent precaution because the mere size of the double pack makes most forms of manipulation extremely difficult.

As further insurance against all the "gaffs" except marked cards, John Scarne suggest that one pack have blue backs and the other red backs. Thus, if a blue card is at the top of the deck and the "mechanic" manages to second deal off the king-sized pack, he is taking a dangerous gamble. Since he can't see his second, he may serve up a *red* card.

This two-pack, two-color game is gaining wide popularity and, like the "stand on 17, hit 16" rule for dealers, is an indication that the play is probably honest.

However, as in most card games, the toughest "gaff" most players face is their own ignorance or reckless disregard of the odds.

That easy 20

For example, regardless of the dealer's exposed card, how many times have *you* stood pat on a 13, 14 or 15 count total? Actually, if the dealer shows a five or under, most authorities will tell you, you should never take a hit on more than 15. It is even prudent to stand on as low as 13. But the lure of perfection—21!—leads most amateurs on to the "bust out."

On the other hand, when the dealer flashes an ace (which can count 11 for him), you are forced to gamble and take a hit even on 17.

How do we figure this out? Simply by analyzing the numbers of possible combinations to make 16 and over on two or more cards and working out the various odds. I don't want to go into all the mathematical minutiae, which would be as laborious for you as memorizing a page out of the telephone book.

But let's hit some of the important odds which you can easily keep in mind.

Not surprisingly, the hardest combo to make with only two cards is a "natural" or 21-point total. (This, they say, is where the name "blackjack" originated; at first, only an ace and a black jack constituted a "natural.") Surprisingly, on the other hand, the *easiest* two-card combo for a total of 16 or higher is the 20!

Thus, in descending order of difficulty from the "natural" are the 19, 18, 17, 16 and 20. But in the first place, the chances against your achieving 16 or more on two cards are approximately 1 to 1⅓. That means there is considerably greater probability that you will get 15 or less—and, being a twenty-one player, you will hit it.

What happens then?

How to win at twenty-one

With three cards, the odds against racking up a 16 or higher are almost 2 to 1, against getting a 21 about 13⅓ to 1. Another way to look at it is this. With a third card, there is more probability of bettering your hand and less danger of busting out *only* if your two-card total is *no more* than 14. At 15, there is slightly more danger of a bust out than of improvement, and at 16 and above, the tilt against you worsens rapidly.

Now let's come right to the point of your chances of victory if you hold 16 or more. The odds against your winning on these hands are: 16, 19 to 1; 17, 6½ to 1; 18, slightly over 2½ to 1; 19, 1⅓ to 1; 20, ⁷⁄₁₀ to 1.

As in its cheating opportunities, as you can see, twenty-one presents many bewildering combinations of odds. You pays your money and takes your choice—and all the time Old Man Percentage is quietly bleeding you.

However, as the result of playing quite a bit of twenty-one in casinos scattered through the West and the Caribbean, I have invented my own technique of play. I won't call it a "system" because I deplore *all* systems as the creation either of Satan himself or the house management. As a matter of fact, I will devote a later chapter to the fallacies of those deluded gamblers who employ superstition, emotion and mathematical "tables" to the inevitable impoverishment of their families.

No, my suggestion is just common sense (which obviously disqualifies it as a system!) whereby you can enjoy an hour's play, maybe losing $5 but more probably winning anywheres from $15 to $25.

You know how twenty-one players sit in a semicircle around the dealer. Get the last seat, that is the one on the dealer's right.

This way, you can't get hurt

These are the seats ordinarily occupied by house "shills" and the last one, at the dealer's right, is especially important. If he is reading the deck, he can signal this "shill" to take an unwanted card that would otherwise force the dealer to bust out. Contrariwise, if it is a low card that will get him close to 21, he signals the shill to stand pat so he, the dealer, will get it.

But the secret of my technique is to stick with low numbers—even as low as 12—and to bet the minimum unit, usually $2.

Let's say you lose. In many variations, most systems advocate increasing your bets as you lose. This prelude to bankruptcy is based on the optimistic but unfounded assumption that luck will shortly turn in your favor and wins on the later, heavier bets will wipe out the smaller, earlier losses.

I recommend precisely the opposite

You have just lost $2. Now bet another $2. You lose again. And again you bet $2. This time, you win. All right now!

Ride the original $2, but now put the $2 winnings in a *separate* bank, either in your pocket or to the right of the original bank. You don't touch that!

Rather, you keep playing with the original bank until it is depleted. Then Bank No. 2—the one you haven't touched up till now—becomes Bank No. 1.

Do you see the prudent beauty of it? You avoid the trap of doubling losing bets which could quickly wipe you out. And you conserve some of your profits by not putting all your win money on the next game.

But remember! The hour's play is up now and you promised that you would leave quietly. If you keep playing, Mr. Percentage will take you just as surely as 22 is an unlucky number.

♠
♥
♦
♣
♠
♥
♦

CHAPTER XV

THE 6-FOR-5 OPERATORS

♠
♥
♦
♣

JUST THE OTHER DAY, I discovered what you might almost call a strange variation of seven-card stud. The operator spreads out seven cards, all face down, and asks the subject to look at and remember one. Then he shuffles the cards and deals them all face up, but tells the subject to answer *No* to each card as it is shown.

This "game" is employed by John E. Reid, one of the nation's great authorities on lie detector tests, when he is giving a polygraph workout to a suspect. Presumably, when the suspect comes to the card he has picked and lies about it, the machine will detect certain telltale reactions. These same reactions would be recorded if he were guilty of a crime and tried to deny it.

Well, I don't want to quarrel with science, but I personally know a few dozen men who, I think, could beat the machine.

Under strong lights and the beady stares of fellow gamblers, they nervelessly fatten their hands by palming or "lapping" extra cards. If they can't manipulate the deck, they miscall. Unblushingly, for example, they will claim a poker "flush" with four clubs and a spade, quickly toss their hand into the discard and rake in the pot. If they are detected, they pass off the incident as an "accident."

"Sorry, fellows. Guess the little woman is right. I do need glasses."

How greedy can a crook get?

But far more adroit and dangerous are the palmers and "lappers" or "6-for-5" dealers, as I prefer to call them. In the financial underworld,

"6-for-5" men are the usurers who exact $1 interest *weekly* for each $5 that they lend out. The "6-for-5" dealers are the usurers of the card table.

In poker, a good "No. 2 man," or second dealer, will "push off" two or three cards, instead of one, into his own hand. Thus, he will wind up with seven or eight which gives him a considerable advantage. In dealing gin, if he is greedy, he may even "push off" twice, thus giving himself as many as 12 or 14 cards instead of the legitimate ten.

A good gin "mechanic" also can lock two cards as one in picking them up. The maneuver, known as "mitting the hand," requires some "shade work." He or a confederate makes a distracting move to divert attention from the crook or, under the pretext of reaching for an ashtray or a drink, physically screens the "gaff" with his arm so the other players cannot see what is happening.

To "queer" this maneuver, make sure that, after the shuffle, the cards are ribbon-spread on the table. You can see exactly how many he is picking up, and he won't be able to lock two as one.

"Lapping" and palming are such dangerous and related black arts that I think I should describe them in some detail. But please don't try to master them! They require months, even years of practice—and, after that, you might find yourself playing against me.

Some 60 years ago, in his classic on cheating titled *The Expert at the Card Table,* E. S. Andrews, the fabulous mystery man of gambling, wrote:

"The art of card palming can be brought to a degree of perfection that borders on the wonderful.

"It is very simple to place one or several cards in the palm and conceal them by partly closing and turning the palm downward or inward; but it is entirely another matter to palm them from the deck in such a manner that the most critical observer would not even suspect, let alone detect, the action."

Perhaps in a few places (such as saying that little cheating can be accomplished with the table riffle), Andrews, or E. S. Erdnase as he called himself in print, is somewhat dated today.

For example, during the process of a riffle shuffle on the table, an expert "mechanic" *can* "crook the deck." He may "peek" the top cards and bring them to the bottom in reserve for the deal. As a matter of fact, he can control any card from the middle of the deck either to the top or bottom in one or two shuffles.

Don't misunderstand me. I am not quarreling with Andrews, alias Erdnase. I respect him as a supreme card craftsman. He had once been a "mechanic" himself, I suspect; he almost comes out and says so, and even now, 60 years later, his book is the takeoff point for anyone interested in the manipulation of cards.

In fact, in tribute to this artist at the table, I first want to dispose of the very common, bungling palmer whom Andrews-Erdnase would heartily despise—on aesthetic grounds alone.

A fish hook strictly for the birds

The fellow I am talking about holds his palmed card with the very telltale "fish hook" grip. His thumb and fingers are curved into the shape of a fish hook because he is so desperately afraid that he will show or drop the card. (Beware the crooked thumb and closed fingers.)

As additional evidence, examine the cards to see if any are bent. The "fish hook" amateur tightly clutches his palmed card and, when it finally gets back into play, it looks as if it had been subjected to an exaggerated bridge. Since he holds it facing him in his palm, the card will be bent upward.

Incidentally, that is the way good crimp men bend cards. The idea is that when the card later lies face up on the table, the doctoring will be less noticeable if the ends curve upward. If they curve downward, the crimp effect can be easily spotted. (Without sounding too much like teacher, may I suggest that if you have forgotten the important distinction between crimping and bridging, you do a little refresher reading of the earlier chapters.)

But when you come to the *artist* rather than garden variety "fish hook" boy, palming does approach "a degree of perfection that borders on the wonderful," as Andrews-Erdnase observed so long ago. This master of misdirection can and will:

Palm one or more cards off the top of the pack while it lies on the table right in front of you.

Palm from the top, bottom or even the middle of the pack while he is dealing.

Palm not one, but as many as five cards at a time. As a matter of fact, he could palm even more and only one thing restrains him. The rest of the deck would then look too suspiciously skinny!

Palm *after* the deal, stealing the extra card from practically under your nose as he drops the pack onto the table and says cheerily, "Well, come on, let's play cards."

Palm a card from his right hand to his left hand (which is known as the transfer).

Caught with the card in his hand

As the story goes, this last clever and helpful maneuver was born in desperation. A "mechanic" had just palmed a card into his right hand when a long-lost friend sauntered over to kibitz the game. He recognized the "mechanic" and shot out his right arm to shake hands!

Thinking faster than an electric computer, the "mechanic" wiped his hands as though they were sweaty—which they certainly were at that embarrassing moment. At the time, he unobtrusively switched the card to his left hand. Then he stuck out his innocent right hand, thereby preserving both an old friendship and his own health.

As I have learned from experience during many lectures and demonstrations, most people seem to think there is one standard way to palm cards and, if they really put their minds and eyes to the job, no slicker can fool *them*.

Figure 75. Author is locking card in right hand for palming maneuver.

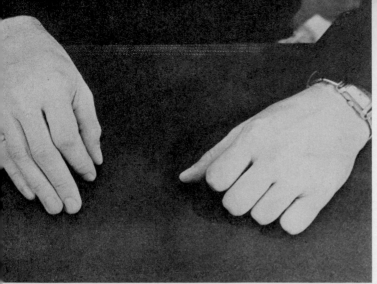

Figure 76. Card "in mitt" lies in most natural position.

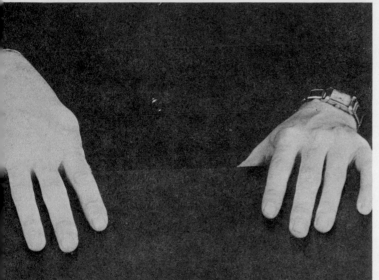

Figure 77. Certainly, with fingers thus spread apart, there can be no chicanery—or can there be?

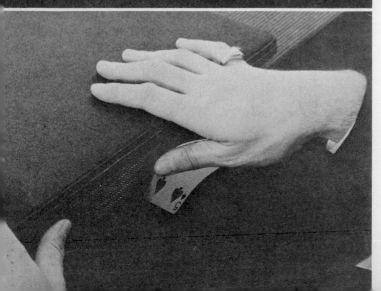

Figure 78. Yes there can. Though fingers are spread, card is being held out in right hand.

On the table or during the shuffle

The only way I have been able to convince them otherwise is to select some "hep guy" from the audience and ask, "What card do you want palmed? Which hand do you want me to use?" Then I palm the card not once, but several times, each time with a different technique.

Perhaps, with text and photos, I can also persuade you that palming is a many-faceted "gaff," with almost as many variations as there are cards in a deck.

First, let's talk about the table palm, a new and revolutionary technique in which the entire action takes place *on* the table. The mechanic riffles the deck widthwise and, as he squares it, he applies pressure with his left pinkie to force the top card into his right palm.

Even if the card doesn't lock in properly, he has a fall-back, "insurance" move. Apparently nervous or impatient, he taps his right palm with his left pinkie using leverage, to force the top card into his right palm.

A variation of the table palm is what I call the oblique palm. After shuffling, the dealer pushes the deck forward to be cut. With his hand thus covering the pack, he picks up a block of cards that he has previously stacked and holds them deeply, obliquely in his right palm. In this position, the stack doesn't show even when he spreads his fingers.

In contrast to the table palms, there are *action* palms which are executed while the deck is being shuffled.

A one-handed "cop"

For example, say there are half a dozen favorite cards at the bottom. The "mechanic" counts them off, then riffle shuffles above them and palms them into his left hand. This is a variation of an old Andrews-Erdnase move in which he counted off the desired number of cards and then, as he turned the deck in his hand, kept the desired ones in his palm.

The telltale sign, if you are sharp-eyed enough to catch it, is a pushing motion of the deck as the "mechanic" gets the "bite" on the palmed stock and separates it from the rest of the pack.

Now, is the following scene familiar?

The dealer is holding the pack in one hand, the thumb underneath, the other four fingers on top with the pinkie flat. The pack, you may also remembers, is slightly beveled. "Come on, fellows!" he says impatiently, waving the pack. "Let's start playing cards."

But he has already started playing. He now has the top card palmed.

Let's do it over in slow motion. The flat pinkie pushes the top card forward. The card pivots and jumps right into the palm position. The principle is like pushing a plank lying on a fence. If you push one end, the other goes up.

Momentarily, so quickly you won't catch it, the hand is in a cramped position with both the thumb and pinkie retracted. But as soon as the maneuver is completed, the "mechanic" can pick up a drink or a cigarette case while holding the palmed card.

This same technique for "copping"—that is, stealing or palming a card—can also be employed after the shuffle as the crook taps the deck on the table to square it.

How not to tell a crook

A staple is the "flat palm," in which the contraband card is held flat right in the middle of the palm. It is "copped" by pressure applied diagonally from the pinkie down to the heel of the thumb and can be easily transferred to the other hand by applying pressure diagonally in the other direction.

However, both for palming and also for switching hole cards, most crooks prefer the "gambler's palm," which locks the card between thumb and pinkie. This hold allows greater freedom for the palming hand, even to the extent of tossing out chips with it.

To palm from the middle of the deck, cheats use what I call the "nip-and-tuck" move. As the deck is cut, the "mechanic" makes sure that the wanted card or packet of cards jogs out three-quarters of an inch from the rest of the pack.

Holding the deck in his left hand, he "nips" the wanted cards (which are injogged, protruding from the back) with his right middle and third fingers. He then pushes his right hand forward, still "nipping" the cards. The desired ones pivot around the left pinkie into the right hand and are securely "tucked" into the palm. While this is strictly an "angle" move, the "nip-and-tuck" is quite effective when properly executed.

Some alleged authorities on crooked gambling will tell you that the way to spot a cheat is by his "squinting" eyes and his "pasty" complexion, presumably the result of long, hard nights in smoke-filled rooms under glaring lights.

Isn't this ridiculous on the face of it! Certainly, all the pros I know are healthy-looking, nicely tanned men and women. After all, most regularly follow the sun to Florida and California—and the rest can at least afford sun lamp treatments.

Three musts *if you want to end in the money*

And, keen eyesight being as important in the profession as non-arthritic, lightning-fast fingers, their eyes are sharp and hard. Once they start squinting, poor fellows, they are *retired* cheats.

No, you can't tell a crooked player by his appearance. If you happen to meet one whose face is pallid, he has probably been ill, and it won't help you to say, "Go get a sun tan, then I'll play with you." That won't change his character.

The only practical precautions *I* know take a little more effort on your part.

First, learn as many of the "gaffs" as you possibly can. Even if you cannot execute them yourself (which is just as well!) you will know what to look for and when.

Second, learn the suspicious patterns that may assert themselves as the game develops. They can be as much of a red flag as a fifth ace.

Third, learn a few simple techniques which, on your part, will forestall or frustrate the "gaffs."

Now to be specific about this threefold advice.

Beware of each of the following players who:

Casually pushes the deck to one side with only one hand (and a bent first finger) or pulls the same move as he seemingly "squares" the pack or as he "absentmindedly" runs his fingers alongside it. These are screening moves for a palm in which most of the "work" is done by the bent first finger.

Holds his hands folded in a crossed position, thus concealing a palmed card.

Sits with one hand relaxed, the other frozen. Most legitimate players follow a pattern in which *both* hands are relaxed or taut, open or closed.

Carelessly tosses the deck toward you. This may indicate the "casual palm" which is accomplished by squeezing the desired card off the top of the deck and into the palm as the toss is made.

Makes quick, jerky, nervous or "busy" movements with his flattened hand. He is probably a poor palmer trying to get the dangerous business over with as soon as possible.

Rests four fingers on the table, with the thumb underneath. If you want, you may charitably assume that he is steadying the table. In my nasty mind, I suspect that the thumb is steadying a palmed-out ace under the table edge.

Executes a hasty pickup of the deck off the table. This ties in with what I said just above. From its position under the table, the thumb quickly slides up atop the deck, bringing the palmed card with it.

Rests his thumb *almost* on top the table but in a cramped position. This position indicates he is holding a card.

Displays a little ball or ridge of flesh in the crotch of the thumb near the first finger. This muscular giveaway occurs when a palmed card is being pinched under the thumb.

Fiddles with his tie and then runs his hand through his hair. He probably is tucking a palmed card in the back of his shirt collar.

Of course, this latter quaint maneuver requires "shade work" on the part of a confederate, and (unless the crook is sitting with his back to the wall) a supporting cast of cheats who, disguised as kibitzers, crowd close behind him to conceal his back.

Obviously, this "gaff" is crude, but to me the most amazing thing about crooked cards is that so many of the "gaffs" are just that crude —and still effective.

In my experience, and please don't feel offended, this is chiefly the fault of the *honest* player. His thinking falls in a rut: cheating is for the cheaters and the sinister kind of characters you see in B movies. Honest playing is for me and the honest people I run into. Ha! This is the same comfortable, but dangerous, assumption all of us make when we read warnings from the National Safety Council against driving on holiday weekends; *we* just couldn't be one of those grim statistics.

Personally, because I know and respect the infinite possibilities for skullduggery at the table, I am suspicious as hell of *everybody* on the rare occasions I play even for fun. Clockwise around the table, I study the characters, meanwhile playing a tight, conservative game that gains me the respect, if not the affection, of any "mechanics" who may be sitting in.

Who's the stranger in this game?

Despite what some gambling authorities will tell you, there isn't a crook alive who can come into a game, take a deck of cards (honest cards, that is) and start doing things with them right away. He has to feel his way along and this, depending on the players, may take an hour or almost the whole night's play.

That is why I play along at the same leisurely pace, but I'm not wasting my time. Meanwhile, I am asking myself questions which I suggest you ask yourself every time you sit in a game.

Which one is the "mechanic"?

Is he alone?

Is he winning—or is someone else?

Is he a peeker, a glimpser, a palmer, a crimper, a bridger, a deck switcher, a marker, a second or bottom dealer, or maybe a holdout man?

Is he a stranger in the game—*or am I?*

No doubt you will have considerable difficulty catching a clever "mechanic" right in the act of "crooking the deck." But remember what I said earlier about the *suspicious pattern* that may gradually assert itself as the game progresses.

If occasionally a particular player distracts you by spilling a drink, sneezing, suddenly calling to a kibitzer or indulging in some other form of "shade work," you are not laboring under a persecution complex to think that, just possibly, he is a cheat or a cheat's confederate.

Readying the runup

Similarly, the player who pulls the impatient routine—"Come on, hurry up, fellows, let's get on with the game!"—is a gentleman to watch. Maybe he is miscalling his hand and naturally he is in a hurry to toss it in the discard before anyone discovers the spades-clubs discrepancy.

At the other extreme, you may gradually detect a dawdling pattern. That is the fellow who handles the cards rather clumsily, paws through the discard, fumbles with the deck—and meanwhile marks the location of the key cards, preparatory to a "runup."

"Runups," which are based on varying mathematical calculations depending on the number of players in the game, will position these key cards in the deck so that they all fall to the same hand. I possess many combinations for two, three, four or five card stock runups, but merely to illustrate how this "gaff" is worked, let me give you the R_x for a two card runup in a four-handed game.

Let's say that the favored cards are at the top and bottom of the deck. Here's the operation:

1. Undercut half the deck, run three cards, injog the fourth and shuffle off the balance, but bring the card originally on the bottom to the top of the deck.

2. Undercut at the injog and run four cards; then run three more cards and again injog the fourth card, shuffling off the balance of the packet.

3. Undercut at the injog and throw on top. Presto! The two desired cards will now be the fourth and eighth in the pack in a position to fall to the dealer.

Just a few simple precautions

Besides looking for any suspicion pattern in the game, you will recall, I suggested that you learn simple techniques to frustrate the "mechanics." Here are just a few examples of what I mean:

To forestall the miscaller, insist that before any hands can be thrown into the discard, they are verified as being what the player claims. If you make this a general rule covering everybody in the game, no one can feel offended.

To prevent a crooked dealer from nullifying your cut of the deck, do the *opposite* of what he suggests. Very probably, when he says "Cut," he will tap a finger to the left of the deck, thus trying to force you subconsciously to cut in that direction. (This makes it easier for him to momentarily slide the two packets under the table, restoring them to their original position.) Similarly, if he taps to have you cut toward him, cut away from him toward the middle of the table.

To make it difficult for the palmer or lapper to dispose of his extra cards, be sure that each hand is spread out and the cards *counted* before the pot is shoved over to the winner.

This is particularly important because the poker player with eight cards in a five-card game or the gin rummy man who is holding 14 cards instead of ten has a pressing disposal problem.

A bug and a beanie

In a careless game, he can quickly slide his bulky hand into the deadwood after exposing only the correct number of cards. (That, of course, is why it is important to spread out and count all the cards.) In a "harder" game with more experienced players, he must try to palm out gradually.

While he is holding out the extras, he may keep them right in his hand, but more probably he will employ the knee holdout (described in an earlier chapter), the "bug" or what I call the "poor man's holdout" because it rarely sells for more than $5.

The "bug," you will recall, is a penny to which a sharp point and a jeweler's watchspring have been affixed. When attached to the underside of the table, the "bug" allows the "mechanic" to tuck four aces flat between the watchspring and the table.

On his deal, as he slides the pack into his hand, he also slides out the four aces to the bottom of the pack—and he is ready to bottom deal himself the four big aces.

The "poor man's holdout," also known as the "beanie holdout," is a rather primitive version of the grand device invented by Kepplinger. A "come-and-go" apparatus, it consists of a hook attached to a rubber-band mechanism; the "mechanic" attaches the held-out card to the hook, releases it, and the rubber band retracts it up his sleeve. The "beanie" is something of an improvement over the old-fashioned clamp that once held cards on the *outside* coat sleeve of cheats, and that's about all you can say for it.

Sitting with two queens in his lap

However, as I have previously told you, many prudent cheats dislike carrying any incriminating apparatus so, rather than using holdouts, they lap their cards.

For example, a poker dealer will quickly let the top card drop into his lap and then openly deal himself the next one. If he is detected, he complains that the cards are "slippery." And here is a new and better "lap" maneuver:

Preparatory to the deal, the crook sees a packet of five cards on the table with—let's say—a queen at the top and bottom. He uses the top queen to casually scoop up the rest of the packet, thus bringing the two queens together. When he drops the packet face down on the deck, the two queens are at the top.

In an apparent effort to scramble the deck, he lifts a top packet and carelessly picks up the two top cards and tosses them in the middle of the pack, then drops the top packet. This creates the illusion that the queens are smack in the middle of the deck.

But what he really did was to toss them right *through* the deck and on into his lap. To allay any possible suspicion, he will hold back a few hands before using them in play.

Except for the first, scoop-up step, this maneuver is practically undetectable when done by an expert. There is, however, a variation of the move which you can detect. The two queens have been worked to the top and, unless he can execute the difficult bottom deal, the "mechanic" pulls this caper to get them both for himself:

A nasty collision

After shuffling, on the pretext of squaring the deck, he places it obliquely and lengthwise on the table. This position gives his opponent a peek at the under card, which so tickles his latent larceny that he completely misses the "lapping" move. This is executed with the "mechanic's" right thumb, which flips the top queen back into his lap. Now he can safely second deal around the table until he comes to himself.

Of course, accidents can always happen, especially when two crooks are trying to work the same game unbeknownst to each other. One such deplorable instance gave rise to that famous gambling tagline,

"You win, stranger—but those are not the cards that I dealt you."
Here is the story behind the phrase.

A deck "stacker" and a deck "switcher," who had not identified
each other through the "Mr. Hemingway" routine, were both struggling
to win the same poker game. Finally, with equal confidence, they came
to the climactic, no-limit pot of the night.

The "switcher" was confident because he had already switched, or
palmed out, the four aces.

The "stacker" was confident because he had arranged four queens
for his opponent and four kings for himself.

He, of course, didn't know that the "switcher" was holding out the
aces. Nor did the "switcher" know that he had been dealt four queens,
for it is the essence of this art that you never look at the cards you
are switching out of the game (to be replaced by those you are already
holding).

The upside-down "cooler"

In this delightful bit of double confusion, the two crooks raised and
reraised each other until all their chips were exhausted.

"What do you have?" the "switcher" finally demanded.

"Four kings."

"Not enough!" He threw down his four aces.

"You cheated!" shouted the "stacker."

"How did you find out?" the "switcher" asked nervously.

"Because those are *not* the cards I dealt you!"

They split the pot.

Another confusion story was told to me by an acquaintance who
has been very helpful in the preparation of this book, though I *still*
make it a practice never to play cards with him. On one occasion, in
what he had thought was a "friendly" game, he found that he was
being hustled, and his professional pride was hurt.

The "gaff" was marked cards and, purely by coincidence, he assures
me, he just happened to be carrying a marked deck himself. The only
difference was that, in his deck, the high cards were marked low and
the low cards marked high.

So he slipped in his upside-down "cooler," and before the other
"paper worker" could untangle the new signals, he raked in enough
pots to make him the big winner of the evening.

Recently, while I was on a cruise to the Caribbean, I heard still a
third confusion story to top all confusion stories.

Not so funny, really

This coup was worked by a "mechanic," who had a little score to pay off with half a dozen of his associates. So he arranged a seven-hand poker game into which he introduced the most peculiarly stacked "cooler" that I have ever heard of. Every hand except his own was stacked as a royal flush!

As soon as it was dealt, he looked at his cards, threw them down in disgust and dropped out of the game. And then the fun began. There were raises, reraises and then raises again, and for all I know, this game may still be going on with the same cards still unplayed. Who calls with a royal flush?

And some day, before they get old and gray and finally do lay down their cards, who will be suspect? Everybody, of course, except the one man who dropped out!

But I don't want to give the wrong impression that crooked gambling is mostly laughs and egg-in-the-beer.

Remember Andrews, alias Erdnase, the master of a thousand cheating tricks at the card table? Surely, if any "mechanic" could have made a big, quick pile and then retired to live happily ever after, I would have picked Andrews for the man.

Actually, so far as I have been able to ascertain, he led a shadowy, haunted life. Where he lived was usually a mystery, and his private life was star-crossed. He had several unhappy marriages. He never got into the big money.

And he ended up—a suicide.

CHAPTER XVI

BRINGING IN THE COOLER

ANYONE WHO KNOWS much about bridge must have been warned against the notorious Mississippi Heart Hand, which I mentioned in an earlier chapter. This cold deck swindle was conceived in sin more than 200 years ago in the days of whist. Down the decades, in its many variations, literally tens of thousands of good, even astute, whist and bridge players have fallen victim to it.

However, what happened to a friend of a friend of mine is unique even in the scarlet history of this deplorable hand.

The victim, whom I will call Hank because his name is Hank, was lounging in the club car of a New York Central luxury train speeding eastward out of Syracuse toward Albany. Two businessmen braced him for a bridge game and Hank, who prides himself on his play, quickly agreed.

Looking around for a fourth, they noticed an elderly gentleman sitting in a corner, quietly reading *The Christian Science Monitor*. His countenance was frosty, he wore a severe black suit, and old-fashioned gold-rimmed spectacles were perched on his nose. But, to Hank's surprise, he agreed to sit in.

"On only one condition, gentlemen," he added sternly. "There will be no gambling. I repeat, *no* gambling. I have deep religious convictions on that point."

Just like a nagging wife

This, of course, was disappointing, but any game was better than none, and Hank decided that he could at least pretend to himself that he was playing for a cent a point. They cut for partners, Hank drawing one of the businessmen, a rather aggressive salesman he didn't particularly like. The other businessman teamed with the stern old gentleman.

For most of the run toward Albany, the game seesawed back and forth. Hank figured he was about $30 to the good (mentally, that is), but his partner put an increasing strain on his usual good nature.

The salesman was one of those post-mortem players who can make bridge such a fretful, nagging game. After every hand, he dissected Hank's plays to show him what he should have done. If Hank had bid prudently and made it, he should have gone for a little slam. If he had bid and made a little slam, he should have gone for a grand slam. And so on. . . .

Finally, 15 minutes from Albany, it was Hank's deal. He shuffled and passed the cards to the old gentleman on his right for the cut. Just as he did, the opponent on his left spilled a glass of ice water onto the table.

Everybody hastily mopped with handkerchiefs and then the old gentleman slid the deck back toward Hank. "No harm done," he said. "The cards didn't get wet."

As Hank arranged his hands by suits, he didn't even bother to conceal the look of triumph that illuminated his face.

Temper, temper, gentlemen!

This was good! So safely good that he would start right off with a grand slam bid and *show* that partner something.

"Seven hearts," he said happily.

"Are you crazy!" exploded his partner.

"Come, come, no temper, gentlemen!" the old gentleman clucked fussily.

"Double," said the opponent on Hank's left.

"Pass," growled the salesman. "Just because this isn't for money, you don't have to make crazy bids."

Hank felt himself flushing angrily, but ignored the insult.

"Pass," said the old gentleman.

Now the bid was back to Hank. He looked at his hand again to make sure that he had made no mistake. No, he really was holding—

Spades	Hearts	Diamonds
Ace	Ace	Ace
King	King	King

Spades	Hearts	Diamonds
Queen	Queen	Queen
Jack	Jack	
	Ten	
	Nine	

And no clubs.

Hank put his cards face down on the table and, staring evenly at his partner, said, "I redouble."

"That does it!" exclaimed the salesman.

The buildup and—

"I told you not to bid like a fool even if there is no money at stake."

Hank could restrain himself no longer. He whipped out his checkbook and wrote a check for $500.

"That's my bet that I make the grand slam," he almost shouted to his partner. "Now you put up or shut up."

Before the salesman could answer the challenge, the old gentleman jumped from his seat and snatched the check from Hank's hand.

"I warned you gentlemen there would be no gambling," he said. Methodically, he tore the check into small pieces. "And there will be no gambling!"

Just then, the train slowed down for Albany.

"Anyhow, I get off here," the elderly gentleman said. "But I hope, young man, you cure yourself of the deplorable vice of betting."

The two businessmen followed without further words and, looking out the train window, Hank saw all three walking rapidly together toward the waiting room. Then he noted that the four unplayed hands still lay face down on the table. He turned over the cards of his belligerent partner first and exposed:

Spades	Diamonds	Clubs
Ten	Jack	Eight
Nine	Ten	Seven
Eight	Nine	Six
Seven	Eight	Five
	Seven	

—the kill

And no hearts.

He swore under his breath. "That old fool shouldn't have butted in," he said to himself. "With four, or at most five plays, I would have cleared out all their trumps."

But the fact that his dummy held no hearts gave him a premonitory twinge, and he turned over the cards of the player who had doubled. This was it—the "Mississippi Heart Hand," in all its lethal beauty.

No spades, no diamonds, the ace, king, queen, jack, ten and nine of clubs—and *all* the remaining seven hearts from the eight down through the two!

Without even looking at the fourth hand, Hank realized that he could have made only his six trump tricks. A grand slam, of course, means taking all 13 tricks. Suddenly, he felt very kindly toward the elderly gentleman who had torn up his check.

But that hadn't happened. A sleight-of-hand crook who can slip in a cold deck while spilled water is being mopped up also can palm a check and tear up a blank piece of paper before your eyes. When Hank got his bank statement at the end of the month, he found the $500 check had been cashed.

As I told you, this story, which was relayed to me by my friend, Donald D. McLennan, of the City Desk of *The News* in New York, is unique. It is the only time I know of that an *unplayed* "Mississippi Heart Hand" claimed a victim.

Serving it practically on a tray

However, on another occasion, my Washington sources have told me, the same hand had an unexpected and rather sad result. A group of newsmen and legislators slipped it to a Congressman who somewhat fancied himself as a bridge player. When he bid into disastrous results, he exclaimed, "If you can't win with this hand, you can't win with *any* hand!"

Whereupon, for a considerable period of time, he gave up card-playing altogether.

There is an infinite variety of ways for "bringing in the cooler," or prestacked deck.

Perhaps a waiter confederate brings in drinks just as the crook, having shuffled the deck and had it cut, is ready to deal. Naturally, the crook puts down the deck to take a drink, and the waiter puts down the tray to serve him. In the process, the waiter deposits the "cooler" which he has concealed under the tray and picks up the honest deck.

Or perhaps the banker in the game, who supplies new decks as players ask for them, is the confederate.

Or perhaps, best and cruelest "gaff" of all, the *victim* is the confederate. The "mechanic," taking him into his confidence, tells him a
switch is being planned and has the victim execute it while the real
confederate isn't "watching." Actually, the cards are stacked so that
both the "mechanic" and victim lose.

Since his "friend" also loses, the victim rarely suspects he has been
double-crossed—and even if he does, he must keep quiet or admit his
own complicity.

Watch that deck! watch that deck!

"Coolers" also can be introduced under the cover of a handkerchief,
paper money or an innocent-looking tobacco pouch or cigar box.
Hence, before the game even starts, you are justified in demanding
that *no* impedimenta of any kind clutter up the gaming table.

There isn't a crook in the world who can say to his confederate,
"We'll switch in the cooler tonight after the third hand." The move
must be worked, almost as a reflex action, at precisely the right
moment when there is distraction, preferably unplanned.

Therefore, always keep your eye on the deck!

If a player spills a drink, if kibitzers are talking loudly behind you,
if there is *any* distracting move or sound, *still* keep your eye on the deck.
That is the moment when the "cooler" will be rung in.

Remember the old-fashioned stage illusionist who, after going
through a lot of preliminary abracadabra, fired a gun? You momentarily blinked and at that moment he pulled his trick. "Coolers" are
manipulated on precisely that principle.

I have so emphasized the "gaffing" of games like poker and blackjack that you bridge players may be understandably smug about the
presumed purity of your particular pastime. I am sorry to tell you that
the "Mississippi Heart Hand" is only one of many ways in which the
bridge deck can be "crooked."

Obviously, since all 52 cards are dealt, holdout "gaffs" are im-
practical, and for an interesting reason, I doubt that much second
dealing is attempted except by master practitioners.

Bridge players, beware!

This is because a dealer establishes a certain rhythm as he deals
out a large number of cards, and any break in his tempo (as he top
deals to himself) might be a dangerous giveaway.

Personally, if I were "crooking" a bridge game, I would prefer to
bottom deal. It is easier to pull off in bridge, but a second deal is by

no means impossible, and I will give you a tip on one thing to watch for.

Sometimes, the second dealer misses his "strike." His thumb, which descends as the top card is being retracted, slips past the slightly protruding second card. It is an embarrassing situation which the "mechanic" can retrieve in only one way.

As though he'd just had an afterthought, he suddenly stops dealing. "Say!" he asks. "Did we add the honors on the last hand?" Of course, everyone did, and he is so told. Reassured, he resumes his deal, making sure this time that he does not miss the "strike."

In bridge and any other card game, any interruption in the process of dealing is per se *suspect.*

I mentioned that second and bottom dealers establish a rhythm as they pass out the cards, and so I must also warn you about the "patriotic gamblers." To get that rhythm, they hum, whistle or sing *Yankee Doodle Dandy* and second or bottom as they hit the beat!

Two other breeds of "mechanics" whom bridge players should especially beware are the "punch dealers" and "knockoff" or "sandmen."

One chance in 150,000,000

The former use the "punch" (which we have previously described) to mark the spade suit with tiny, identifying pricks. To develop that delicate sense of touch demanded of a safecracker or a "punch man," they practice by covering their hands with a newspaper or a handkerchief.

On the other hand, the "knockoff" or "sandmen" place barely perceptible markings by roughening the edges of the cards with a little sanding strip affixed to one finger. (Enough strips for 50 games cost only about $2.50 from any gambling supply house.)

Thus, controlling the distribution of the spades on their deals, both breeds of "mechanics" play a formidable game which they modestly attribute to close study of Goren. There is only one way to beat them. *Don't* play bridge with characters who must wear a bit of adhesive tape because they have accidentally "cut" a finger. Wait till the wound has healed.

The bit of tape is your only clue. These "mechanics" would never be so crude as to deal themselves more than four or five spades. After all, as they know, a perfect hand containing all 13 cards of one suit is a rarity that occurs once in about 150,000,000 times.

In passing, let me tell you about a ladies' bridge game that took place recently in Frankfort, Kentucky. Mrs. E. L. Scott *did* get all 13 spades—and each of the other three players drew all the cards of the

other three suits. Mathematically, that is one chance in 2,200,000,000,-
000,000,000,000,000,000, or one in two octillion, two hundred sep-
tillion.

A game in which reneging is the worst crime also offers many helpful opportunities to the stacker-dealer.

Garcia's gaff-killing cut

With so few hands to watch, he can easily memorize the location of
each spade trick as it is laid on the table. When he picks up the cards
for the deal, he stacks a few high spades for his own hand.

To frustrate him (or a stacker or "switcher" in other games), I suggest the Garcia variation on the Scarne cut, as follows:

1. From the middle of the pack, extract two separated packets and
put them in a separate pile, one atop the other.
2. Place the remainder of the deck atop this pile.
3. Now cut the deck again.

This procedure will take somewhat longer than a conventional cut,
and the other players (especially the stacker!) will cluck impatiently.
Let them! Be a turtle! The Garcia cut hopelessly strews any stack all
through the deck, and what you lose in time you will save in money.

I also recommend this cut for Banker and Broker, a game that can
be too easily "gaffed." In addition to careful cuts, I would suggest
that in B and B, you watch out for the "intentional 'unintentional' peek."
Apparently by "accident," the dealer lets his victim glimpse the bottom
card.

Of course, at the payoff, it isn't there. But that isn't all. Again, the
"mechanic" gives him a peek. But now the victim is both wise and
angry. He didn't dare squawk after the first peek because he would
have implicated himself. "But he won't catch me a second time," he
says to himself.

Then, this play, the peeked card *is* left at the bottom.

19 ways to switch a hole card!

A neat, cruel bit of psychology based on the ancient principle that
you never give a sucker an even break!

When a "mechanic" himself wants to peek at the bottom card and
is not the dealer, he can do it on the cut. As he lifts the top packet
off the deck, he pushes with his middle finger. This bellies out the
bottom card of the packet so that he can glimpse it, and when the cut
is completed, of course, this card is at the bottom of the deck.

Figure 79. First move in a two-handed method for switching the hole card. Card to be switched can be seen in open right palm.

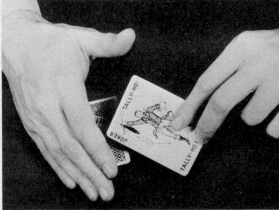

Figure 80. As legitimate hole card is picked up with left hand, notice that right hand is extending palmed card slightly forward.

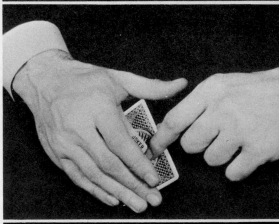

Figure 81. The legitimate hole card is now tucked into the right hand and locked into palmed position.

Figure 82. Maneuver completed. Legitimate card is concealed in right hand, and "mechanic" shows palmed card. Entire switch takes about half a second.

In contrast to those crooks who think big and switch in 52 card "coolers," there are many dainty specialists in miniaturization. They prefer to switch just one card, usually the hole card in stud poker or blackjack.

This maneuver can be accomplished with one hand or with two, the latter being known as the "Chicago move," probably because it is taught at a "school for cheats" located in the Windy City. Many "wise" players think that exhausts the subject. As a matter of fact, I myself know eight ways to switch hole cards.

And one day, as we stuffed ourselves on Chinese food, that amazing friend of mine, Dai Vernon, showed me 19 distinct methods, one after the other, each better than the preceding one!

In my book, Dai is the greatest living exponent of sleight-of-hand or natural card handling in the world today. Many of the techniques I know and practice I owe entirely to him, and I would conservatively estimate that American cardplayers are at least $1,000,000 in the black simply because Dai is an honest man.

His knowledge is profound and his dedication to his art is absolute. Sometimes, when he wants to practice up on a certain technique, he will lock himself in a room and, for the next several days, without eating or sleeping, tirelessly repeat the move in front of a mirror. As an incidental hobby to cards, he is one of the ten top masters of the vanishing art of silhouette cutting. You'd like the guy.

It wouldn't particularly enhance public honesty for me to itemize all the hole card switches I know, but I do want to tell enough so you can at least be on your guard if you come up against one of these *artistes*.

Here, it's the crook who doesn't peek

Ordinarily, players immediately lift one or two corners to get a peek as soon as their hole card is dealt. When you see a character first cover his hole card completely with his hand before lifting it for a look, he probably is palming.

While covering the card on the table with his hand, he has managed to slide a second card concealed in his palm under the legitimate card. Thus, the palmed card becomes the hole card and the latter is palmed off.

To facilitate this maneuver, so that the palmed card can be more easily slid under the hole card, the legitimate card is given an upward wave, widthwise. So a corollary clue is to watch for a "nervous" player who absentmindedly waves his hole card before covering it with his whole hand and picking it up.

A disarming variation worked by an adroit "mechanic" goes like this. With his entire hand, he covers the hole card and then spreads his fingers. The other players see the back of the palmed card (which they assume to be the hole card). The "mechanic" then draws back his hand, drawing the hole card back, too, and lapping it before he picks up and studies the palmed card.

Again, the best clue is the covering motion. After all, how many players are so cool and restrained that they will pass up that first, quick, hopeful peek!

I think I should clarify one point. In describing the various "gaffs," I cannot always pinpoint them to a particular game. All I can do is to describe as many techniques as possible and leave it to your judgment which ones apply to *your* game.

Snipsnapsnorum or plain Oh Hell

From auction bridge to Zioncheck, there are, all told, at least 200 different card games played by Americans. They range from coon can (ancestor of the whole rummy family which is played with two full packs, plus two jokers) to hasenpfeffer, a variation on euchre developed by the Pennsylvania Dutch. A player dealt the joker may well be *"hase im pfeffer"* (which is, roughly, the German way of saying "in a pickle"). Hence the name.

Just in canasta, there are some nine to ten variations, including the gargantuan Pennies from Heaven, played with four decks plus eight jokers for 20,000 points. Some people like Spit in the Ocean, Klabberjass or Snipsnapsnorum, while others prefer Stealing Bundles or plain Oh Hell. And our friends in the Philippines have recently come up with a heady, abbreviated poker that dispenses with deuces, treys and fours —and lets each player use his lowest pasteboard as a wild card.

No, I couldn't begin to tailor all the "gaffs" to all the games, nor, frankly, could I or anyone else anticipate all the "gaffs" themselves, so many of them being spur-of-the-moment creations. I can only emphasize, again and again, that you must assume all plays, all cards, all movements (even the most natural-seeming) are suspect until proved otherwise.

For example, one deplorable character made a practice of betting on a high spade whenever he played stud poker. The odds are 3 to 1 you won't catch a spade at all, but he considerably shortened them by regularly holding out the jack of spades. Then, on his deal, he would drop it atop the pack and retrieve it by second dealing till he came to his own hand.

The indigestion move

But one night, just as a waiter came in with a tray of drinks and sandwiches, a heavy and suspicious loser suddenly stopped the game.

Roughly, he demanded that all the cards be counted. When the jack of spades proved to be missing, he pulled a gun and even more roughly demanded that every player be searched.

In the only natural way he could, our deplorable character preserved his health. Using the "hole card switch" move, he palmed the jack into his sandwich.

Then he ate it.

CHAPTER XVII

♠
♥
♦
♣
♠
♥
♦

THE FALLACIES OF <u>ALL</u> SYSTEMS

♣
♠
♥
♦

THERE ARE LITERALLY millions of system players (including many well-educated men who ought to be ashamed of themselves) and thousands upon thousands of systems. But the players and their mad dreams break down into only three or four general types. Even before describing them, I want to make one flat statement.

No system works. Not one of them.

Who broke what bank?

I say this at the risk of being proved wrong by one of the great computers at MIT or some other seat of mathematical research. However, I calculate this risk as roughly as probable as the moon going berserk and knocking the sun out of the universe. So I will say it again:

No system works. Not one of them.

Oh, I know what you are going to say! *Your* system, the one you personally worked out with a pair of drugstore dice, has been practically perfect in a couple of thousand test runs. And the "secret" system bought by a friend of a friend of yours from a hustler who got it from a dying gambler works even better.

Admittedly, on paper or as the hustler describes it, every system looks good and, in practice, many systems seem to come tantalizingly close to success.

On occasion, I hear stories that I am sure are true about a system gambler enjoying a successful night's play—even as you and other non-

THE FALLACIES OF ALL SYSTEMS

system men. I even still hear that misleadingly titled old song, "The Man Who Broke the Bank at Monte Carlo," but why do I so rarely hear the epilogue?

That the "lucky" Englishman, Charles Wells (who actually won something less than $200,000 at one table), ill-advisedly paid a return visit, whereupon the bank practically broke him.

That the year 1891 when he made his coup brought great profits to Monte Carlo—the casinos somehow never suppress stories of lucky killings—and that 35 years later, when Wells died broke, Monte Carlo was still flourishing, as it is today.

Nor, except for a sad little paragraph in the newspapers, do I hear of the many thousands of system players who go home, or wherever it is they sleep nights, and quietly cut their throats.

What ever happened to the rabbit's foot?

The first kind of system is so patently absurd that we can dismiss it out of hand. It is devoutly—I should say superstitiously—followed by the "hunch" player who bets on "lucky" numbers. How does he ascertain the intentions of fate?

Maybe he plays his wife's birth date, or the license plates on his car, or the hour and minute of some important event in his life. Maybe he consults dream books to find the mathematical interpretation of what that late welsh rarebit last night did to his slumber. It's somewhat egotistical, though, to believe that numbers with some personal association will influence the speed of a horse or the roll of a roulette wheel.

And, in the case of the "hunch" player, pride sure does go before a nasty financial fall!

Of course, I won't deny that if you play $1 every day of your life on the basis of such a sorry system, you may win something sooner or later. (Especially if you carry around double-whammy loadstones to control the good and evil spirits. Don't rely on a rabbit's foot; thinking "hunch" circles say the rabbit's foot no longer has its old-time luck potency.) But any winnings will be coincidence, or the tardy workings of the laws of probabilities, and you won't begin to get back what you misinvested over the years.

For example, the newspapers not long ago related the story of a spry little man aged 76 in Sault Ste. Marie, Mich., who had never lost his faith in dreams. One night, Morpheus whispered to him that the program numbers of the winning horses in next day's daily double at Hazel Park Race Track in Detroit would be 10 and 3. So he rushed by plane to Detroit with a sizable wad and slapped it all down on O'Riley in the first and Cosmic Wish in the second.

It's twenty-two skiddoo

Sure enough, the Irishman and the cosmic thought romped home first, paying $134.40 and $19.40, respectively. Just on the five $2 daily double tickets at the rate of $1256 for $2, highest daily double payoff of the Michigan racing season, the aged dream believer collected $6,280. He refused to say how much additional winnings he collected on heavy separate bets on the same horses.

It's quite a success story in its own offbeat way, and I predict that for years it will be making the rounds of "hunch" players, giving them false comfort. The only thing the little old man *didn't* say was how many times previously he had thus flown madly about the country in pursuit of his dreams—and how much luck he'd had at it.

If this is a fair sample of his system for playing the ponies, there is only one mystery. Where on earth did he get the scratch money for the plane ticket and the track tickets!

Corner bookies, their underworld bankers, the casinos, both legit and "gaffed," love publicity about such blue-moon killings, and there is good reason to believe that they often plant the news. However, one thing should be obvious. The mere fact newspapers play up these stories proves they are enormously rare; otherwise they would not be considered news.

Now look at a system player who doesn't make the public prints. I have an otherwise rational friend who consistently plays the number 22 at any opportunity in any game. He was born on June 22, 22 years after the birth of a half-brother on June 22 and was the 22nd grandchild of a grandfather born on June 22.

All his life—he is now 50—he has accepted the gracious invitation from Lady Chance to make his fortune on 22. With what result? Has 22 ever come home for him?

One nice thing about "mechanical" systems

"Only now and then at blackjack," he tells me sadly. But he still plays it. It's a disease with him—as with any "hunch" player.

Now let's look at precisely the opposite kind of system. This is pursued by stern, no-nonsense men, often engineers or do-it-yourself practitioners, who look for some mechanical sleeper or flaw in the operation of gambling equipment.

Going back to Monte Carlo again, and this time we have to reach way back to the Eighties, a British engineer named Charles or Edward Jaggers hit the house for something between $100,000 and $350,000. The story is that, after laborious calculation of the winning plays, he located one erratic wheel that favored certain numbers.

Gambling historians are generally agreed that Charles or Edward really did win $100,000 or $350,000, but we must add that the costly and painful lesson was not lost upon the casino proprietors. Today, in all gambling houses (except where they have already "gaffed" the wheels in their favor), the equipment is calipered daily and sometimes the wheels are changed hourly or every few hours.

I can't deny that maybe, possibly, somewhere, a mechanical snafu might not bring a windfall to a gambler of an engineering turn of mind. But, in general, I must agree with Darrell Huff who says in his excellent book, *How to Take a Chance* (W. W. Norton & Co. Inc., New York, 1959):

"The main profit in mechanical systems, however, is the money you don't lose while you are too busy observing and tabulating to bet."

Of course, we live in a wonderful age, and maybe electronics will yet come up with some newfangled system more successful than the poor brain of man has ever been able to devise. I certainly had a bad turn the other day when I came across an ad for an electronic handicapper for horse players, priced at $20.00.

According to this system, you simply enter five readily-available past-performance facts and presto—the electronic circuit tells you whether or not you can bet safely.

Las Vegas, say hello to IBM

Considerably more formidable is the system which a young mathematician at MIT has worked out—with an assist from an IBM-704 computer—to beat the house at twenty-one or blackjack.

First off, the player memorizes a chart that uses conventional statistical probabilities to classify his hand as "favorable" or "unfavorable." He also keeps tabs as the various fives are used up in the series of deals off the same pack. When the four are gone, the pack theoretically favors the player.

Now, if a player gets a hand that is "favorable," according to the chart, he bets the limit. However, when his hand and the "five situation" are not favorable, he rides with minimum bets.

The creator, Dr. Edward O. Thorp, thinks his system is 99 per cent foolproof, though he believes a prudent bettor should have at least $3,200 capital to weather a possible losing streak. This amount, divided into $40 betting units, should return long-range winnings of $10 hourly. In the $500 maximum units allowed at Las Vegas, $40,000 would bring profits of $125 hourly, by his estimate, and obviously the casinos would have to give up twenty-one.

Now, as to the foregoing, I only know what I read in all the news-papers about Dr. Thorp's system. However, I must add that you can still get a game out in Vegas any day, any night.

Four tests of any system

I want to treat Dr. Thorp with due respect because he is a serious mathematician, and it is the mathematicians who have traditionally tried to educate us laymen about the complicated business of proper odds and improper systems. Matter of fact, as far back as the 1600s, those two great mathematical scientists, Galileo and Pascal, straightened out an Italian nobleman and a French chevalier, both of whom had dice-odds problems on their minds.

So, leaving Dr. Thorp's system to the judgment of the ages (and Las Vegas), let's get on with our little essay about the fallacies of formulas that turn chance into a sure thing. Offhand, I know some 50 systems, and every one flunks at least one of the following tests. And that's all that need be flunked!

1. It misreads the "law of averages."
2. It overlooks the house percentage on each game.
3. It forgets the house rules on maximum size of bets.
4. It assumes the game is honest in the first place.

To most of us, the "law of averages" represents a rhythmic swing of luck between "winning" and "losing" streaks. When you are "hot," you ride your winning streak, and then you pull out because the tide must turn and a long losing streak follow. In any game, this is a complete fallacy, but we can most simply demonstrate this by coin tossing which is uncluttered by complicated odds, house cuts or "gaffs."

You take tails, I'll take heads, and we will flip a hundred times. Theoretically, we should break even because it's a 50-50 chance whether the quarter will land heads or tails. Actually, *anything* could happen on those hundred throws because the 50-50 odds are calculated on infinity, and infinity is a very large number.

Heads I win, tails you lose

Even the fabulously wealthy Mr. Onassis, who now controls the gambling at Monte Carlo, could get wiped out if he went so far as to forget himself and tried to fight infinity at his own tables.

We can go further. Suppose I really scorch you by tossing 20 heads in a row. After all, such runs are possible. The Desert Inn at Las Vegas publicly displays the dice with which a player some time ago made 27 successive passes. And, in the last century, when a British gambler bet

£1,000,000 against £1 that no one could roll an ace ten times in a row with one die, do you know what happened? A patron rolled *nine* aces! (He gallantly rejected the offer of a handsome settlement by the perspiring gambler and missed on his last throw.)

So if I flip 20 successive heads (and you have not been pursuing some suicidal doubling-up system of betting to recoup your losses), you are actually enheartened. Ah-ah, you say to yourself. Now we are due for a run of tails, and I can start betting heavily on them.

Which is 100 per cent dead wrong.

The mathematicians have said it till they are blue in the face, and I hope they won't mind if I repeat them. Coins, roulette wheels, dice can neither remember nor look ahead. Our coin doesn't *know* that, having fallen heads for 20 times, it had better get busy and straighten out the odds. On the 21st toss, the chances are *still* 50-50 that it may fall either way, and perhaps this run of a hundred tosses just isn't going to come out even-Stephen.

Secondly, systems inevitably rely on long plays to iron out such ups and downs—but now the house cuts in with its varying percentage.

The cut that kills

At Monte Carlo, the one-zero roulette wheel gives the house a modest edge of 1.35 per cent for the "even-money" bets put on the odd-even or red-black numbers. This has built a glittering casino and provided a beautiful life for Princess Grace (Kelly), but the American roulette proprietors want considerably more. They make it a double and sometime triple zero wheel, pushing their edge up to some 5¼ per cent and higher.

Naturally, the more the wheel spins, the more you play, the more you pay.

No matter which way you turn—to craps, cards, horse racing, lottery or football pools—the house cut or merciless tilt of the odds will kill any system that can't guarantee you quick winnings. And none, of course, can do that.

Further, with systems premised on the siren's song of doubling losing bets till you eventually win, you collide head on with the house rules on maximum bets. That is, even if you are rich and game, you will reach a point where you must double beyond what the house allows —and right there, the system goes blooie.

And we still have not taken into consideration whether the game is honest in the first place. Let me make just one depressing observation along these lines. In many cases, because of the lack of demand, honest roulette wheels cost more than the popular "gaffed" wheels which can be manufactured practically on an assembly line basis!

Right here, I think I see a larcenous gleam in your eye. If so many wheels are "gaffed," you are thinking to yourself, all I need do is ascertain who the big money victim is—and play opposite him. That's been thought of. The house may even tolerate you as a sort of non-salaried shill if you don't get greedy with the size of your bets.

A $635 investment returns—$5 profit

On the other hand, that ex-pug who looks so uncomfortable in black tie might toss you out on your ear. So this is not so much a system as a chance.

Probably the most ancient and ineffective system, which has misled gamblers for some 400 years, is the "martingale." The martingale is premised on that tidal flow-of-luck theory. Whatever your betting unit, you continue it so long as you win, putting aside your winnings. Each time you lose, you double the bet. Thus, when the tide runs again in your favor, you have recouped your losses and go home with the earlier winnings.

Simple, isn't it?

Of course, the martingale violates all the rules which we postulated earlier, and just watch how the money vanishes with a moderate run of bad luck. You have just lost your betting unit—let's say $5—and the system demands you now double, betting $10.

If you lose five successive tosses, rolls, spins or whatever, you drop $10, $20, $40, $80, $160. Besides the original $5 that triggered the disaster, you have now lost a total of $310 on these doubled bets. So now you must bet $320, and if you win, you take in $640, less the $320, less the previous $315 loss—for a net gain of $5!

In a giddier variation of the martingale, not only are the loss bets doubled but $5 (or whatever the betting unit) is also tacked on following each loss.

By comparison, a sort of inside-out martingale seems as downright commonsensical as putting your money in Government E Bonds. Here, you set yourself a goal (say, five successive wins) and keep doubling that original $5 till you lose or achieve your goal. Then, in either case, and this is a divine flaw in the system, you are supposed to go home pronto.

Ascot is as Ascot does

Let's look at this kind of martingale through rose-colored glasses. With your original $5, you pull five successive wins, your profits thus being $5, $10, $20, $40 and $80 for a total of $155.

I ask you! What redblooded American sitting there with $160 in chips in front of him ($155 of them representing house money) would tamely cash in and go home?

Many systems are a jungle of numbers, and their devotees need not only faith but also sharp pencils, plenty of paper and the knack of adding, subtracting and betting between rolls, races or spins.

For example, the "Ascot," which was supposedly sired at the famous British track, starts with the figures 3, 6, 9, 12, 20, 25, 45, 50, 75, 125, 200. The number 25, being sixth, is dead center, and that is the fanatic's opening bet.

(Of course, for the big boys, we could double the units to 6, 12, 18, 24, 40, 50, 90, 100, 150, 250, 400, which would clean the rented limousines out of the track parking lot earlier, but let's stick to a "safe" $25 opener.)

Now, if he wins, his second bet is $45 and, winning that, he then bets $50. Here he loses, so he drops back to $45 again. And so he goes all afternoon, playing a game of musical numbers. We are, you see, back to the hoary old "streak" theory, the "Ascot" fattening the bets as luck runs with the player, decreasing them as luck "turns" against him.

But you still gotta pick the winner!

Let's say Mr. Ascot Bettor hits four out of eight races (all for the sake of argument at even money), winning the first, third, fourth and seventh. His sheet for all eight races then goes like this: plus $25, minus $45, plus $25, plus $45, minus $50, minus $45, plus $25. Or, $120 in winnings against $140 losses for a $20 net loss.

Look what you can do, no hands!

Not too bad, but you and I could do about the same without all that pencil-and-paper figuring.

And, frankly, I am not sold on its supposed protective features. Let's assume an unhappy but not untypical situation. Mr. Ascot Bettor drops all first six races, thereby losing 25, $20, $12, $9, $6 and $3 for a total of $75. He wins the last two, picking up $9 for a net day's loss of $66.

You, on the other hand, are just a stubborn, no-particular-system bettor. You play $25 a race and let your winnings, if any, ride. At that rate, on the first six races, you drop a total of $150 while Mr. Ascot Bettor is losing $75.

But now you begin to pick up. You bet another $25 on the seventh, win and slap the $50 on the eighth. You win again, taking in $100. You have lost $150 on the first six and put another $25 on the seventh, making a total investment of $175. But your $100 win reduces the day's loss to $75, only $9 more than Mr. Ascot Bettor.

In other words, you have been penalized $1.12½ per race for not going through all the abracadabra of the "Ascot" system.

Or suppose you both drop the first five and win the last three. Mr. Ascot Bettor loses $25, $20, $12, $9 and $6 for a total of $72, and wins only $3, $6 and $9 for a total of $18. He is still out a total of $54.

You lose $125 on the first five, invest another $25 on the sixth race (making your total investment $150). You get back $50 on the sixth, $100 on the seventh, $200 on the eighth. That $200 wipes out your $150 investment and leaves you with a net *gain* of $50 for the day.

Don't misunderstand me! I am not recommending a system of steady bets and ride-your-winnings. I am just trying to show that, under many circumstances, it can be as good or better as the touted Ascot.

What ruined the ONE good system?

In my library, I have a quaint, yellow-paged book entitled *PROTEC-TION—The Sealed Book* which, a good half century ago, deplored the system obsession. One system for roulette, then being peddled at $5, consisted of this magic stew:

After the first, second and third 12, the bettor places a chip on the two that have won most. If one 12 wins, he keeps playing; if he loses, he doubles. Following five consecutive losses, he changes one of the 12s for another and begins again with one chip.

The author, Joseph E. Meyer, reported that "a sport" had told him this "F.C.K." system brought him a killing; but then Meyer could get no reply to repeated inquiries. "Finally, however, I learned from a mutual friend that the sport was seen taking a 'blind baggage' for parts unknown," he added drily. "Evidently the system went wrong."

On an honest roulette wheel, Meyer concedes, a week's close observation of one croupier might disclose that he inadvertently turned up the same winning number several times in an hour. Playing this "system," a player could realize a nice steady profit daily—"but where there are roulette wheels run fair, the croupiers are changed every hour, thus putting the ONLY system out."

Many systems, especially those for horse players, are a confusing hash of sound advice on trying to pick the winners mixed with unsound mathematical formulas. Practically all have some progressive or doubling ingredient to recoup losses—and none takes into consideration the cruel "handle" of some 15 per cent or more that goes to the state and the track.

But the more you dress up a "martingale" or "Ascot" in fancy mathematical formulas, the more you obscure their basic fallacies and, with each new system, the dreamer can dream on.

Just a game of Tick tack toe

Another one of these mathematical numbers games, even more complicated, goes by various names such as the "Labouchere," "Closed Book," etc., but I like to call it the "ticktacktoe system." That's what the devotee's scratch pad looks like as he keeps adding and x-ing out the magic numbers.

It starts out with a deceptively short and simple formula, the numbers 1, 2, 3 which indicate your betting units. Let's say you are a $5 bettor and translate the formula into your own terms. It now becomes $5, $10, $15.

Your opening bet is calculated by adding the first and last figures. In your case, that is $20. If you win, you x out the $5 and $15, and bet what is still left of the formula. That is $10, and if you win again, you x that out, and your game of "ticktacktoe" is over. You have won a total of $30 (six of your original $5 betting units), and that is the entire goal of the "Labouchere" or "ticktacktoe," that you will eventually win six units.

However, this has been the quick and easy part of it. Let's say that you lose the first two bets instead of winning them. How does the "system" work? Your first bet, of course, is the same $20 (the total of the first and last figures in the formula). But you lose the $20, so you add that figure to your original formula without any x-ing out. The formula now reads $5, $10, $15, $20.

Your second bet becomes $25 (the first figure, $5, plus the last figure, $20). You lose again and the formula stretches out to read $5, $10, $15, $20, $25. Thus, if you are beginning to get the hang of this crazy thing, you can see that your third bet will have to be $30 (representing $5 plus $25).

What more can I say?

Now I am going to assume optimistically that you win the $30 bet. So you cross out the first and last figures you had previously written down ($5 and $25). The magic numbers now read $10, $15, $20. You bet $30 and, if you win, you eliminate the $10 and $20. You bet the one remaining number, $15, and, if you win again, you cross that out. The game is over. Though it has taken longer than in our first example, you have again wound up with six winning units.

Of course, I could just as easily assume pessimistically that you would sustain a long series of consecutive losses. In that case, the formula would grow and grow until you ran out of scratch paper for further calculations and green paper for further financing. Take pencil and paper, borrow some of your wife's trading stamps for your betting units and play this system for yourself, assuming ten straight losses.

If you want to give yourself a healthy scare, I also suggest, pretend that each stamp represents a $100 betting unit.

As I mentioned earlier, I know some 50 systems, many of them ingenious variations of the ones I have already described. I am not going to bore you by explaining them in detail, because they all come down to the same thing. They are gallant, futile attempts to circumvent the demonstrated shortcomings of the Ascot, "Tick tack toe," etc. Under the four-point acid test, they all collapse.

If you are ever tempted to buy, borrow or devise a system, I most strongly urge, subject it to this test! And please don't think that I am just a mean young man who hates dreamers. In a national magazine (*The Saturday Evening Post,* November 21, 1959), Professor Philip G. Fox, an authority on statistics and gambling odds, told writer Stanley Frank:

"Before I am deluged with sure-fire winning 'systems,' let me point out that I have studied most schemes ever concocted, and I never have seen one that gave the player a remote chance to break even in an honest game, much less show a profit. I have read some 500 books rehashing fanciful stories of spectacular killings in gambling houses and, with rare exceptions, I do not believe they represented more than temporary conditions.

"I have seen documented proof of consistent winnings over an extended period of time only twice."

(One was a GI who won only because he was able to get even-money bets against a dice shooter making his point if it were six or eight. The right odds are 6 to 5. The other instance was the Jaggers coup in Monte Carlo.)

I am sorry to say it, but systems must be lumped in with the alchemists' formulas for making gold out of base metals, the con man's wonderful box for "printing" $5 bills, the buried treasure maps obtained from "the Spanish (or Mexican) prisoner" now languishing in jail and unable to dig up the stuff himself.

Systems, thus, are just another pathetic symptom of that incurable disease so widely prevalent among mankind: that, somehow, somewhere, there is a magic "secret" for making a fortune without having to work for it.

CHAPTER XVIII

♠
♥
♦
♣
♠
♥
♦

BEWARE THE "BEWARE" BOYS!

♣
♠
♥
♦

THE OTHER DAY, through the mails, I received some "books" I had seen advertised on the subjects of cards systems and the control of fair dice. I was scarcely prepared for what my $15 had bought. The "books" turned out to be rather poorly printed pamphlets with smudgy illustrations and, among all three, a total of just fifty-two pages of reading matter.

They even cheat the cheat

However, it is not their cost which concerns me but their content— or rather their lack of content. Schooled in such reading matter, the apprentice card cheat can never become more than just that. Some of the designs "exposed" in this literature are so old that he would be instantly suspect if he used the decks in any cardplaying circles outside the society of antiquarians. My eyes are sharp and reasonably expert in detecting marks, but thanks to the blurry illustrations, I could scarcely spot them.

Biggest fraud of all, the nameless author warns of a breakthrough in the technique of luminous card marking that has resulted in work which is beyond detection. His conclusion . . . "BEWARE."

Curiously, he does not point out the obvious—that in any reasonably sophisticated game the use of visor, tinted glasses or even contact lenses (which can be detected) is like a badge stating, "I use luminous readers."

Just maybe, I can guess the reason for this omission. The same supply house that peddles these over-priced pamphlets will also sell all the costly paraphernalia for luminous work. To any crook who has paid for the "book," the message must seem plain. Any luminous mark that defies detection is for him.

Oh, I realize that those "correspondence schools in cheating" outrageously cheat the pupil. (I once sent away for a dice "exposé," which consisted of two sheets of mimeographed paper. The first sheet listed the odds incorrectly and gave skimpy instructions on how to switch in crooked dice. The second sheet contained several muddy photographs supposed to illustrate switches and this cheerful advice, "If you practice faithfully, one day you will become adept. Good Luck!" That was all I got—for $5.)

Actually, I don't much care if the big sharks eat the little sharks; that is not the important point. With their tempting wares, those houses fan latent larceny in men and women who might otherwise play honest cards. And if they master just one technique, however crude or dated, they can cruelly "gaff" almost any "friendly little game."

More than anything else, I despise the hypocrisy of the "gambling supply" houses. On the one hand, in their catalogues, they offer every conceivable crooked device for fumble fingers who never could master an Erdnase cull or a "Hudson" shot in dice. On the other hand, with their false cries of "Beware!," they profess to "expose" in over-priced brochures the very wares they are selling.

As I write, I have before me a catalogue of a "sport" supply house located only a loaded-dice throw from the neon lights of Times Square. Let's look at it, because it typifies the kind of double-dealing that is the stock in trade of these places.

First, the firm attests that it specializes in precision dice-casino equipment. Then it lists two varieties of "perfect dice" (concave spot and flush spot), several sizes of rattan dice sticks and other gambling equipment, all perfectly legal, of course, where gambling is legal.

But also itemized are two dozen varieties of crooked dice, marked cards in the form of readers, strippers and sorts, line and shading ink, daub and palming fluid.

But don't misunderstand their purpose! The order blank carries a line for the signature of the purchaser—declaring that he wants the goods for "legitimate" purposes only.

Maybe I am too cynical. If a "mechanic" promises on his Boy Scout honor to use readers only for the education of the laity, if a "magician" wants "passers" or "miss-outs" for his act (and you know how many magicians use dice routines), how could this "sport" firm—or the many others like it—possibly suspect bad intentions?

Don't let the Feds hear about this

Where the professional crook is concerned, the supply houses are dangerous. Like the underworld gunsmiths who used to arm the gangs back in Al Capone's heyday, they furnish him with finest handwork in "gaffed" cards or dice, custom-made to his specifications.

All told, from my own experiences, there are more than a dozen of these cheating factories scattered from New England to California, with concentrations in New York City and Chicago. Some profess that they are engaged solely in making perfect dice and chips that cannot be counterfeited for the casinos. Others are dedicated to making "magical" and "sleight-of-hand" devices for the apparently millions of Houdinis, Thurstons and Blackstones throughout the country.

Actually, of course, except for a very small handful of legitimate houses, this is a blind. So long as cash or money order accompanies the letter, you can order by mail without corroborating reference from a fellow "magician." You can even walk in off the street and, in the furtive tone of a man ordering French art photographs, get any "gaff" you desire.

What I cannot understand is this. The United States Attorney General is dedicated to a purge of all racketeers, the Postmaster General worries ceaselessly about the purity of the U.S. mails, and every state in the union has education laws that govern even kindergarten teachers, let alone "correspondence schools."

Yet, so far as I know, there is *no* prosecutory agency at the federal, state or local level even mildly interested in these outfits that teach and sell cheating techniques and devices.

Or, possibly, am I cynical?

CHAPTER XIX

♠
♥
♦
♣
♠
♥
♦

HOT DICE AND COLD HEARTS

♣
♠
♥
♦

FOR DAYS MY FRIENDS, the New York police, who wage unending war on gambling despite almost impossible odds against them, had been hearing the rumors. Someplace in the heart of the city, near one of the major railroad stations, a high stakes dice game was floating from one respectable hotel to another.

That was all they could find out. Their informants didn't know, or feared to tell any more.

In brassy, crowded mid-Manhattan, with its hundreds of hotels, the game might come to rest in any suite, and among the thousands of sharply dressed men streaming in and out of the lobbies, who were the gamblers? Hunting for one needle in two haystacks would have been an easier job.

But, as I happen to know personally, New York detectives can be very stubborn, *and* they know how to back up that stubbornness with the shrewdness of long experience.

So, one spring night, two attractive, smartly dressed girls—a petite redhead and a shapely, six-foot brunette—casually drifted in and out of the milling lobbies. Escorting them were two smooth-looking gentlemen. Though they took pains not to show them, all four were carrying shields.

Their mission: "Watch for the characters in the $300 summer silk suits and see where they congregate." Like military reserves, a deputy inspector waited for the word in the nearby railroad station with 11 detectives and plainclothesmen.

Finally, shortly before midnight, the word came. The two couples had ferreted out the game in a $76-a-day air-conditioned suite high in one of the city's most respectable hotels!

Even a burglar has to relax

So important was the game that, as the reserves moved in, the first deputy police commissioner took personal charge of the raiders. And then, to the dismay of the fluttering hotel management, the fun began.

One of the house detectives, the cops said, tried to shout a warning. He was a beefy 230-pounder, but no match for the brunette police-woman.

With a headlock, she threw him to the floor, using a bit of judo to flip him over on his face. Out of wind and suffering from modesty (the seat of his pants split in the tussle), he subsided.

From inside the luxuriously decorated seven-room suite, one of the suspected gamblers tried to make a break for the elevators.

Figure 83. How about a little action with the ivo-ries? You can't *possibly* win, you know!

Now the little redhead wheeled into action. She tackled him in the corridor, applied a judo wristlock to throw him on his back, and dragged him back.

The detectives counted their catch:

Forty-five expensively dressed men with $70,000 in their possession.

Four pretty girls in form-fitting cocktail dresses who, the cops said, were prepared to entertain any of the players who became bored with dice. (There were also two bartenders on hand to provide liquid refreshment.)

A baize dice layout, ten pairs of dice and a large quantity of very blue chips, ranging in denomination from $50 to $200.

What interested me most were the dice. One had two fives, another two threes. In fact, my detective friends told me, seven of the ten pairs were crooked.

Oh, yes, and one other thing. As the raiders had stormed in, they'd heard the crash of something being thrown out a window. On a setback below, they found a set of *burglars'* tools.

$211,000 profit—in two nights

This true story drives home the point that I hope to make again and again, for your sake, in this section. *Dice and honesty just don't mix!*

Oh, I know the stories you constantly hear, and sometimes even see in print. Except for the fast, pickup games in which "single-os" operate and the notorious "bustout joints" that are dice clip joints and nothing more, dice games are largely honest—the theory goes. As the optimists gravely explain, the house can "afford" to be honest because of the 5 per cent cut it takes on every winning bet and the law of averages that is always working in its favor. Don't believe it!

Aside from the legitimate, licensed—and inspected—casinos, I think an honest dice game is almost as hard to find as the 30th of February on your calendar.

And for three very good reasons which I hope I can spell out convincingly.

First, again excepting the licensed houses, practically every dice game in the country, fixed or floating, is controlled by individual hoodlums or the organized underworld. Even if they could financially "afford" to offer untilted odds, unloaded dice and an unjuiced shooting area uncontrolled by powerful electric batteries, they wouldn't *dream* of doing such a silly thing! Except for their conscienceless greed, they wouldn't have been hoodlums in the first place.

For example, let me tell you a little about the background of one of New York's steepest, oldest "floating" games—now permanently at rest, I believe, and good riddance! A player needed $10,000 to be socially acceptable and, after that, anything went. On two successive nights, a wealthy garment executive walked out with $86,000 and $125,000 in winnings.

Why stop at murder?

No stall, no protest. In fact, courtesy of the house, two husky bodyguards accompanied him both nights to make sure he got his bundles of green safely home. Sounds like a cosy, exclusive, rich men's club, doesn't it?

Well, fact is, the operator was a hoodlum with a long and rapacious police record. (Even his own dice manager quit because he often unexpectedly dropped in on the game and grabbed $20,000 to $30,000 for walking-around money.) And he was using the game's inordinate profits to finance his long-drawn-out appeal in the wanton murder of a Negro carwasher. Eventually, he lost and went to prison for life. Would you trust somebody like *him* to manage your game for you?

Second, when a game is allowed to operate more or less openly because of protection, the delivery of "ice"—graft payoffs to the politicians and police—is a budgetary item that the *player* pays.

Sometime ago, a dice ring engineered the practically wholesale corruption of enforcement officials in a small town between New York and Albany.

The cops closed their eyes to the sudden influx of strange cars, so many that the dice game had to have its own parking attendant. They pretended not to see the taxis that brought players (without charge) from as far away as Times Square in New York and even from Pittsfield, Mass. When there were rumors that some characters from out of town were going to stick up the game, the cops turned out indignantly, afoot and in prowl cars, to *protect* it.

In return, of course, there were payoffs, not only to cops but also to politicians—at the rate of $2,500 monthly minimum, according to later sworn testimony. Yet the dice operators netted $70,000 monthly profit! Does it figure that profits, payoffs and ordinary business expenses (including a staff of 15) *all* came out of a 5 per cent cut and the workings of the law of averages?

A little action between funerals

Third, where a game is constantly on the run, the overhead involved in always finding new locations and the intermittent shutdowns necessitated by police raids make the operation even costlier. And since at any moment the cops may come marching in, there is every incentive to make hit-and-run killings.

These are the games that flourish fugitively East Side, West Side, up in the Bronx and out in Queens far from the neon lights of Times Square. Actually, they could—in fact, they *do*—similarly flourish in Boston, Detroit, Chicago, south to Houston and out to LA, not excluding *your* home town. The geography is unimportant, here are the *patterns*.

It is, seemingly, just another modest apartment on New York's teeming lower East Side. And then, with raiding axes, the detectives open the front door to discover:

A windowless room, its walls and ceilings paneled with special acoustical material to deaden sound . . . an elaborate vent system to provide fresh air . . . large fluorescent lighting fixtures . . . recessed ashtrays . . . bolted to the floor, a padded 5x12-foot dice table equipped with rubber sideboards . . . *and* $10,000 in cash.

Up in Harlem, detectives tail "mourners" as they slip quietly into the rear door of a funeral chapel. Inside, the small altar has been pushed off into a corner to make room for a big dice table with a foam rubber "kickboard," and 35 men are dicing. This funereal game has been attracting $20,000 nightly play.

Out in Queens, I listen sympathetically in court as a dealer in religious goods explains to the magistrate, between sobs, how he happened to be caught in a barn with 29 crapshooters. He had accidentally heard about the game, he says, and hurried to the scene, hoping to sell some of his inspirational literature to the ungodly.

Fun in the woods

Instead, the police arrived and arrested *him* along with the impious, even confiscating $1,400 he happened to have on him. He sobs again and I think uneasily that maybe my friends, the cops, made a mistake this time. The magistrate is unmoved.

"You are," he says coldly to the wet-eyed defendant, "the worst liar I've seen in all my years in public office."

Then he fines him $500 and orders the $1,400 permanently confiscated, at which the defendant sobs violently. As a matter of fact, the cops explain to me later, the "religious goods dealer" was the captain of the floating game.

It is close to midnight and, far up in the Bronx, northernmost part of the city where there still are pastoral patches of trees and greenery, the warm July air is heavily scented. Suddenly, a group of husky men materialize out of the dark, grab a frightened idler and force him to guide them through thick woods.

Silently, like Indians, they slip among the trees until they come to a rock glowing in the dark. The guide hesitates a moment, then leads them along a path to the left. They come to a tree similarly marked with fluorescent paint. Now they turn right where some bushes have been pushed aside.

In a few moments, they reach a woodland glade (which has been thoughtfully sprayed with bug repellent. There, under strong lights powered by an auto battery, a large crowd of rustics is happily shooting craps on a pingpong table. Did I say rustics? This proves to be a $200,000-a-night operation!

To show you how highly organized such games are—and what a "nut" must be supported before the house begins to make money—let's you and I drop in together on one of them.

Only the driver knows

Limousines to the out-of-town "action" spots used to leave from the Times Square area, but I think the police have pretty well cleared them out. Best thing, we'll grab a cab up to Madison Square Garden and mingle with crowds coming out after the fights. Some steerer should recognize me and "give us the mitt," or information.

Ah, see that shabby little man walking toward us? Don't stare at him, just listen. As he passes, he says out of the side of his mouth, "Forty-seventh, north side near Eighth, black sedan, Jersey plates." We stroll over, the driver nods, and there's just room to squeeze us in with four other sports.

We cut into Eighth, which is one way northbound, drive a couple of blocks, then make a long circle to the right that brings us back to Eighth again. This time, we keep north, threading our way through Columbus Circle, and head up Broadway.

I figure the driver is making for the George Washington Bridge, but at 72d Street, he cuts left, heads for the West Side Highway and turns *south,* taking us to Jersey through the Lincoln Tunnel. Nobody protests.

You see, the driver is a very important man. Except for the house employees and operators who are waiting for us, he is the *only* man who knows the location of the game. His job is to get us safely there without being tailed by police or stickup mobs.

In half an hour, we reach a roadhouse set back from the road, drive behind it and get a reassuring wave from a lookout that the coast is clear. We get out of the car and go into a long, low, nondescript building some 50 yards behind the roadhouse.

Through the powder-blue haze of cigarette smoke, we can see maybe a hundred men clustered around the tables. The atmosphere is strange and difficult to describe to anyone who hasn't actually visited a "bootleg" dice house.

Complete to a portable pawnshop

Unlike the casinos, there are no elegant touches, no gayety and, except for the drone of the calls, surprisingly little noise. Almost like an intricate dance, you see a pattern of motion and arrested motion: the snake's tongue move of the four-foot rattan stick that flicks back and forth as the stickman rakes in money and dice . . . the hurried movements of the houseman as he walks about to match money bets by the players . . . the slower-moving loan shark (who has paid for the concession) examining watches and jewelry offered by "tapped-out" players . . . the checker frozen on his high stool, only his head turning as he watches for "agents," who may be working with crooked house employes, and "movers," who try to change their bets after the toss.

Except for the sandwich men who move among the players with platters and a makeshift bar in the corner, there are no frivolous extras and yet, as you can see for yourself, this is an expensive operation. Besides all the house employes, don't forget the several lookouts protecting you from raids, legal or criminal, or the steerers and drivers.

Yes, it's a sizable payroll, and you must add in, too, the exorbitant rent demanded by the roadhouse owner because his neck is way out, too, if there ever is trouble. Considering the hours, the risks, the complexities of this business, *I* know I would want a bigger profit than honest application of "the law of averages" could possibly yield.

But you've seen it now, so judge for yourself. . . .

In the following chapters, I want to tell you some of the dice "gaffs" used by the houses and individual sharks to make you seven out. I hope that I also can make a few illuminating remarks about *correct* odds and sucker bets. Even many experienced dice tossers, I have found, have the wildest misunderstandings of the right odds and thereby systematically cheat—themselves.

A policeman's lot is not, etc.

But, for the moment, let me return briefly to something I mentioned right at the beginning of this chapter. That is the almost impossible odds, practically and legally, that the police must buck in trying to stamp out illegal dice games.

In the first place, the players, most of them otherwise law-abiding and often business and civic leaders in their communities, *conspire* with the hoodlums against the police. It's a sad replay of Prohibition when, thanks to the patronage and protection of the decent element, the underworld first became firmly entrenched as a national menace.

Only on the very rare occasions when they suspect they have been taken by crooked dice—and most of them naively go through life supposing the underworld offers "honest" craps—do the players voluntarily cooperate with the police. Even during a raid, they remain silent as the housemen and operators protest they themselves are "only players" and, for lack of evidence, can be charged only with the misdemeanor of disorderly conduct.

In court, the magistrates tolerantly consider dicing no more heinous than spitting on the sidewalk and fine accordingly. Once, I recall, a lawyer for 34 dice players caught in the act pleaded them not guilty and protested strenuously that their civil liberties had been grossly violated. It seems they had suffered the indignity of being fingerprinted.

This was simply too much for Inspector James McDonald, one of the most decorated cops in the New York Police Department, which does not hand out decorations like the Cuban army.

Face flushed, controlling his voice with difficulty, he arose to address the magistrate.

It's your roll, brother!

"The Police Department is always in the middle on these dice cases!" he exclaimed. "Must we always remain mute and silent!"

Then he told of the police manhours that had gone into successfully smelling out and raiding that game. In the laborious job of checking out each of the 34, he added, his men had discovered that many of the players lived upstate and out of state. They had come to New York expressly for this "action."

In other words, here was no "friendly" neighborhood game that had gotten a little noisy and out of hand. It was a professional operation by undesirables to attract more undesirables into the city.

The defense lawyer was deeply impressed. So much so that he changed the pleas of all 34 to guilty. The magistrate was impressed, too. Sternly, he meted out fines to all—of $5 each.

I am not trying to make out a special case for the cops or against the courts. And I am not going to discuss legalized gambling, which is a big, complicated (and somewhat dull) subject.

All I want to say is this. So long as there *are* laws against gambling, so long as they *are* so widely flouted by the public, only the hoodlum profits. And the reverse side of that big shiny dollar is that only the public pays—inordinately.

So whichever you may feel, that the present laws should be obeyed or that new laws should be enacted, the final decision is up to *you*.

CHAPTER **XX**

♠
♥
♦
♣
♠
♥
♦

COME ON, JOE COLLEGE!

♠
♥
♦
♣

WITH ALL DUE RESPECT to the Dekes—and some of my best friends belong to this quiet, studious fraternity—probably the most flagrant cheating at dice (and cards, for that matter) takes place among the brethren of the various Greek letter societies.

Now before DKE and all the other campus lodges pass resolutions denouncing me for being unfair to organized fraternities, let me make myself perfectly clear.

I do not accuse the Greek brothers of being any more unethical than the average uninitiates on the campus. On the other hand, I frankly cannot credit them with *more* moral fibre than the average student. And they do possess that delightful added advantage of having their own house, which is certainly not a home, where they can play with a minimum of tedious interference from the school authorities.

Not surprisingly, the presidents and deans of our some 1,250 colleges and universities (I am omitting the junior colleges and theological school) maintain a stately silence on this awkward subject. Only when their basketball stars are indicted for "shaving points," do they make brief, shocked comment to the press, after which they shut up as quickly as they can.

So maybe they don't know what is going on under their noses. I wouldn't be surprised because, after all, who is going to tell them? But through professional gamblers who resent the intracampus competition with their own games and through the students themselves, I have made my own survey of this hush-hush subject.

These "mechanics" go to college

So far as I know, it is the first investigation of its kind, and it's an eye-opener! Already, I can hear the thundering denunciations of the college editorial writers and plaintive parental cries of Say-it-ain't-so, Frank! But gambling investigation is my job, so here goes!

Conservatively:

Averaging out the big schools against the small ones where, obviously, opportunities are sharply limited, there is at least one student in every college who is working his way through as a cheat. That's a total of 1,250 (again I am excepting the seminaries and junior colleges).

In each school, there are two more who can be called "Frenchies," in gamblers' argot. That is, they ordinarily play an honest game, but know one or two "gaffs" which they fall back on to recoup losses or to take an especially tempting pot or dice bet. Add another 2,500.

Finally, in each college, there are another three students who systematically profit through "sucker bets," inveigling their less mathematically astute classmates into wagers at unfair odds. True, this is an ethical shadowland but, in my book, and among gamblers generally, it is considered a form of cheating. Add another 3,750.

So we come up with a total of 7,500 collegians who are fully or partly working their way through college as gambling cheats!

I might add that since this represents ¼ of 1 per cent of the over-all enrollment, the figure, on the face of it, is conservative. Nonetheless, it is shocking to realize that, interspersed with their studies of philosophy, religion and social justice, *7,500* college students are stealing money from their best friends.

Three ways to cheat at dice

Moneywise, I frankly can't pretend to give an accurate estimate of the yearly "loot." The subject cries for research in depth by one of the grants-dispensing organizations, but they seem to prefer safer, duller and often far less immediate problems. Anyhow, the presidents and deans would probably throw me right off the campus if I ever showed up with a foundation handout and began asking questions.

Similarly, game-wise, I can't give a breakdown on whether bridge, poker, blackjack, gin or dice is most heavily "gaffed." I suspect dice because it is fast, furious and ideally adapted to the college schedule and college temperament.

After the football games, on the long party weekends, after the ladies of Vassar, Skidmore and Simmons have been respectfully ushered

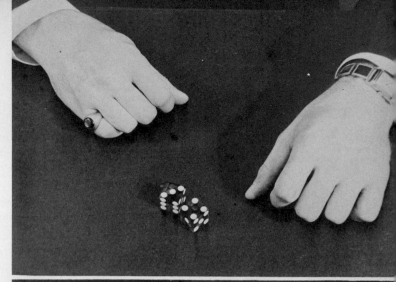

Figure 84. The honest dice are on the table. Notice closed position of "mechanic's" right hand. He must be holding something.

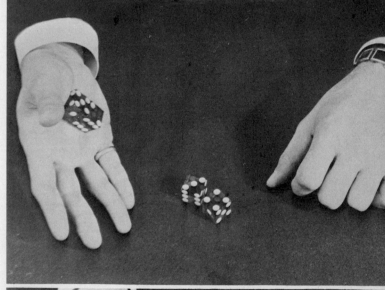

Figure 85. Oh, oh! Tucked beneath the thumb and against his palm are a pair of loaded dice. Now watch the switch . . .

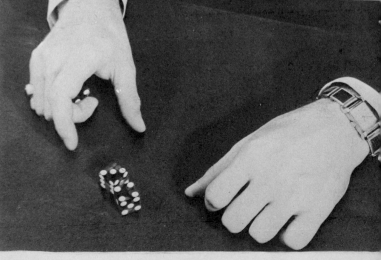

Figure 86. With the loaded dice held at base of the fingers, he opens thumb and forefinger of right hand to grasp dice on table in a casual, sweeping motion.

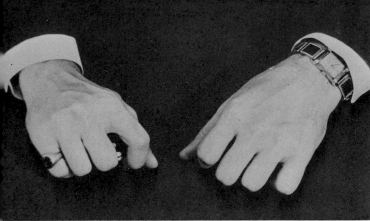

Figure 87. Right hand continues to pick up the honest dice and then switches them for the "gaffers."

Figure 88. "Ungaffed" dice are palmed in thumb crotch position (which you ordinarily would not see, of course).

Figure 89. Switch completed, victim fleeced . . .

home, what is so refreshing as a game of craps! The situation is heaven-sent for the cheat.

There may, just possibly, have been a bit of drinking or, anyhow, the brethren are tired and inattentive. Between 1:00 A.M. and dawn, any good liberal arts hustler can make his mid-semester fees if the game is big and well heeled.

How does he do it?

Whether he is a collegian or a full-time pro, he must resort to one of three general techniques.

First, switch crooked dice in and out of the game—and when I tell you how many varieties there are, your head will reel!

Second, manipulate honest dice by false tosses. One of the most notorious of these is known as the "Greek roll," but I want to add hastily that the name does not derive from the Greek letter societies, but rather from that country on the Mediterranean.

Third, know the right odds but never bet them, which would be a fair gamble.

In the next chapter, I will go into the business of odds so, for now, let's talk about crooked dice and crooked throws.

When I first learned to roll 'em, most dice were of about the same size and design—the familiar, old-fashioned, black-spot-on-white-cube "ivories." Today, there are almost as many varieties as in playing cards.

From a quarter of an inch to three quarters, you can get them in some 14 sizes, and even larger dice are becoming popular (because cheats find them almost impossible to manipulate). The spots may be flush with the surface of the die or concave. They may be just dots or "eyed" in prettified designs called "ring eye," "bird eye," "double ring eye" and "special bird eye" spots. And, as the home furnishings stores advertise, available in all colors.

There are three broad classifications of dice: "perfect" cubes which will pass a caliper test as true to 1/10,000 of an inch or finer; "drug store dice," the ordinary cheap dice available at any store which may be considerably off (and thus, in effect, unintentional crooked dice), and deliberately made crooked dice.

The important thing to remember is that whatever the size, color or design, crooked dice are made that simulate the honest ones. Even those reassuring transparent dice can be loaded!

Unethical ivories usually are "gaffed" in one of three ways, each of which has a number of subdivisions.

They may be *loaded,* just a little to give a modest but comfortable "percentage" over long play, or so heavily that they become known as "first flop" dice. (Later, I'll tell you of some remarkable recent strides in metallurgy that have been adapted to loaded dice.)

Tap, tap, who's there?

They may be *shaped,* or rather misshaped, out of the true to favor certain numbers or combinations, thus becoming "flats," "floats," "trip dice," etc.

They may be *misspotted,* in which case they become "busters," "door pops," "tops and bottoms."

First, let's study the "peeties" or "loaded blocks," as gamblers describe dice that carry a lopsided burden. Originally, some were known as "tappers," because their bellies concealed a load of mercury or some similar substance. If the load remained dead center, the die was legit, but if the "mechanic" casually tapped it, the load would shift to the side he wanted down, and you would tap out.

"Tappers" are feasible only in opaque dice, so the growing popularity of transparencies posed a grave and challenging problem to the best metallurgical brains of cheatdom. In all fairness, I must report they came through nobly, from their point of view.

First, they discovered that a mercury-like substance could be concealed within the spots as a permanent, nonshifting load. True, you could not tap these dice from fair to foul and back to fair again but, in experienced dice circles, tapping has become a pretty transparent device in itself.

Figure 90. Notice how author grips "slick cup" containing five dice. He tosses with downward sweep, as though cracking a whip. Dice settle on favored numbers (in this case, "dead sixes").

Figure 91. Throwing them out on the table, the author rolls all sixes. This game is particularly popular in Chicago.

Next, they found that 24-gauge gold fills in the spots were even more effective and, after that, they noted that 24-gauge platinum would produce "a very strong percentage."

How "strong"?

In one form, as "miss-outs," one die is made to come 1 and the other 6 and 2, thus bringing up the numbers 3 and 7 and showing "a handsome percentage for the Banker at all times," as the ad attests. As "passers," the dice are admittedly not "quite as strong," but they can be filled to favor 4, 6, 8 and 10. In either form, they are rather expensive at $35 per set (compared to $15, $25 and $30 for the mercury-like substance, gold and platinum, respectively). However, a matching set of fair dice is also thrown in.

For about $50.00 you can acquire three of the wonder-fill dice, plus two fair ones, the advantage being that two of the filled dice are the regular old stand-by missouts, Ace and Six Deuce. The third filled dice is a strong filled Deuce Four and when used with the Deuce Six makes the points 4,6,8, and 10 the favorites. Or so says the catalogue.

No danger of mixups

Or, for the same price, you can get a three-way combination consisting of a "dead Deuce," an ace-five and a three-five, plus two matching honest dice. The "dead Deuce" simply means that the five on the opposite side has been heavily loaded to insure the deuce coming up.

With the ace-five, this deuce makes a fast missing combination to seven 5-2. On the other hand, the ace-five and three-five used together become passers, favoring points 4, 6, 8 and 10.

225

Thoughtfully, the supplier states that whichever three-way combo you prefer, the filled dice carry a secret mark to avoid the possibility of mix-ups.

The claims of a rival house offering a similar combo of passers and miss-outs at a slightly lower price are considerably more frank. The brochure tells you that these dice are extra strong against the shooter on the comeout, and seven out fairly fast after a point is obtained. When the third dice is used, they make a good passing set. . . .

So much for all the gambling house pretense that they offer wares for magical and "exposé" purposes!

In all the foregoing raptures about the new alloy fills that are so round, so firm, so fully loaded, I don't want to give you the impression that "tappers" have become obsolete. Far from it!

There also have been refinements in this form of "gaff," and you should always watch and listen for the casual tap. Today, instead of mercury, oil or other fluids, a solider, more dependable substance is used for the load. Yet ingenious ways have been devised so that the bones' interiors will not rattle suspiciously.

Burn it, cut it, nothing shows

As you can judge merely from the price, the latter-day "tappers" must be popular in some sets (most probably in "friendly" neighborhood and college games which are not the "hard" games of the professional gambler). These dice cost $40 a pair, or $75 for sets of both passers and miss-outs. Matching fair dice are not supplied, but they really aren't necessary. After all, the tap makes the "tappers" themselves momentarily "fair," doesn't it?

Another very recent advance has been what its proud creator calls the "cabalistic transparent weight." This secret substance will provide a "mild" load to red or green transparent dice, and do it very cheaply, too. This invention can be had for under $8.00 a pair, with matching honest dice thrown in.

But the real beauty of the "cabalistic" cubes is that they can be even burned or cut open without disclosing any evidence of weights. In "gaffed" dice, this is very important for the continued good health and facial appearance of the hustler, as you can readily understand.

(A little further on, after describing the various other types of crooked dice, I want to tell you about the tests to detect them. There are a number of ways, some elaborate but many quite simple, in which wary and experienced gamblers always examine strange dice.)

Obviously, if the masters of controlled chance can load the transparents, ordinary white dice are child's play for them.

And now, a reverse load

The many same, happy combinations of miss-outs and passers are available, as in transparent dice, but the loads are stronger. One $35 set, will show 6, 8, 9, 10 and 11 about *five times* as often as ordinary dice. Craps come up rarely, and the hustler may make as many as six passes before throwing a seven.

A rather recent innovation in the use of loads has been to combine a fair die with a "peetie," usually to make a miss-out pair. For example, an ace-deuce used with an honest die will favor the numbers 2 and 3, forcing the victim to crap out.

"Floats" or "floaters" are what you might call loads in reverse. That is, the interiors are hollowed rather than weighted. If the hollow spots are made beneath the ace and 6, these numbers will show most frequently, and again we have a miss-out pair that favors the 7. (You can buy "floats," with matching fair dice, for only $10 a set.)

Even a bit of heavy metallic paint will transform ordinary dice into "percentage" cubes with a mild load. On the opposite sides from the numbers that are to be favored, the spots are delicately deepened or widened with a tiny drill, and the paint applied. While the load is too light to satisfy greedy hustlers, "paint work" dice are sometimes used by the prudent because they are difficult to detect.

As I mentioned previously, the second major form of dice "gaff" is the misshaped cube but, before we get to that, there is a variety that falls somewhere between loads and misshapes. These are "capped" transparent dice, in which the favored sides are shaved off and a "cap" of nonslip material, identical in color, substituted.

The replacement cannot be easily detected, the "caps" will not fall at the critical moment, and yet the "rubber balls," as they are sometimes called, make strong passers and miss-outs.

Gaff 'em as you roll 'em

The softer "cap" material has the effect of forcing the dice to spin *off* the treated sides and come to rest showing the uncapped numbers. In a variation of surface capping, certain edges may, instead, be capped. While not as strong, capped edge work is even less detectable than ordinary capping. Whichever way you like them, capped dice are modestly priced at about $7.50 to $10 per set.

Do you remember, back when we were discussing cards, I talked about the "cosmeticians" who use different concoctions to mark them during play? These hustlers have cousins in the dice-cheating fraternity who use pastes and liquids to achieve a capping effect on honest dice.

One $5 product for use on transparent dice is a liquid, which, according to the manufacturer, penetrates the die surface, causing a change in the chemical composition of the material. But you must pay twice that amount for paste which will "gaff" any kind of cubes, making them "honey dice."

From what I have learned, I doubt that many college cheats use these concoctions.

However, there is another form of loaded dice with which an amateur cheat can make *very* sure how the bones will bounce. While they cost more than $25 per pair, the insurance makes them worth it for the novice manipulator. These are transparents that have not only been capped but also weighted in the spots.

If we can believe the purveyor, they are the strongest transparent passing or miss-out dice set made and can be counted on in fast company.

Now, gentlemen, wouldn't you agree that any dice fit for fast company should be standard equipment for dormitory or fraternity games?

And now the "flats," "shapes" and "sucker dice" which have been shaved, sanded or otherwise abraded out of the true. The best work, of course, comes from the professional suppliers, but often down-and-out grifters make their own "flats" by spitting on the dice and sanding them down with a slow, circular motion on a pumice stone or the stoop of a browstone rooming house. The results are surprisingly passable, too.

Look out for the belly rollers!

"Flats" are a form of "shapes" in which one die is shaved to favor points 3 and 4, the second to favor 2 and 5. Hence, together, they are passers, being very partial to numbers 5, 6, 8, 9. Or both can be shaved to favor the 1 and 6 which add up to the miss-out numbers, 2, 7 and 12.

Even stronger are "two-way flats," only $3 per pair, in which the 1 and 6 are made 10/1,000 of an inch off, and the 5 and 2 of the second die 5/1,000 off, with an added, invisible bevel on the 2.

Bevel brings up still another form of dice "gaff" which you should know about. The favored numbers are left flat and untampered with, and the other sides beveled into a bellied shape (shaving from the center toward the edges). Results are fairly predictable. The dice tumble away from the bellies, favoring the flat sides. You can bevel either miss-outs or passers—and then load them, too!

Just as we have seen that the hollowed "floats" are the opposite of "loads," bevels" also have their opposite design. These are suction dice, in which some of the sides are made concave rather than convex or protruding.

If the ace is hollowed out, the suction will make the die settle on the ace, with the 6 showing. Concave both the ace and 6 on two dice, and you have a miss-out combo that favors 2, 7 and 10.

Conversely, of course, you can make passers by having the suction apply to numbers 1, 3 and 5 which will make 2, 4 and 6 the points that show most often. Simple arithmetic tells you that a pair of such suction passers will favor 4, 6, 8, 10 and 12, the latter not a desirable number —but then even a crook can't have everything rolling for him.

However, what he can, and frequently does, do is to bevel the sides which are not concave. Between spin and suction, he now enjoys a sizable investment—in your pocketbook.

And a horse on you!

I would like to report cheeringly that we have about exhausted the dice "gaffs," but unfortunately a square shape fascinates a crooked mind. We have quite a few "gaffs" still to go. May I suggest that, purely for the care and feeding of your bankroll, you now follow closely?

In the old days, hustlers roughened and buffed the little tools of their trade in the belief that such roughness made the dice tumble until they landed on a smooth side, whereupon they slid along until they stopped. The old-timers had something, too, which has now been refined in several interesting ways.

Easiest, probably, is merely to leave the rough little burrs on the wanted numbers at the time the spots are drilled during manufacture. On cloth, the burrs tend to adhere to the surface, thus making the dice tumble, polished side down, burr side showing.

In "trip dice," also known as "slick dice," the *edges* of favored numbers are raised so these sides have a larger surface, or are cut at a broader angle than the other edges. For only $2.75 per pair, "edge-work dice" that favor either ace-6, ace-2-6, ace-2-5-6 or 4-5-6 can be purchased in the following variations:

Raised edge trip work, made with square corner, feather turned edge or slightly turned edge; razor edge convexes, square corners only; split edge work, slightly turned edges only; cut edge work, feather turned or slightly turned edges; cut edge and corner work, the same two choices; saw tooth edge, made with slightly turned edges.

Probably the most unblushing fraud is the use of "tops and bottoms," or "horses," as they also are called. Impudent hustlers only dare use them in fast, confused games—the very kind of games you find in college circles.

Some very fast horses

"Horses" are neither loaded, hollowed, concave, convex, or edged. They would pass the most searching ordeal of fire, cutting open or calipering, but flunk the easiest test of all. If you tried to match them, you would see that the various sides don't total seven all around as honestly spotted dice do. In fact, they won't seven at all!

"Tops and bottoms" are misspotted dice in which the same three numbers are repeated twice on each die. Thus, what is called the "old style 4 to 11 tops" will total *only* to the numbers 4, 5, 6, 8, 9, 10 and 11 and *never* come up craps (2, 3 or 12) or 7.

Other "tops and bottoms" sets consist of 1-3-5, 1-4-5, 2-3-6, 2-4-6, 3-5-6, each appearing twice on each die. None of these can possibly total 7, but each carries the hazard of one possible crap (either the 2 or the 12). However, each combination also offers either four or five safe points, and if the crook gets past the first roll without crapping out, he *can't* lose because he can't 7.

An even faster "horse" consists of three "special" dice, as the "gaff" mongers like to call their wares. Two of them will make only the even points, 2, 4, 6, 8 and 10. Now substitute the third "special" for one of the pair, and the combination will show only the odd points, 3, 5, 7, 9 and 11.

Most lethal are the "door pops." So lethal, in fact, that you are most apt to find them in "soft" or quasi-amateur games, such as collegians play. Among more sophisticated circles, these dice which will 7 or 11 on *every* roll (or, in another combination, 3, 7 or 11 without fail) are too, too perfect not to be suspected and promptly examined.

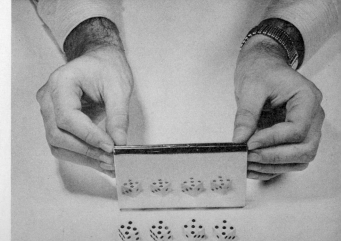

Figure 92. Mis-spotted dice, known as "tops and bottoms," or "tees," from the author's collection.

Figure 93. Expensive magnetic dice (about $35 a pair) are loaded with magnets and controlled by electrical current.

Figure 94. Even transparent dice can be "juiced." Here author is testing transparents with fairly strong magnet. Notice how die clings to magnet.

But even this doesn't begin to exhaust the variations of misspots!

There are double number dice (with two 5s and no deuce; two 3s and no 4, etc.) . . . "California 14s" (two ordinary and two "specials," the latter showing all numbers but favoring 6 and 8 rather than 7) . . . Eastern tops (two ordinary and two special, each spotted 1-6 and double 5 and double 3).

Beware of electrical burns!

I have saved the worst for the last.

These are the "electric" dice controlled by magnets, either ordinary or electromagnets, which may be concealed on the person or under the field of play. By loading the nonfavored sides with steel slugs, the operator makes them cling to the magnetized surface so the dice will show the desired numbers.

231

Two-way magnet dice, ranging in price from $10 to $30 per set, come in several combinations: 6-1 to show 2, 7 or 12; 5-2 to show 4, 7 or 10 and 4-3 for 6, 7 or 8. "Dead number" magnet dice, which will give a double combination on one pair, run from $25 to $60.

Magnetic dice shakers and spin shakers, complete with magnetic dice and a small magnet that can be concealed in the hand, cost $50. (By contrast, a fair shaker is only $5.) There are small magnets (1x2x⅜ inches) that cost only $30, but thereafter, the prices rise steeply because you are beginning to play with the big boys.

Or, more accurately, the big boys are beginning to play with you.

Take that "friendly" ginmill owner who will extend credit to the end of the month when the next allowance arrives from home . . . the proprietor of the "college" cigar store who goes to all the football games . . . the "nice guy" who operates the off-campus snack shop where you can take a date . . .

Each of these guys enjoys a little action with the cubes, doesn't he? Maybe on the bar or the counter, a few quick rolls for the tab, for the change left after you've paid the tab, for a fast $5 or $10.

Come to think of it, though, how *often* have you won against him? I hate to disillusion you about such a swell character, but very probably you will notice that all the action takes place on one area not quite 8x8 inches.

For only $70, he can buy all the necessary equipment: a pair of two-way dice, magnet, wiring and switches, along with four dry cell batteries. Or he can dispense with the batteries by hooking a "special rectifier" to a 110-volt line, but the rectifier will cost another $125.

(To control a larger surface, he can buy extra units and wire them together but, by now, his investment is getting rather steep. Not that you or I care—except that the bigger his investment, the more often will he turn on the juice against you to be sure of reaping a "fair" return. After all, he's a businessman.)

And here's how to tell the "gaffs"

There are also table magnets controlling slightly more than a 10x10 inch surface and, for the "single-o," a magnet belt (at $150) which will control the lead-slugged ivories through two inches of material. But the granddaddy of them all will magnetize an area 28x40 and is so powerful that it requires not only a rectifier but also *three* wet cell storage (auto) batteries! This leviathan of electronic loading costs *$1,200*—and offers a far better explanation than "the law of averages" of why the dice houses get rich and the patrons go broke.

Back in Chapter Six, I gave a few of the simpler tests for detecting crooked dice. Now that you *really* know what you are rolling against, let's spell these out in some detail.

If you were a full-time pro, you would invest in such testing apparatus as the dial micrometer or micrometer caliper, which show variations to 1/10,000 of an inch, but cost $35 and $25, respectively. You might also invest in a slide caliper ($12), a balancing caliper ($6) or the knife edge square ($12.50).

All of these are praiseworthy instruments of scientific detection but, aside from an ordinary slide caliper (which you can pick up for less than $12), they are not necessities for the average player.

Instead, let's apply the following observations and tests to the various dice "gaffs":

Tappers—You watch for the tapping motion, of course. You can usually expect to find these dice only in ⅝ inch size in white or opaques, never in transparents. Tap them yourself and then apply the pivot test (by holding two corners loosely with thumb and first finger) or the water test (by dropping them in a glass of water). If they are tappers, the favored numbers will continue to show as the tests are repeated.

Cut, burn, saw

Transparent loads—Though they are made in various sizes, you most probably will encounter them in the ⅝ inch size and on a smooth hard surface. To accommodate the extra weight, the spots are drilled deeper than in fair transparent dice. If you compare an honest transparency with a suspect one, you can tell whether the latter is loaded. Slightly rounded corners are another indication that they may be phonies.

Ordinary loads—Also usually encountered on a smooth hard surface. Apply pivot and water tests. Or, as I also mentioned in the earlier chapter, burn the dice. Phoenix-like, the load will survive the flames.

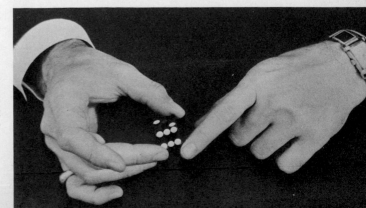

Figure 95. Holding die loosely in thumb and forefinger or middle finger, author is applying the pivot test to determine if it is loaded.

Figure 96. Another way to detect loaded dice. Here author is applying the water test.

Figure 97. Treys on two pairs of dice to the right slant correctly. Pair on left has been "gaffed" with trey running wrong way—as signal to confederates that loaded dice are now in play.

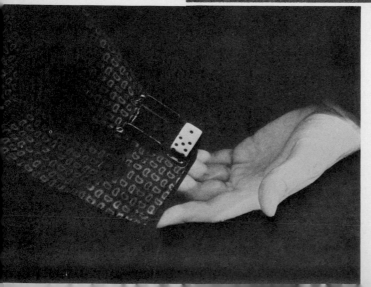

Figure 98. Sartorial must for the dice "mechanic." A $12.50 dice holder that will fit snugly beneath jacket to store "gaffed" dice.

"Floaters"—If you apply the water test, the light side will float face up. More destructively (which is what "floaters" deserve) you can saw the die in two, thus exposing the hollowed-out section. These dice usually are $\%_{16}$ inch or larger.

"Paint work" loads—Use pivot test, but repeat a number of times as the load is mild and may not be immediately detected.

"Cabalistic transparent" loads—While burning or cutting won't tell you anything, appearance may. They come only with flush spots, only in size $\%_{16}$ inch and larger.

Capped dice—If you dig your fingernail against all the sides, you will leave a distinct mark on the capped areas. Another test is to rub the dice together on all sides. You may notice that some of the sides seem to stick together or don't rub as smoothly as the other sides.

"Flats," "Shapes," etc.—Here you could make use of calipers to determine that all sides are of the same size. However, you could also make a test by putting two dice together on a flat surface and making sure all the sides square.

"Bevels"—Placed against a perfect die, the bellied-out "bevel" will wobble slightly. Or if a perfect die is laid atop the suspect, and the two held toward a light, the "gaff" shows. But try all sides.

—And a few more tests for honesty

Suction dice—A ruler laid endwise to the die will show up the concavity if held toward a light. Often, merely with your fingers, you can feel the scooped-out section.

"Edgework" dice—Usually made $\%_{16}$ inch or larger for best results. And usually used on cloth-covered surface, rubberback canvas being preferred. The "work" in such dice lasts only a few hours of play. Cut edge work can be detected by making sure that all angles are the same degree. Raised edge can be felt by running fingernail over all the sides.

"Burred" dice—Finger will detect the protruding burr or, if you rub the dice together, you may notice the same sticking effect as in capped dice.

Misspots—The most obvious test of all, which is merely to make sure that the two dice, on all sides, total seven. (A variation which I had not previously mentioned is that sometimes the 3 is spotted to run diagonally from the left upper corner down to the right lower corner. Correctly, the spots should run from lower left to upper right. Usually, this misspot is applied to dice "gaffed" in some more serious fashion and is merely intended as a silent signal from the switcher to his confederates, "Here comes the load!")

"Electric" dice—Shrewd players carry pocket magnets disguished as "lucky" pieces which they rub against the dice to "bring them luck." If the lucky piece sticks to the dice, they know luck is against them. A small compass also will react violently when the juice is turned on but, in a land-going game, who has a compass?

(Note: In any of the foregoing, where double "gaffs" are used, such as "suction" dice that are also beveled, some authorities advise employing both appropriate tests. But once you have found one "gaff," what greater prompting do you need—to say goodnight!)

The tap test for "mittmen"

When an accomplished cheat pulls his "rip," that is, switches in crooked dice, there's almost no possibility of detecting him. Very often, he wears a "cummerbund," the inside of which is a hidden apron to store half a dozen pairs of different sizes and colors. (Obviously, his switch-ins must match the fair dice already in play.) Or he may carry the "gaffed" dice in his pockets, for that matter.

An absentminded tug at the cummerbund, the casual act of reaching into a pocket for a pack of cigarettes is all the cover that he needs. Rather than trying to catch him in the act, I suggest you watch his throwing hand.

In the act of switching, his hand will be in a cramped position and, of necessity, he has to hold the dice lightly in his palm. Under some such pretext as "Come on, let's have some action!" reach over and impatiently tap his hand with your finger. You will knock the concealed dice right onto the table!

Once in a Nevada casino, I recall, a "mittman," as gamblers call dice switchers, suffered a major catastrophe. Somehow, he dropped *three* dice on the table. Luckily for him, the dignity of a licensed, respectable house must always be preserved. The stick man, with a withering glance at the incompetent, took one die and pushed the other two back to the hustler.

"Go ahead and shoot," he said. "Your point is *18*."

Which reminds me of a similar story; one of those fascinating snatches of street dialogue you occasionally overhear.

"We had a little trouble at the club last night," one flashily dressed character confided to his companion.

"Yeah, what happened?"

"Fellow made a 9 the hard way."

How not to crap out

"Yeah, how?"

"Rolled three 3s."

Of course, such accidents rarely happen, and a really good dice manipulator won't even switch in the first place. Like the accomplished bottom dealer at cards who scorns dangerous mechanical contraptions, he prefers to control honest dice.

This can be achieved by such "gaffed" throws as the old Army or blanket roll, also known as the soft or pad roll; the Hudson, sometimes called Navy Twist, the English or the Spin; the Indian, the Pique (or Peekay) and many others. Often, he controls only one of the dice, which at least insures that he won't crap out on the first roll with a 2, 3 or 12 and increases his odds for making his point.

In the Pique, for example, the one controlled die, with the favored number up, is merely slid along the surface without tumbling. This is a hand shot, usually on a hard surface like a bar, and the dice are not rattled as the tosser is holding them one above the other. Thus, he can "kick off" the top die with his third and fourth fingers while making the bottom, favored die slide. As you can see, there are several telltale moves in this technique, once you know what to look for.

On the other hand, the famous old blanket roll controls both dice and, as the name suggests, works best on a softer surface, such as a blanket or bed. The hustler favors different point combinations by placing two *unwanted* points (say 1 and 1, for example) on their sides.

Holding the dice somewhat loosely between the first and little fingers, he can make them "cackle," but they are locked into position and do not actually revolve. He throws quite close to the surface in a level, almost flat toss so they tumble end over end, with the aces remaining safely on their sides.

Are you safe if "they hit the board"?

Best advice I can give is the oldest: "Never shoot craps on a blanket with a stranger!" Or on a bed, rug or similar surface, for that matter. Or to shorten it a little, never shoot craps *any place* with a stranger!

In contrast to the blanket roll, the Hudson controls the dice by spinning them sidewise. The dice are tossed with the favored numbers up, and they remain up because they don't tumble, all the motion being the side spin or "English." Thing to watch for is the strong, almost abrupt way the hustler pulls back his hand as his two middle fingers are putting on the spin.

There are a couple of variations of the crooked roll whereby one die can be controlled even when the dice must hit a backboard. The essence of these techniques is that both the backboard and the bottom playing surface are hit evenly and simultaneously by the two dice, one atop the other. Then the bottom one will remain face up as it left the hustler's hand.

In other words, don't be lulled into a false feeling of security that "hitting the board" insures an honest toss—any more than a dice cup necessarily guarantees an honest shake. *Only* a trip dice box which has a protruding lip inside near the top insures that the dice will really tumble.

Otherwise, using a "slick box" in which the inner surface is smooth and highly polished or a small-diameter cup (the maximum *should* be two inches), a hustler can produce a reassuring noise without tumbling the dice. As in a controlled hand shot, they emerge just as he placed them.

Or he may ring in a "Chinese dice box," which costs only $5 or $6 and, properly, should be considered a magician's trick. With it, he can 7, 11 or toss any other point at will.

Even put and take is loaded!

Because the player is so peculiarly vulnerable in dice, whether to the cubes themselves, the throw or the cup, I hate to tell you that there is yet another "gaff" of which you must beware! Clever manipulators can hold out and conceal one die in their hand while using a cup. On the toss, just as the other dice drop from the box, they slide it forward—favored side up, of course.

For a Dekes' quiet night at home, for a bit of relaxation while cramming for mid-years, I would recommend top spinning even over tiddlywinks. After all, in tiddlywinks, you might come up against a sharpy with long practice, but top-spinning, I had always assumed, had to be a fair contest. Anybody can spin a top, and I was somewhat cheered the other day, while leafing through a supply house catalogue, to come upon an ad for this simple, old fashioned, "gaff"-proof game. What could be more childishly innocent than a Put & Take Top?

Then I noticed that this toy available in white and red transparent celluloid for $3, was described as "fair" (a dainty word for "honest"). And to round out the ad, an identical top was offered, with instructions, at $7.00.

In other words, they're even loading put and take today!

Do you know the "gaff"? Spin the top one way and you always win, spin it in the other direction and you lose. (For $14, you can get a matching pair, one guaranteed to win, the other to lose, no matter which way you spin them.)

I also saw ads for attractive, Renaissance-style chess sets in a plastic simulating wood grain that cost from $6.50 to $17.50, and a dizzying thought overwhelmed me.

Gentlemen of the campus, I appeal to you. I have told you all I can about the many, devious ways in which you can be taken. Now, if possible, please tell me something.

Is chess honest?

CHAPTER **XXI**

♠
♥
♦
♣
♠
♥
♦

HONEST DICE—FOR A CHANGE

♣
♠
♥
♦

LIKE THE FELLOW who bets the stock market, the dice player is constantly being deluged with expert advice on odds and percentages —to the point of total bewilderment. So I propose to strip this chapter down to the bare essentials. Here is only what you *must* remember, and I want to keep it short so that you will remember it all.

First, a table showing the number of ways the various points can be made. Seems fundamental, I know, that you make a 6 with 1-5, 2-4 or 3-3. But since *each* die has a 1, 2, 4 and 5, you can also make this point 5-1, 4-2. So, actually, you can 6 with any of five different combinations.

Here is the table:

Point	2	3	4	5	6	7	8	9	10	11	12
Number of ways	1	2	3	4	5	6	5	4	3	2	1

One easy method for remembering the table. Up through 7, there is one less way of making the point than the point number itself. Above 7, you keep subtracting an additional 1 for each number.

Now to translate the table into odds. In all, on one toss, there are 36 possible ways listed above for the dice to show. Among them all, however, there is only one way to make a deuce (1-1) or a 12 (6-6). Hence, the odds against your rolling "snake eyes" or "boxcars" are 35 to 1.

The same odds apply that you won't make "doubles" (that is, two 2s, two 3s, two 4s or two 5s) because there is only one 2, 3, 4 and 5 on each die.

Thus, properly, on "come-out" bets or on one roll, the odds on the above are rightly 35 to 1, but most well-run gambling houses will pay only 30 to 1.

Paste these figures in your mind!

If we keep on translating the table by finding how many ways a given point can be made out of the 36 total possibilities, we get these other correct odds on the "come-out":

17½ to 1 against making 11 or 7 in a *specified* way (1-6, 2-5 or 3-4) or 3.

11 to 1 against making a 4 or 10.

8 to 1 against making a 5 or 9.

6⅕ to 1 against making a 6 or 8.

The odds against *any* crap is 8 to 1, against *any* 7 (not specified), 5 to 1.

Now, let's go a step further. Say the tosser didn't 7, 11 or crap out on the first throw. He rolled some point between 4 and 10 and his problem is to roll it again before he sevens. The true "point bet" odds against him are:

4, 2 to 1; 5, 3 to 2; 6, 6 to 5; 8, 6 to 5; 9, 3 to 2; 10, 2 to 1.

Burn those odds into your mind!

I say this because hustlers traditionally offer the following sucker bet odds: even money that the thrower won't make his point if it is 6 or 8; 6 to 5 against his making a 5 or 9; 3 to 2 against making a 4 or 10.

Even many honest players, having heard them so often, think these "sucker bets" are the correct odds and may give you an argument. Tell them you got the message from Garcia—not from an overpriced dice book that gives odds favoring the hustler.

"Even money" has a very reassuring ring to it, but no hustler ever made an *honest* "even money" bet in his life. He may offer "even money," for example, that he can throw a 5, 6, 7 or 8 in one roll. If you look back at the table, you will see there are 20 combinations out of the 36 which will give him one of these points, so his chances actually are 5 in 9, which is better than even money.

A long formula and a short cut

Other standard, but very lopsided "even money" bets are that a tosser will come up with a 6 or 7 or a 7 or 8 in two rolls; that with a 4, 5, 9 or 10, he will not get more than three rolls (a 7 on the third roll counting for the hustler); that he will throw a 7 in four rolls.

Let's take that 6, 7 or 8 routine in two rolls and work it with reference to the table. Either combination, 6 or 7 or 7 or 8, can be made 11 ways. Right? Hence, out of the 36 possibilities, they *cannot* be made in 25 ways. In two rolls, multiplying 25 by 25, they cannot be made 625 ways.

This sounds pretty awesome, but wait a minute. For two rolls, we also must multiply 36 by 36 to get the total number of possibilities, which comes out 1,296. Now if you subtract 625, the number of ways these points cannot be made, from the 1,296, the over-all total, you will get the number of ways the points *can* be made. This is 671. And 671 to 625 is an *even* money bet?

I don't want to go into further mathematics to prove the other "even money" bets are just as cockeyed or more so. You can either take my word for it, or use the same formula to work them out to your own satisfaction.

You (a) establish the total combinations by which the offered points can be made and subtract that figure from 36. You multiply the result by the number of rolls involved in the proposed bet (two, three or four). You also multiply 36 two, three or four times, depending on the rolls. Finally, subtracting the total number of ways the points cannot be made in *x* number of rolls from the total possibilities, you get how many times these points *can* be made.

Frankly, the simplest thing to do is just forget about "even money" bets altogether!

300 *years later, this advice holds good*

Another misleading (but honest) proposition in casino dice is the house's offer that you can "play the field" after any roll of the dice. Usually, you are given the numbers 2, 3, 4, 9, 10, 11 and 12 for a one-roll bet, while the house takes the numbers 5, 6, 7 and 8.

If one of the field numbers shows, the house pays even money, except for the 12 or 2 on which it pays double the amount of the bet.

To most players, the propositon seems attractive because he has seven numbers on which he might win, against only four on which he can lose.

Now look at it another way:

You can make	The house can make
2—1 way	5—4 ways
3—2 ways	6—5 ways
4—3 ways	7—6 ways
9—4 ways	8—5 ways
10—3 ways	
11—2 ways	
12—1 way	

Add 'em up and you will find there are only 16 possible ways for the seven field numbers to be made—while there are *20* possibilities for the four house numbers. In other words, out of every 36 rolls, the house has a four-roll edge. But, remembering the player gets paid double on 12 and 2, you have a problem in calculating the odds right to a "t"!

I merely want to point out that *unless you constantly refer back to the table of probabilities and make calculations accordingly,* you will fritter away money on seemingly tempting but actually tilted odds.

I told you I would keep this chapter short, and now I am signing off with a bit of advice from Pascal. In an earlier chapter, you may recall, I mentioned that the great French philosopher and mathematician came to the aid of the anguished Chevalier de Mere, who'd had a nice little dice proposition running for him. He bet he could come up with one 6, anyhow, in four rolls of a single die.

Using the formula we just studied, we can determine that the chevalier had 671 possibilities in his favor against 625 adverse ones. However, the chevalier suddenly offered the boys a new proposition he could 12 once in 24 tosses of two dice. And now he lost.

When you carry these figures through all the multiplication and subtraction, you find the reason. These odds are slightly against the player, as Pascal informed de Mere.

But the important thing about the episode (aside from the fact that it got top brains interested in probability) is what Pascal said to a friend about the chevalier. A gentleman and all that, but definitely not a mathematician.

"This is, as you know, a great fault," he added severely—which certainly applies to dice players.

CHAPTER **XXII**

♠

♥

♦

♣

♠

♥

♦

WHY ZSA ZSA COULDN'T WIN

♣

♠

♥

♦

EVEN FOR FREMONT STREET in Vegas, where the neon signs and lights outdazzle Times Square, where the roulette balls tirelessly roll for 24 hours of the day, where you can buck cards, craps, wheels or slot machines at 6:00 P.M. or 6:00 A.M., this night was crazy, *crazy.*

In and out of the casinos, laughing, gambling, losing and only laughing more, darted a beautiful woman superbly gowned even by Vegas' rich and sophisticated standards. Her game was twenty-one, at $500 per unit, and as one croupier dealt and a second raked in the chips, she lost, lost, lost—$10,000 in all.

A few nights later, I caught up with her on the Jack Paar TV show. She knew she hadn't been cheated, she told me, because she had played in the legitimate licensed casinos, and she didn't mind losing the money because it had been *such* a fun night. But, in my professional experience, what did I think was wrong with her play?

Even she—Zsa Zsa Gabor—could not impress the huge court that is held in Vegas twenty-one, I explained. There, they play the game not with one or two decks, but with seven. When you figure there are 16 court cards (four each of ace, king, queen and jack) in every pack, that comes to 112 in all—plus 28 tens!

No twenty-one player alive can keep track of *140* cards and yet, if you don't intelligently follow the fall of the cards, you don't win at twenty-one. Seven-deck twenty-one is too "court-sized" for me.

I am not criticizing the Vegas casinos because obviously a county which reaps more than $100 million yearly in gambling revenues has too much at stake to tolerate crooked gambling. So do the casino operators.

If the dealer is crooked . . .

But even in the best casinos, you are, as they used to say of faro players, "bucking the tiger."

The house odds and commissions will get you, even if your own system doesn't. The classic case on the record is a marathon game in which that fabulous expert, "Nick the Greek," participated—and lost because the 5 per cent house take eventually frittered away his stake.

When you come to casinos that must pay heavy "ice" or protection money, to hotels that unwittingly let their gambling room concessions to hoodlums, you are *sure* to be taken. This can be done gently by heavy house takes and unfair odds that load the games against the players—or by downright frauds and "gaffs" in "bust-out joints."

For example, the Tropicana in Havana (at least when Americans were more popular there) would offer a $10,000 prize on the night's first and last bingo games. That is, *if* the card were entirely covered in 50 plays.

This means that every other call would have to be one of the numbers on your card and, while I don't say that is totally impossible, the odds against you are astronomical. I know that, in some eight visits there, *I* never saw a $10,000 card.

But I saw something almost as curious. An entertainer on our ship won with a card that wasn't filled out. A house shill came over to him, took the card and shouted excitedly, "We have a winner here!" They paid him off, too, just to prove that such animals exist—occasionally.

I hate to disillusion grandma, but like *any* wheel or cage game, her bingo can be gaffed. Maybe some of the balls are "copped out" so no one can win. Or the numbers may be miscalled to give the winning boards to stooges in the audience.

$1 back on each $6

But let's pretend the game is honest. What are grandma's chances when she bets her Social Security check?

Sometime ago, bingo parlors ran wide open in Venice, the little seaside community in Los Angeles. Theoretically, you paid to take part in games of "skill" which entitled you to "free" bingo. When the Los

Angeles Police Department decided to clean out the parlors, their researchers and statisticians came up with a very interesting estimate.

They figured that for every $6 bet on bingo, the customers received the handsome return—of $1.

More recently, New York State has been gingerly experimenting with licensed bingo. Leaving out a few unsavory episodes that popped up, let's concentrate again on the customer's chance.

In something less than three years, almost 25 million New Yorkers poured almost $85 million into the newly legalized games and collected back $60 million in prizes. Thus, between them, the state (which collected at the rate of $5 per game) and the operators who took in everything else skimmed some 29 cents out of each bingo dollar.

And, for the sake of argument, I am now assuming that all the $60 million went to *legitimate* winners rather than house shills.

By more than coincidence, many, many dealers at one time were crooked gamblers. So, if they find themselves in a tight spot, they can pull a "gaff" or two. Of course, this talent can be turned two ways— against the house as well as against the customer.

So the crooked casinos which are so busily fleecing their patrons must employ special watchers to make sure their dealers don't fleece *them*. I rather enjoy this bit of irony.

If you like twenty-one, red dog, "shimmy," read on

If a house dealer employs a large "shoebox" which can hold up to seven packs at a time, you can rest assured that you are getting a square deal. But if he is using one of the following boxes, beware! Better, *be gone* as soon as possible.

The first is a rather small dull box of German silver known to the trade as a "tongue-tell" or "sandtell," which originally was perfected for faro—the crookedest gambling game in American history.

The high cards having previously been punched and marked, the dealer can feel the blister on them and, by manipulating a hidden tongue or protrusion, hold them back and deal the second cards. Or he can play a "legitimate" game, but know precisely which cards are out.

"Sandtell" no doubt derives from an interesting variation of the same "gaff." If the backs of the low cards and the faces of the high cards are sanded, they will lock together as one when pressure is applied. If the dealer uses no pressure, you are dealt a low card.

In faro boxes, the handy little devices which enable a dealer to pass out tops or seconds at will are known as the "walk" and the "retard" or "sneak." And please don't think I'm being an antiquarian when I tell you all this. While still called faro boxes in tribute to the old-time stovepipe hat crooks, these machines are being widely used today in blackjack, red dog and *chemin-de-fer*. Like old soldiers, old "gaffs" never die.

A slightly more expensive variation of the crooked box (which costs $65 to $75 compared to $40 or $50 for the faro machine) is the "second dealing box" in which the top card is always under control.

Finally, in contrast to these dull finish boxes, there is a dealing machine of highly polished chrome plate which actually deals tops! However, this bit of honesty is overcome by the high polish. As he deals each card, the operator "peeks" its reflection from the extended base at the bottom of the box.

Like most everything else today, they don't make phony dealing boxes the way they used to. Back in the river boat days when faro was the game, these devices were individually crafted, often with great artistry.

More important, no two boxes were made to operate exactly in the same manner, and only the purchaser knew the secret of their manipulation. Matter of fact, I own one which I prize as an antique, but I can't yet operate it.

There is another form of vanished artistry which I rather deplore, at least aesthetically. As you no doubt know, any unethical electrician can probably "gaff" a roulette wheel by hooking up concealed wiring under the table. Two sets of magnets will control the reds and the blacks, the odds and evens. Reportedly, with enough juice, some roulette wheels even can control specific numbers.

But I remember "Pop," a gruff, whiskered ivory cutter, who somehow could load an ivory roulette ball with a tiny piece of metal, leaving absolutely no indication on the surface that it had been tampered with. For each of these controllable, undetectable balls, he demanded and got anywhere from $100 to $200.

To the dismay of the trade, "Pop" has retired without passing on his secret, but every time I drop into a casino, I have the same uneasy thought.

This game was on the house

How many of his perfect little creations, I wonder, are still obediently spinning and stopping as they are directed? After all, ivory lasts a long time, especially when treated with the proper, loving care.

(To detect magnetic roulette balls as they also test for "electric" dice, profesional gamblers carry their own magnets concealed in a "lucky" piece or their belt buckle. As I mentioned in the dice section, they rub the suspect ivory for "luck" to make sure that it doesn't conceal a magnetic load.)

Of course, despite the most elaborate mechanical and professional precautions, the casinos can get hurt, too.

At intervals during the night's play, they change the 20-pound roulette wheel. They examine the spindle or axle that tapers to a sharp point, making sure that because of friction it isn't favoring the red or the black. If a wheel suddenly becomes "hot," the croupier can have it changed at will and, as an obvious precaution, the croupier himself often is changed, too.

Yet, every so often, as in the old days at Monte Carlo, a sharp-eyed player makes a quick buck on an erratic wheel.

Again, in such a game as twenty-one, you would assume that by now nobody could tell a casino *anything* about its ramifications. Quite recently, however, at Lake Tahoe, half a dozen men hit one of the houses hard with a perfectly legitimate caper.

Casually, one by one, they drifted to the same table and then, after about an hour's play (as you have the right to do when losing), they demanded that a new deck be produced. As they were removed from the case, the cards were in sequence, either ace down or deuce up.

Just a memory . . .

After the jokers had been removed, the pack was butt-shuffled a couple of times and then cut—which left the deck "stacked" in high-low combinations.

All the players made the maximum bets, scorned "insurance" bets and stood pat on the 13, 14, 15 or 16 that they almost invariably drew. Because of the way that the high-lows came out, the dealer just as often came up with a 16.

Under the rules, he had to hit himself—and, almost always, he then "went bust" with a court card.

With a half dozen players thus ganging him and playing the top limit, the dealer was shelling out $1,200 (plus the players' original investment) each time the caper was pulled.

Not surprisingly, there was quite a commotion when the casino discovered how it was being taken. But don't waste your money on an airplane ticket to Nevada. Precautions have been taken to prevent the same thing from happening again and, among the dealers, the episode is just a memory.

A contented crook

Not even the worried casino proprietors could tell you how many "crossroaders," working "single-o," are living off them. The good lone wolves hit the same casinos only a few times yearly so they don't become marked men and they hold their winnings short of suspicion.

For example, there is a mousy, retiring little New Yorker who recently caught the card act of a magician friend of mine. Among the men, honest and crooked, who manipulate cards, there is a certain professional camaraderie, and after the show "The Irishman," as I shall call him, expressed admiration for a certain false shuffle.

My friend offered to teach it to him. "The Irishman" politely declined. "I like what you do, but I don't need it," he explained contentedly. By occupation, "The Irishman" is a hole-card switcher. One of the top pros in the business, he lives by occasional, discreet trips to the "shimmy" and twenty-one tables in Nevada.

Quite frankly, I am not overly concerned about the business risks of the casinos; like all good businessmen, the proprietors take them into consideration in fixing their prices. Nor, if the games are honest, am I worried about the casino clienteles. For the most part, they are made up of well-heeled gamblers who can afford the ride and tourists who for years will bore their friends with reminiscences of that cra-azy week in Vegas, Reno, Tahoe.

Not long ago, my friend, New York *Daily News* columnist Charles McHarry, flew out to Vegas for a long weekend with a party of more than 100 wealthy restaurateurs, real estate operators and garment executives. One of the crowd offered Charley 5 to 2 that it was "the richest, swingingest load of passengers a plane ever had." He knew his fellow gamblers intimately and estimated their combined worth at $2 *billion*.

One chance in 390,000

In no time, a couple of games of twenty-one were underway with bets of $20 to $200 a hand, and then one dealer impatiently announced no limit, and the bets soared to $500. These were men who craved action, got action and, most important, could *afford* action.

Unfortunately, gambling is a universal appetite—the third appetite after food and love—and I *am* concerned about those who cannot afford it. They are forced to play penny-ante games, bucking wildly unfair odds that yield penny-ante returns. That is, *if* they win, *if* the game was honest in the first place.

Nobody can even estimate how many counterfeit Irish Sweepstakes tickets are peddled yearly. If you are lucky enough to lay hands on a genuine one, no one can precisely calculate your chances of winning because the Sweeps proprietors are so notoriously close-mouthed about their operation. Some authorities put your odds against taking home a top prize at 390,000 to 1.

In football pools, the genius who can pick six in six winners should be rewarded at 63 to 1 odds; usually, he gets about 25 to 1. If you pick a number from 000 to 999 and win, the numbers racketeer should pay at 1,000 to 1 odds. You receive $50 for your dime and have to give the collector $5 out of that, so the payoff is 450 to 1.

Slot machines are gimmicked to give you one chance in 2,000 of hitting the jackpot if the man behind the one-armed bandit is being "reasonably fair." He can, of course, make the payoff much smaller, and you'll never, you'll never know.

Maybe this is where you came in—but stay

We have previously discussed the heavy track "handles" that the horse bettor must buck and, if he does business with a bookie, he must take an "insurance" bet to get the track odds whenever he is playing a long shot. Forgetting the "handle," if you lay 100 bets, the chances are about 120 to 1 that you won't win ten of them.

Most of all, beware the cheap grifts, the old grifts that never die!

More than a century ago, the granddaddy of the three-shell game was played with cored-out apples or potatotes instead of walnuts to cover the elusive pea, and later thimbles were employed. (The term "thimble rigger" once was common American slang for a cheap crook.) Old, whiskery, corny, you say. *I'd* never fall for that.

Don't be too sure! There must be some sound commercial reason why the "gambling supply houses" still peddle the three-shell game at $3.50 per set (compared to the 50 cents that legitimate magicians pay in legitimate magic stores). And refinements in this ancient fraud are constantly being made. I myself own the latest, known as the "mystery shell," which has been "gaffed" so that I can show it empty or produce the pea—all without strings or mechanical devices that may get out of order. (I don't think it would serve any useful purpose to disclose the "gaff.")

Similarly, "tossing the broad," or three-card monte, and its big brother, six-card monte, are so old and still so good.

Figure 99. The start of the search. Author shows three shells and that elusive pea used in three-shell game.

Figure 100. Having covered pea with middle shell, author moves shell forward.

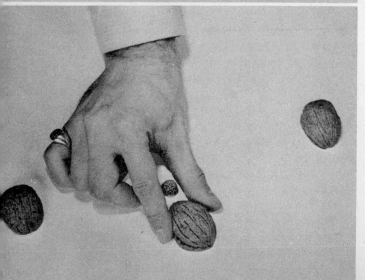

Figure 101. Author has executed the "kickout move," and in this exposed view, you can see pea being held out. He can feel free to load it under any shell.

Figure 102. Sometimes, ostensibly as an added precaution, a cocktail glass or whisky jigger is used to cover the shell. My advice is, Never play this game!

Figure 103. And here's why. The pea is covered with the shell, and the shell moved forward and covered with the glass. But you can see the author doing the "kickout move" (the pea is in his right hand) before the shell goes under the glass.

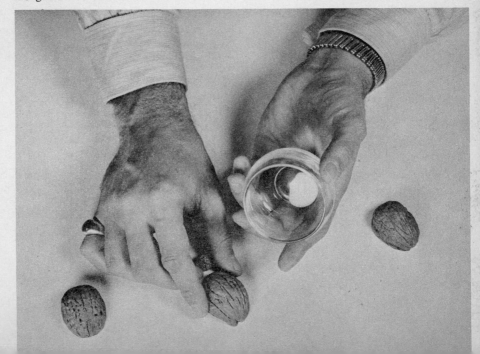

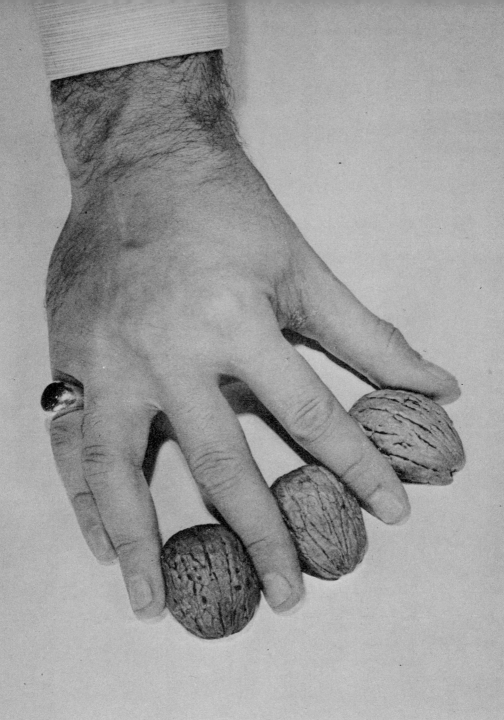

Figure 104. In this "Escobar move," notice that the shells are held with only one hand. Nonetheless, the pea can be maneuvered under any desired shell.

Follow the ace, follow the queen—I dare you!

Not long ago, when I was traveling through Europe for the Air Force, I met a sergeant, a seemingly "hep" cardplayer, who had gone for $300 trying to find the spade queen (the "broad" in three-card monte). I don't care if you have the sharpest eyes in a regiment of sharpshooters! The chances are 999 to 1 against catching a good monte man whether he is executing the two-handed game or the one-hand "sucker move."

Though the grift may seem small, monte demands such expert card manipulation that perfectly legitimate magicians often master it for the practice it gives them. Incidentally, my good friend, Jay Ose, is one of the greatest three-card monte men in the world. Dai Vernon, who can do more things with cards that Beethoven could with chords, agrees.

In the photographs that illustrate the two-handed caper, the ace represents the card you are trying to follow. As the first four photographs demonstrate, it is scooped as the under card in my right hand. Now look closely at Figure 109 which demonstrates the "hype move."

Seemingly, I am throwing down the bottom card, the ace, but actually I am pushing out the top card with the tip of my first right finger and throwing *it* first. To confuse the action, the left hand comes over to drop its card, and then I drop the card still in my right hand—which is the ace.

In the photographs that illustrate the one-hand "sucker move," the black queen represents the card you *think* you are following. As you can see, I first pick up the ace, flash it, then do the same with the queen, chanting almost hypnotically, "Remember the black queen, remember the black queen."

Six-ace monte

As I am talking, in Figure 110 I execute the same "hype move" that you saw in Figure 109 of the previous set. The top card, the ace, is thrown, and I still have a lady queen in my hand.

In either the one-hand or two-handed game, there is a variation in which a shill bends the corner of the desired card, apparently while the operator isn't looking. However, rest assured that when the cards are finally turned over, the "broad" will be miraculously intact, and one of the other two cards will display the bent corner.

When you encounter this caper, *don't* bet the bent card, and you will stand a 50-50 chance of winning. Or perhaps I shouldn't be so optimistic. In the rare instances where a player accidentally wins, the shill

Figure 105. Start of one of the many variations of three-card monte. Two Queens are on the outside, Ace of Clubs in middle.

Figure 106. Author is ready to execute "flip move." An Ace often is used as the favored card because, if accidentally exposed, it will not "flash" as much as a court card.

Figure 107. Both hands are here closing in on the ace.

Figure 108. Ace is turned over, and the right hand, already holding one Queen, picks it up.

Figure 109. Watch this "hype move" closely. The Queen is being thrown rather than the Ace, as you would think.

Figure 110. The left hand approaches toward the left with the second Queen, and puts it to performer's extreme right.

Figure 111. The right hand supposedly containing the other Queen places it between the other two cards. Actually, this is the Ace.

Figure 112. Invariably, the victim would bet the leftmost card to be the Ace. After the bet, the Ace is shown in the middle.

quickly tips over the playing surface and calls a misdeal. Then they get you next time.

In six-card monte, as Figure 24 shows, we have six cards, reading upward from my hand as ace, six, seven, five, four and eight. Your problem is simple. When I turn them over and shuffle them rapidly back and forth, keep your eye steadily on the ace.

But, wait, why are the six *all* aces in Figure 25? Figure 26 explains. Each card is doctored at one end with false pips that make it a different denomination. So even if you can follow the ace, the operator extracts any of the other cards and, covering the false pip, shows it as the ace.

There are so many of these cheap, mean, fast grifts!

Match odd-man-wins with two strangers, and chances are one has a double-head or double-tail quarter. . . . Bet even money that in 20 passing cars, half will have license plates that end in the same two digits and you are accepting what should be a 7 to 1 bet. . . .Try to stick a pin in the center of a rolled belt in "the endless chain game," and you will never achieve it (the belt is manipulated.). . . . Play the corner punchboard game and, chances are, the proprietor paid the gaming supply house a small premium for a key locating the winning numbers and has already removed them.

Anybody seen the postoffice?

I could go on and on, but the way I feel is wrapped up in the story of the small-town businessman who had been mulcted time and again by grifters. One day, in the usual opener to such a pitch, a well-dressed gentleman briskly asked my friend, "Pardon me, I'm a stranger in town. Could you direct me to the postoffice?"

For a few moments, the businessman just stared and then said slowly:

"I can't find the queen of spades.

"I don't know the center of the belt.

"I can't find the pea under the shell.

"Ask somebody else where in hell the postoffice is!"

Both from reading about the "gaffs" that flourished even before Rome fell and from my own experiences, I am sadly convinced that in gambling matters, man is a persistently credulous animal. All I have tried to do is to open your eyes to the cheats around you and offer some advice on how you can play a *better* game of cards or dice.

But, in the final analysis, whether you play expertly and enjoyably, or desperately, illogically, superstitiously, depends on *you*.

As a final word, I would like to offer the 13 words of advice given by America's most fabulous gambler. John W. ("Bet a Million") Gates gambled on *everything*—stocks, horses, cards. With him, bridge was a $1,000-a-point game, and he once backed a poker hand with $50,000. When a small-timer tried to get into one of his games with $500, Gates said coldly, "Give him *a* chip." As relaxation, he flipped pennies for $1,000 a toss.

In the end, though, the market almost bankrupted him, and his gambling gains were largely gone. Not long before his death half a century ago, he gave this remarkably modern bit of advice:

"Don't play cards.

"Don't bet on horse races.

"Don't throw dice.

"Don't gamble!"

♠
♥
♦
♣
♠
♥
♦

MAYBE I CAN DEAL <u>YOU</u> FOUR ACES

♣
♠
♥
♦

I WANT TO MAKE a unique offer that perhaps will do some mutual good.

For the price of a stamped, self-addressed envelope—exactly that and not a penny more—I will answer any questions you may have about cheating methods and analyze your gambling problems.

Of course, I cannot undertake to instruct you on *how* to cheat, nor can I offer any "system" or method of play that will insure winnings.

What I can do, however, if you make your problem clear, is to point out the specific way in which some cheat may be operating in your "friendly" game. And another thing. There are an amazing number of fallacies, misconceptions and dangerous half-truths about cards, dice and betting. If you are laboring under one of these delusions, having heard it from a friend who got it from a friend, I can probably give you the simple, money-saving facts.

So, to you, the *honest* player—businessman, commuter, housewife, serviceman, collegian, high school student—I make this offer.

If you think that I can help in some way, write to me in care of: *

> PRENTICE-HALL, INC.
> EXECUTIVE OFFICES
> ENGLEWOOD CLIFFS, N.J.

* Of necessity, I reserve the right to withdraw this offer at any time.

GLOSSARY

ABYSSINIAN POLO—A dice game.

ACE—One dollar.

ADA FROM DECATUR—Eight in dice.

AGENT—A cheat who works with a casino dealer.

ARMY ODDS—Reputedly, the correct odds.

BAIL THE KALE—To bring out the money.

BANKROLL MAN—Dice game banker.

BARRACUDA—A cheat.

BASE DEALER—Card cheat who deals from bottom of the deck.

BEARD—Someone who lays down bets for another person.

BEND—To fold a card slightly to facilitate various cheating tricks.

BERRIES—Money.

BET AROUND THE HORN—A single craps bet on the 2-3-11-12.

BIG DICK—Ten in dice.

BIRD CAGE—Box for storing dice; also cage used in Chuck-a-Luck.

BLANKET ROLL—Dice tossed on a blanket in a controlled throw.

BLAZE—Five-face-card hand in poker.

BLISTER—To fix a card deck for some cheating technique.

BLOW—To make an exit.

BOBTAIL—In poker, a four-card straight or flush.

BONES—Dice.

BOTTOM DEALER—Same as base dealer.

BOUNCE SHOT—A crooked dice toss in which the cubes are slithered.

BOXCARS—Two sixes in dice.

BREAD—Money.

BREEZE—Same as to blow.

BRICKS—Dice that have been tampered with.

BULL—Policeman.

BURNT OR BURIED CARDS—In blackjack, cards that are turned face up and then put at bottom of pack.

BUM STEER—Bad information.

BUMBLE—A dice game.

BUNDLE—Money.

BUSTERS—Dice that have been misspotted.

CABBAGE—Money.

CAPPED DICE—Dice in which one side is more "bouncy" than the others.

CAP OR COP—To Palm.

CASE NOTE—Last dollar.

CELLAR DEALER—Same as base dealer.

CENTER BET—A wager between tosser and those who bet against him.

CENTURY—One hundred dollars.

CHICKEN FEED—Loose change.

CLUB STAKES—Stakes fixed by agreement before play starts.

COCKED DICE—Dice which hit an obstacle in the roll and stand on end.

COME-ON—An inducement to a prospective victim.

CONGO—A dice game.

COOLER, OR COLD DECK—Prestacked deck slipped into play.

COURT CARDS—King through jack in any suit.

CRICKET—A dice game.

CRIMP—To bend the end of a card.

CROUQUET—A dice game.

CROSSROADER—A cheat from outside who steals from the casino.

CUCUMBER, CUKE—An ignorant or naive victim.

CURSE OF SCOTLAND—Nine of diamonds.

DEVIL'S BOX—Same as bird cage.

DEVIL'S BEDPOSTS—Four of clubs.

DICE KNIFE EDGE—A little square to measure dice.

DICK—A detective.

DON'T PASS LINE—Place on dice layout to put bets that the tosser won't win.

DOOR POPS—Dice misspotted to show only sevens and elevens.

DO-RE-MI—Money.

DUNSKY—A victim.

EIGHTER FROM DECATUR—Eight in dice.

EIGHTY-SIXER—A tightwad victim.

FADER—A gambler who bets against the thrower in dice.

FIVER—Five in dice.

FILL—Three or more casino employes working together to steal from the house.

FIELD—Place on dice layout for field bets (2-3-4-9-10-11-12 or 2-3-5-9-10-11-12).

FIN, FINSKY—Five dollars.

FIRST FLOP DICE—Dice that have been heavily loaded.

FLATS—Dice usually favoring six or eight because sides are shaved.

FLOP—A toss of the dice.

FLOATS—Dice which are hollowed out at corner.

FLUSH SPOT DICE—Spots are not indented, but are stamped or painted on cubes.

FRENCHY—A gambler who plays an honest game but cheats on occasion.

FROG—One dollar.

G-NOTE—One thousand dollars.

GAFF, GAFF OF THE MAGILLA—A cheating technique.

GIMMICK—The same as gaff.

GLIMMER—A mirror-like device known as a "shiner" by which the cheat gets a peek at the cards, usually on his own deal.

GLIMWORKER—A peeker.

GOING SOUTH—To palm an object (usually a card or pair of dice) away from the table toward the pocket.

GOLF BALLS—Dice.

GRAND—One thousand dollars.

GREASE THE PALM—To spit on the dice, or blow on them, preparatory to tossing them.

GREEK SHOT—A cheat's way of controlling the dice on the throw.

HARD WAY—Making point in dice with same numbers (as two fours to make the point of eight).

HEP, HIP—Aware of, "wise to."

HIT ME—In blackjack, asking the dealer for another card.

HITS—Dice which will not roll sevens.

HUSTLER—A card or dice cheat.

IN THE KICK—In the pocket.

INSURANCE BET—A wager to insure against losing a second, larger bet.

IVORIES—Dice.

JACK—Money.

JOHNNY LAW—A policeman.

JUICE JOINT—Any gambling establishment that is crooked.

KEISTER—The backside.

KICKER—The highest indifferent card in a poker hand.

KOMAPA—Counterfeit (as money).

LAMB—A victim.

LARRY—The player with the final turn.

LAYMAN—The same as lamb.

LAYOUT—A dice betting surface with various areas for different types of bets.

LETTUCE—Money.

LITTLE JOE—Four in dice.

LOADED BLOCKS—Dice loaded so as to favor the tosser.

MAKE THE PASS—False cut or nullification of an honest cut.

MARBLES—Dice.

MARKER—A victim.

MARTINGALE—A venerable system for doubling up losing bets.

MECHANIC—A card or dice cheat.

MIDDLE DEALER—A cheat who can deal from the middle of the deck.

MISSES OR MISS-OUTS—Crooked dice which will roll fewer wins than craps on first throw, or seven thereafter.

MISSOURI MARBLES—Dice.

MITT—The hand.

MOOCH—A victim.

MOOLA—Money.

MOVER—A casino cheat who waits till the roll has started before placing his chips.

MOUTHPIECE—A smooth talker.

NATURAL, ALSO A NICK—Number seven or eleven on first toss.

NEVADA LETTUCE—One thousand dollar bill.

NINETY DAYS—Nine in dice.

NO RUMBLE—No trouble.

NOTE IN THE HOLE—Last dollar.

OAKUS—A wallet.

OLD POT—Old-fashioned, old hat.

OLLA PORDIDA—The same as old pot.

PAPERWORK—Bending, crimping or waving the cards; also premarked cards.

PATSY—A victim.

PEEK—To get a glimpse of the cards.

PEETIES—Same as loaded blocks.

PEG OR PUNCH—To prepare the deck for some cheating maneuver.

PHOEBE—Five in dice.

PIG—A wallet.

PIGEON—A victim.

PIKE—To peek.

PIP—The spot on a card.

PONE—Player sitting to dealer's right who cuts.

QUEER—Counterfeit money.

QUEER PUSHER—A person who passes counterfeit money.

RABBIT—A victim.

RIGHT BET—Wagering that the dice will pass.

RIP—Switching in crooked dice.

SAND PAPER—Cards marked by sanding the edges.

SAWBUCK—Ten dollars.

SECOND DEALER, NO. 2 MAN—A cheat who deals the second card from the top of the deck, reserving the desired top card for himself or for a confederate.

SHAPE—A formed of crooked dice that has been shaved out of true.

SHARK—A cheat.

SHEKEL—A dollar.

SHELL GAME—An ancient cheater's game in which the victim tries to guess which pod the pea lies under.

SHILL—A house or cheater's employe who pretends to be a player.

SHIMMY—*Chemin-de-fer*.

SHINER—A mirror-like device that enables the cheat to "peek" at the cards.

SHOVER—Passer of counterfeit money.

SIGN ON HIS BACK—A gambler known to be a cheat.

SIMOLEON—One dollar.

SINGLE-O—A cheat who works without confederates.

SIXTY DAYS—Six in dice.

SKIN—One dollar.

SKIN GAME—A rigged game in which an honest player always loses.

SKIN THE DECK—To palm cards from the pack.

SLICK CUP—A dice cup with polished insides to help control dice.

SLICK DICE—A dice toss in which one die is legitimately bounced and the other slid in such fashion that a desired number will come up.

SNAKE EYES—Two aces, in dice.

SNAKE—To wave a card.

SPLITTER—A crooked die which "splits up" a pair of crooked dice. Thus, a "splitter" used with a passer may become a miss-out pair or, used with one miss-out, may become a passer pair.

SQUARE JOHN—A victim.

STEER JOINT—A crooked gambling establishment to which victims are brought by a steerer who gets a percentage of the take.

STICK MAN—A dice house employe who rakes in the dice with a stick after the throw.

STONEWALL JACKSON—A tightwad.

STORE DICE—Ordinary cheap dice, often also called drugstore dice, which may not be perfect.

STRIPPER—A card so doctored that it can be easily extracted from the pack.

SUB—A belt or arm device for holding palmed cards.

SUBWAY DEALER—Same as bottom dealer.

SUCKER—A victim.

SUCKER DICE—Crooked dice which have been made concave.

SWITCHER—A cheat who switches dice, cards or entire decks of cards into the game.

TABLE PASS, HOP, HIPE OR JUMP—To get the deck back into its original position.

TABLE STAKES—Agreed betting limit made before the game.

TAKE—Gross receipts in gambling.

TAKEOFF CRAPS—Players pay fee based on size of betting units.

TAP OUT—Lose the last of your money.

TAPPERS—Dice which have been loaded with mercury or a similar substance that shifts inside when the cubes are tapped.

TENSKY—Ten dollars.

TIP THE MITT—To give away information.

TOP THE DECK—To palm cards from the pack.

TOPS, ALSO KNOWN AS TOPS AND BOTTOMS—Dice mismarked so that they have two faces alike.

TRIP DICE—Dice in which the edges have been tampered with.

UPHILLS—Dice made to roll high scores.

VALLE CARDS—Cards that have value.

VEAL CUTLET—A victim.

VIGORISH—The 3 percent to 5 percent cut of the pot taken by the operator.

WAVE—Same as to "snake" a card.

WILL-O'-THE-WISP—The middle deal.

WORK THE TUBES—A gambler who operates aboard steamship.

WORKER—A hustler.

WRONG BETTOR—One who wagers that the thrower will lose.

YAPPER—A talker.

YARD—One hundred dollars.

YARD AND A HALF—One hundred and fifty dollars.

YUCK—A victim.

BIBLIOGRAPHY

(Books starred are especially recommended)

. . . and a Pack of Cards, Jack Merlin (revised and edited by Jean Hugard, assisted by John J. Crimmins Jr.). Max Holden: New York, Boston, Philadelphia, 1940.

Association of American Playing Card Manufacturers. Material from files.

Basic Statistics, George Simpson and Fritz Kafka. W. H. Norton & Co.: New York, 1952.

Dice. (Author not listed.) Fox Enterprises: Las Vegas, Nev., 1959.

Elements of Psychology, David Krech and Richard S. Crutchfield. Alfred A. Knopf: New York, 1958.

* Fools of Fortune, John Philip Quinn. The Anti-Gambling Association: Chicago, 1892.

Gambling and Gambling Devices, John Philip Quinn. J. P. Quinn Co.: Canton, O., 1912.

How It's Done, A. E. Wilson. Los Angeles, Calif. Copyright (no date).

How to Play Poker and Win, Sidney H. Radner. Key Publishing Co.: New York, 1957.

How to Spot Card Sharps and Their Methods, Sidney H. Radner. Key Publishing Co.: New York, 1957.

Lotteries, Laws and Morals, Judge Francis Emmett Williams. Vantage Press: New York, 1958.

* *Playing Blackjack to Win,* Roger R. Balctwin and M. Burroughs. Barrows Co.: New York, 1959.

Protection—The Sealed Book, Joseph E. Meyer, Author and Publisher. Milwaukee, 1911.

Roulette and Other Casino Games, Sidney H. Radner. Key Publishing Co.: New York, 1958.

* *Scarne on Cards,* John Scarne. Crown Publishers: New York, 1949.

* *Scarne on Dice,* John Scarne. Military Service Publishing Co.: Harrisburg, Pa., 1945.

Secrets of Gambling, Al Price. Trend Books Inc.: Los Angeles, 1958.

Sharps and Flats, John Nevil Maskelyne. Longmans, Green and Co.: New York, 1894.

Shoot the Works, Edward Marlo. Published by L. L. Ireland: Chicago, 1943.

Something for Nothing, Clyde Brion Davis. J. B. Lippincott Co.: Philadelphia and New York, 1956.

The Big Gamble, Charles Graves. Hutchinson & Co. Ltd.: London, 1951.

* *The Education of a Poker Player,* Herbert O. Yardley. Simon and Schuster: New York, 1957.

* *The Expert at the Card Table,* S. W. Erdnase. Copyright 1902 by S. W. Erdnase. Entered at Stationers' Hall, London.

* *The Fireside Book of CARDS,* edited by Oswald Jacoby and Albert Morehead. Simon and Schuster: New York, 1957.

The Official Rules of Card Games, Albert H. Morehead, editor. The United States Playing Card Co.: Cincinnati, 1950 (47th edition).

The Pocket Book of GAMES, Albert H. Morehead. Pocket Books Inc.: New York, 1944.

The Psychology of Gambling, Edmund Bergler, M.D. Hill and Wang: New York, 1957.

* *You Can't Win,* Ernest S. Blanche, Ph.D. Public Affairs Press: Washington, 1949.

INDEX